Priests &
Politicians

TSEHAI
Publishers & Distributors

PRIESTS & POLITICIANS

*Protestant & Catholic Missions
in Orthodox Ethiopia
(1830-1868)*

Donald Crummey

TSEHAI
Publishers & Distributors

ለርብቃና ፡ ማቴዎስ

TSEHAI
Publishers & Distributors

Priests & Politicians: Protestant & Catholic Missions in Orthodox Ethiopia (1830-1868)

Tsehai Publishers and Distributors
P. O. Box: 1881, Hollywood, CA 90078

www.tsehaipublishers.com
info@tsehaipublishers.com

ISBN: 10: 1-59907-021-9
ISBN: 13: 9-781599-070216

Publisher: Elias Wondimu
Marketing and Sales Director: Sara Gezahegne
Cover Design by Yoseph Gezahegne
Production Manager: Wondimu Bizuneh

Second Edition

First Edition - Published by Oxford at the Clarendon Press (1972)

Library of Congress Catalog Card Number
A catalog record for this book is available from the Library of Congress.

British Library Cataloguing in Publication Data
A catalogue record for this book is available from the British Library.

1 10 9 8 7 6 5 4 3 2

Printed in the United States of America

Preface

Priests and Politicians first appeared in 1972, thirty-five years ago. The book explores the activities of European missionaries during four decades in the middle of the nineteenth century, when the modern Ethiopian state began to take shape in response to a rapidly changing world, which pressed on it with increasing intensity. The missionaries mediated between Europe and the Ethiopian rulers, who sought access to the technology, mostly military, which was so salient a feature of Europe's growing imperial presence. To Ethiopian elites, the missionaries also represented the European culture, which underpinned the technology, and so they became part of Ethiopia's early grappling with modernity.

The book was written during the last years of the reign of Haile Sellassie. Looking back, from that point in time, one could see a continuous, if halting and slow, process of Ethiopia's adjusting to modernity. Only two years after the book's appearance, the political framework of that process was radically disrupted by young Ethiopians, who, inspired by the European revolutionary tradition, set out to transform their country. Ethiopia's first experiment in accelerating development and modernization, launched in 1974, failed within fifteen years, and dissenting members of the same age group, which had launched the experiment of 1974, launched a fresh experiment in 1991. It is still unclear whether the leaders of Ethiopia in the later twentieth and early twenty-first centuries will prove more successful in grappling with modernity than those who preceded them a century before.

Three themes of *Priests and Politicians* are of continuing relevance: Ethiopia's search for modernization and development; the country's domination by political elites; and the importance of religious belief and practice. Looking back now, over the intervening century and a half, the sense of continuity, apparent in the 1972, has re-emerged. The striking disparity between the living conditions for most of its citizens and the conditions promised by contemporary technology remain a central challenge to Ethiopia. The struggle to forge a national identity and create organic political institutions is ongoing. Politics remain authoritarian. Orthodoxy is still a touchstone of identity for many Ethiopians, as is Islam. Protestantism and Catholicism are still important pathways to modernity and national identity for yet other Ethiopians.

I have chosen not to change the text as it appeared in 1972. While there have been relevant advances in scholarship, they do not seem to me to have invalidated what I originally wrote.

So many of the people, who were important in my graduate study and early career, are no longer with us—my parents, Richard Gray, Richard Caulk, and Sergew Hable Sellassie. Others have continued to enrich my life many times over—Taddesse Tamrat, and, most importantly, Lorraine. The book was originally dedicated to our elder children, Rebecca and Matthew. The birth of their sister, Naomi, coincided with the party planned to celebrate the book's publication. I would like to repeat the dedication, including now Naomi and our grandchildren—Zoey, Siobhan, Valentin and Willa. May they ever enrich the lives of others!

Urbana, Illinois   Donald Crummey

May, 2007

PREFACE

MISSIONS are well established as a branch of African history. In many respects the following simply adds detail from another corner of the continent. The necessarily unique factor is an indigenous Church. Unfortunately, we lack sufficient Ethiopian texts to make this a genuinely three-sided study of Protestant, Catholic, and Orthodox. Ethiopian attitudes towards missions have largely to be deduced from missionary accounts. Nevertheless, I have limited the book's scope to 'Orthodox Ethiopia', by which is intended those areas which from medieval times had preserved their Christian identity in its least modified form: Shawā, Gojjām, Bagēmder, Semēn, and Tegrē. As these provinces were the last components of the eighteenth-century state, before its disintegration, some coherence is given by common culture, religion, and political aspirations. Excluded are the Muslims, pagans, and peripheral Orthodox groups in Gurāgē, Kafā, and the remaining south-west. The Gāllā, Ethiopia's largest ethnic group, appear only inasmuch as they had become assimilated to national politics, or as an object of missionary strategy.

A system of transcription has been adopted for Ethiopian names and terms which tries to represent their Amharic values. Its principles will be clear to the knowledgeable, others can safely ignore it. However, the bar over vowels ('ā') represents openness, rather than length; and the sublinear dot ('ṭ') an almost explosive quality. The spelling of place and proper names has been assimilated as closely as possible to indigenous spelling, although this too varies. In quotations and footnotes I follow the aberrations of my sources, in European as well as Ethiopian words. One common misusage does not appear: *Abuna*. This form should never be used independently, but only in a construct relationship with a proper name: '*Abuna* Salāmā'. The correct form, *Abun*, is rarely used locally, and I have preferred such terms as bishop or metropolitan.

Acknowledgements, however habitual they have become, are both necessary and pleasant. They stress what has long been a fact: the communal nature of scholarly life. My indebtedness is very wide: to the Canada Council and the Central Research Fund of the University of London who provided financial support for my research; to the patience and acuity of the supervisor of the doctoral thesis in which much of the following material was first presented, Richard Gray; to Professor Roland Oliver for encouragement; to the keepers of the several archives and libraries central to the study, for their uniform co-operation and kindness; to my colleagues in the History Department, Haile Sellassie I University, especially Sergew Hable Sellassie, Taddesse Tamrat, and Richard Caulk, for general stimulation and many detailed points of advice; to my father, for my initial interest in history, and much subsequent support; and to Lorraine, to the fruits of whose labours this book is dedicated.

DONALD CRUMMEY

Addis Ababa
Masqal 1971

CONTENTS

LIST OF PLATES

I a. King, abbot, and bishop. Detail from a canvas mural in the Māryām Church, Darasgē, depicting the church's founding (probably painted 1840s)

b. The Eçhagē Bēt, Gondar. Undoubtedly nineteenth century, or earlier; possibly the house in which Gobat conversed with Eçhagē Filpos
facing p. 18

II a. Johann Ludwig Krapf as a young man. From the Basel Mission Archives

b. Samuel Gobat, Bishop of Jerusalem. Originally published in his autobiography, reproduced from the CMS archives *facing p.* 38

III a. *Abuna* Salāmā, *c.* 1860. From H. Stern, *Wanderings among the Falashas* . . . (London, 1862). Probably a good likeness, for Stern travelled with a camera

b. *Dajjāch* Webē in the early 1840s. From Th. Lefebvre, *Voyage en Abyssinie* . . . (Paris, 6 vols., 1845-8)

c. Webē. A stylized portrait from the Māryām Church, Darasgē
facing p. 66

IV a. Bishop Justin de Jacobis. From J.-B. Coulbeaux, *Vers la lumière* . . (Paris, 1926)

b. The young Bishop Guglielmo Massaja. From E. Martire, *Massaja da Vicino* . . . (Rome, 1937) *facing p.* 80

V a. The Church of Gwālā, near Addigrāt. The first modern Catholic parish in Ethiopia

b. The bell tower at Darasgē Māryām. Built by an associate of the Lazarist Mission to house a bell from Pope Gregory. Local tradition holds that Tēwodros was crowned here, and not in the church *facing p.* 110

LIST OF MAPS

ABBREVIATIONS AND SHORT REFERENCES

Archival

AG, OFM	Archivum Generale, Curia Generalizia, Frati Minori Cappuccini (Rome).
APF	Archives of the 'Propaganda Fide' (Rome).
—— *SRC.AC*	*Scritture Riferite nei Congressi. Africa Centrale.*
BN, *Éth.-Abb.*	Bibliothèque Nationale (Paris), *Fond Éthiopien-Abbadie.*
CGL	Curia Generalizia, Lazarists (Rome).
CMS	Church Missionary Society Archives (London).
IO	India Office Archives (London).
—— AOC	*Abyssinia Original Correspondence.*
—— BSP	*Bombay Secret Proceedings.*
MAE	Ministère des Affaires Etrangères (Paris).
—— *Corr. pol. Ég. Mass.*	*Correspondance politique. Égypte. Massaouah.*
—— *Mém. doc.*	*Mémoires et documents (Afrique).*
PRO	Public Record Office (London).
—— FO	Foreign Office.
Spittler-Archiv	Staats-Archiv des Kantons Basel-Stadt, *C. F. Spittler Privat-Archiv 653.*

Ethiopian Documents

'Cronaca Reale'	'La Cronaca Reale Abissina dall'anno 1800 all'anno 1840', *RRAL*, S5, xxv (1916).
'Nuovi Documenti'	'Nuovi Documenti per la storia d'Abissinia nel secolo XIX', *RRAL*, S7, ii (1947), with document number.
'Vicende'	'Vicende dell'Etiopia e delle missioni cattoliche ai tempi di Ras Ali, Deggiac Ubie e Re Teodoro . . .', *RRAL*, S5, xxv (1916).

Periodicals

Annales	*Annales de la congrégation de la mission* (Lazarist).
Intelligencer	*Church Missionary Intelligencer.*
Record	*Church Missionary Record.*
Rev. his. miss.	*Revue d'histoire des missions.*
RRAL	*Rendiconti della Reale Accademia dei Lincei.*

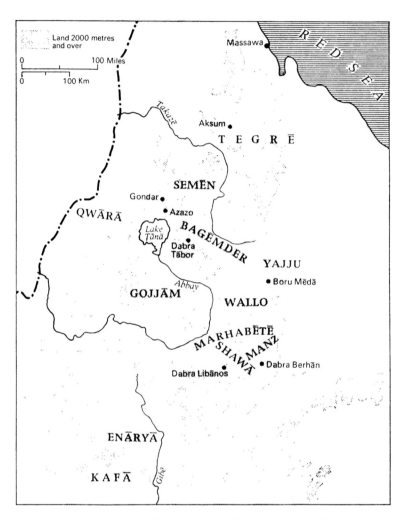

MAP I. Christian highlands and south-west Ethiopia.

CHAPTER I

Priests and Politicians

FEW themes of modern history are so important as Europe's interaction with the rest of the world. Christian missions have played a
vital role in this story; perhaps nowhere more so than in tropical
Africa. Here missionaries generally had precedence amongst Europeans in establishing permanent connections with indigenous
societies.[1] Their stations became a major focus for much of rural
life; centres from which flowed avidly sought education and medicine.[2]
Here, too, was a rare place of intimate contact between European
and African. The Church soon developed into a prime instrument of
social advancement; and religion served as an early vehicle for
nationalism.[3] On the other hand, in their encounter with proponents
of Christianity, Africans sometimes met with contempt or belittle-
ment; their response to the Gospel thwarted by the distorting framework of imperialism. In short, missions were integral to the formation of contemporary Africa.

Ethiopia is unique in the black world. Decidedly African, she also
belongs to the Middle East.[4] One of the oldest Christian states, her
development has been marked by an often exaggerated, but real,
isolation. She is the only African nation to escape prolonged alien
domination; yet her society is indeed backward, measured by such
indexes as literacy, *per capita* income, spread of public health, and

[1] See the recent symposium edited by C. G. Baëta, *Christianity in Tropical
Africa. Studies Presented and Discussed at the Seventh International African
Seminar, University of Ghana, April 1965* (London: O.U.P., 1968).

[2] H. B. Johnson, 'The Location of Christian Missions in Africa', *The Geographical Review*, lvii (1967), 168–202.

[3] E. A. Ayandele, *The Missionary Impact on Modern Nigeria 1842–1914.
A Political and Social Analysis* (London: Longmans, 1966), Chap. VI. See also
R. Oliver, *The Missionary Factor in East Africa* (London: Longmans, 2nd ed.,
1965); J. F. A. Ajayi, *Christian Missions in Nigeria 1841–1891. The Making of a
New Élite* (London: Longmans, 1965); and R. Rotberg, *Christian Missionaries
and the Creation of Northern Rhodesia 1880–1924* (Princeton, N.J.: Princeton
University Press, 1965).

[4] E. Ullendorff, *Ethiopia and the Bible. The Schweich Lectures of the British
Academy 1967* (London: O.U.P., 1968); and E. Haberland, *Untersuchungen zum
äthiopischen Königtum* (Wiesbaden: Franz Steiner Verlag, 1965).

cadres formation. Both independence and social backwardness are, in part, functions of Ethiopia's relations with Europe, although, in this case, negative ones.

Protestant and Catholic missions have played significant roles in the development of contemporary Ethiopia. In our period they helped generate the diplomatic situation which culminated in the British Maqdalā campaign. Again, as major representatives of the European presence, they were highly influential in moulding Ethiopian attitudes towards the external world. In more recent times they have been involved in education, medicine, and élite formation. Two vital factors, however, have lessened their final importance compared with the rest of tropical Africa: the existence of the Orthodox Church; and the absence of European colonialism. Still, until the later nineteenth century missionary activity throughout the continent was broadly similar; slight in social impact, but deeply involved in diplomacy and politics.[1]

The Secular Framework

Often unwittingly, the missions served as fore-runners of European aggression, and herein lies their greatest significance for our period. Elsewhere, the consummation of imperialism in colonial rule led to the second, social, phase of their activity: its frustration in Ethiopia has been largely responsible for the meagre modernizing weight of missions there. Despite much recent controversy surrounding the subject it seems unnecessary to argue that the relations between Africans and Europeans throughout the nineteenth century were dominated by the development of a new imperialism, or that the essential cause of this phenomenon was the rise of industrial capitalism in Europe.[2] Whatever the forms expanding European influence took, and however kaleidoscopic the motives of explorers, missionaries, consuls and statesmen, all were conditioned by their rapidly evolving domestic economy. The unique character of modern imperialism is surely derived from the tendencies to subjugation and exploitation inherent in the economic system of the North Atlantic

---

[1] Ayandele, *Missionary Impact*, Chaps. I–IV; Oliver, *Missionary Factor*, Chap. III; and D. A. Low, *Religion and Society in Buganda 1875–1900* (Kampala: East African Institute of Social Research, n.d.).

[2] The leading revisionist statement is by R. Robinson and J. Gallagher, *Africa and the Victorians. The Official Mind of Imperialism* (London: Macmillan, 1965); but see the criticisms in G. Barraclough, *An Introduction to Contemporary History* (London: Penguin Books, 1967), 55–64.

world. While it is true that these tendencies expressed themselves in rather different forms, as the century progressed, their essence was not modified. It is not, then, an anachronism to talk of imperial trends in the early nineteenth century, nor to apply the concept to those missionaries who in their political activities sought to hasten the advent of European rule in order to establish the pre-conditions for their proselytizing activities. Nor is it illegitimate to see in these 'imperialist' activities a connection with the subsequent extension of direct European rule throughout tropical Africa. A number of examples will be discussed in succeeding chapters.

What is really required is to see the missions of the nineteenth century as one factor in a three-sided process of religious impulse, African society, and European government, each component of which maintained its autonomy of interest, but whose driving force lay in the European economy. This placed the bearers of the Good News, given a complete singleness of spiritual purpose, in the position of using, and being used by, not only their metropolitan rulers, but also African societies. However, their intentions were rarely undivided. Baëta has remarked: 'In principle the object of mission is simply to make God known wherever He was previously unknown. . . . But this primary purpose appears to have been purely and solely the moving force in the missions of apostolic and sub-apostolic times.'[1] Recent European religious enterprise has been deeply imbued with western culture, just as, in earlier times, Christianity presented itself to Ethiopia in a Hellenistic guise to be transformed by the Afro-Semitic values of the highlands. Again, the missionary expansion of the medieval Ethiopian Church was embedded with secular aspects.[2] It is, perhaps, natural to an expanding society to feel the superiority of its own culture. Nineteenth-century missionaries certainly did, and, moreover, often attributed it to religion.[3] Thus, they generally believed that conversion to Christianity entailed some adoption of European behaviour and attitudes. This led directly to the second factor in the process: Europeans were not

[1] Baëta, *Christianity in Tropical Africa*, 13.

[2] Taddesse Tamrat, 'Church and State in Ethiopia 1270–1527', unpublished Ph.D. thesis (University of London, 1968), Chap. IV.

[3] M. Warren, *The Missionary Movement from Britain in Modern History* (London: SCM Press, 1965), 42. See also H. A. C. Cairns, *Prelude to Imperialism. British Reactions to Central African Society 1840–1890* (London: Routledge, 1965), 199 ff. For several relevant contributions on the classical European Church, see G. Cuming (ed.), *The Mission of the Church and the Propagation of the Faith* (Cambridge: C.U.P., 1970).

alone in paying tribute to their ascendancy. Africans eagerly sought
the fruits of a more-developed economic order; and, viewing the
missionaries primarily as representatives of the European system,
tried to exploit them in a host of directions. Thus, the secular dimension was inherent both in the missionary approach and in the African
response.

The final factor was power politics. Most frequently, African
rulers sought to use missionaries as bridges to their home govern-
ments. Missions, on the other hand, turned to their protecting nations
in times of trouble, and naturally channelled the African desire for a
European connection in the direction most favourable to themselves.
Missionary diplomacy, however, was not inherently imperialistic.
Indeed, the pioneer work of the early and mid-nineteenth century
entailed a commitment to indigenous political structures, and it was
often only when these became undermined by the secular pressures of
imperialism (or less frequently by religious ones) that missions helped
ease the establishment of European rule. Ultimately, both Africans
and missionaries were the pawns of external powers, their relations
to be transformed by the swelling tide of the partition. Although
some brave individuals breasted the current, most were swept
along by it; for nationalism was not only proper to men of the age,
but was also intricately linked with sectarianism. Until mid-century
the alignment was relatively simple: Protestants towards Britain;
Catholics with France. The unification of Italy and Germany, along
with Belgium's new aspirations, complicated the picture, without
changing its essentials. Where Catholics and Protestants converged,
historic fears and suspicions sometimes produced action which
placed their deeper attitudes in fresh perspective. Ancient reflex was
at work. But it laboured to reveal just how prevalent assumptions of
aggressiveness and domination were. While few recognized these in
themselves, they perceived them in sectarian rivals. Whether these
tendencies were intrinsic to missionary activity, or simply part of the
European personality, is probably irrelevant. They existed.[1]

The Missionary Approach

The Orthodox Church was a unique problem for missions in
Ethiopia. A fine line existed between service to Christianity in the
country, and the imposition of alien forms and prejudices upon it.

[1] See below the example of J. L. Krapf in Shawā in the early 1840s, Chap. III,
pp. 47–8, 53.

Here the intermingling of religion and secular culture was particularly complex and acute. Three modes of Christianity met, confused by two distinct civilizations. Criteria for judging the validity of missionary activity in this theatre are elusive; yet such activity cannot be dismissed out of hand. It would be patronizing to suppose that individual Ethiopians could have no interest in new expressions of the Gospel, or that their Church might not profit by emergence from its isolation. For guidance we must turn to the Apostolic model and seek signs of openness, flexibility, and, above all, of humility and the desire to serve (1 Cor. 9: 22–3; Phil. 2: 5–8; Acts 17).

Given the limitations of their outlook, most missions adopted flexible and enlightened approaches. The Orthodox Church was initially taken by both Catholics and Protestants as the cornerstone of their strategy. A revitalized Ethiopian Christianity was seen to be the key to the conversion of the 'pagans' of Africa. Although this might have implied a considerable interest in the Africanness of the Ethiopian Church, in fact, with some exceptions, European conditioning generally prevented such an appreciation. In our period, Protestants explicitly repudiated any attempts at proselytization, and sought to stimulate an indigenous Reformation. As they were of mixed backgrounds—mostly Calvinists and Lutherans working under Anglican sponsorship—they were further prevented from imposing any specific Protestant pattern. They were, thus, much freer than the Catholics when it came to the details of Church organization or practice. In theory, the problem of interfering with the 'style' of indigenous Christianity ought not to have arisen. The Evangelicals' intention was the worthy one of sharing with a sister Church their own experiences, undoubtedly of great relevance to the new world pressing on the remote highlands. Literacy in the Scriptures, personal piety as opposed to ecclesiastical formalism, and new concepts of individual and social morality could all help to enrich and renew the life of the Orthodox Church. Moreover, the Protestant skill in, and love of, religious dialectic was a strong point of contact with educated clergy. Also, in Ethiopia, more than anywhere else in Africa, the individualism of the Evangelicals could strike a responsive chord. It is true that the desire for an Ethiopian Reformation entailed hostile judgements about the existing spiritual condition of the country, but it also implied a recognition of its essentially Christian nature. However, Pietist hostility to liturgical devotion, fasting, and veneration of the saints, countered its openness towards form.

For Catholics the question was more vexed. Organizational problems could scarcely be avoided, as the Church was held visibly to be
one. Moreover, there were variances both in doctrine and practice.
Dogmatic differences were the more intractable, stemming from the
Council of Chalcedon (AD 451),[1] and constituting a formal relationship, not merely of schism, but also of heresy. Variations in
practice, once so important, were now rather less so. From the
standpoint of the Latin Church, the customs and forms of Ethiopian
Christianity were distinct indeed: observation of the Sabbath,
dietary proscriptions, circumcision, liturgy, calendar, canon law—
all these separated the two. However, many, if not all of these
divergent usages were prevalent elsewhere amongst the eastern
churches, both Greek and 'Monophysite'. Despite an earlier phase
of aggressive Latinization, tolerance, or at least flexibility, characterized our period. Nevertheless, the distinction between doctrine and
usage was often blurred, and both circumcision and observance of the
Sabbath were held, by Catholics, as heretical or superstitious. At its
highest, Catholic missionary activity in Ethiopia sought to bring
indigenous Christianity out of isolation into living communion with
the Universal Church, and to reform abuses and irregularities which
were, at times, an affront to the apostolic faith. Perhaps the two
strongest points of the Catholics in Ethiopia were the discipline of
their clergy and the intensity of their sacramental life, while their
concept of the nature of the visible Church, liturgical and episcopal,
was closer to the Orthodox position than was the Protestant. This
formed an important point of contact leading to the conversion of
men of real standing.

The Jesuit Aftermath

Catholic success was won in the face of a disastrous precedent.
From 1555 to 1633 the Society of Jesus had worked for the conversion of court and country.[2] Almost fifty years without effect were

[1] A. Harnack, *History of Dogma* (New York: Dover Publications, 1961), iv.
212–26; F. L. Cross (ed.), *The Oxford Dictionary of the Christian Church* (London:
O.U.P., 1958), 'Chalcedon', 'Monophysitism'; and for a statement from a
'Monophysite' position, V. C. Samuel, 'Proceedings of the Council of Chalcedon
and its Historical Problems', *Abba Salama. A Review of The Association of
Ethio-Hellenic Studies*, i (Addis Ababa, 1970), 73–93. The same distinction
applied to the Protestants, but was less important as Pietistic and Evangelical
doctrines were stressed more than Conciliar ones.

[2] Some of the finest historical writing on Ethiopia deals with this subject.
B. Tellez, *The Travels of the Jesuits in Ethiopia* . . . (London, 1710); J. Ludolf,

dramatically changed by the conjunction of two extremely remarkable men with a profound political crisis: the missionary Peter Paez; the Emperor Susenyos (1607–32); and a succession struggle following 1596 which had threatened to tear the country apart. There followed a revolution at once political and religious. Susenyos drove towards a more complete form of absolutism, while Latinization sought to eradicate the country's distinctive Christian customs. Paez died in 1622, to be succeeded in 1626 by the Patriarch, A. Mendes, a man of less tact and flexibility. Faced with mounting resistance, court and mission began to drift apart. Mendes was unable to retrench. Over ten years of pretty constant, bloody, civil war led in 1632 to Susenyos's capitulation, and the collapse of Catholic enterprise. Their most fundamental mistake was uncharacteristic of the Jesuits: hostility to indigenous usages. Not only were such practices as circumcision attacked; the missionaries went so far as to encourage the eating of pork, abolish the Ethiopian religious calendar, and import the Latin liturgy, their only substantial concession being the use of the Ge'ez language. A far stronger state would have strained to impose such a revolution, so intemperate and unnecessary. The consequences for Ethiopia were serious: a radical isolation from Europe and bitter internal divisions.[1] Catholicism had discredited itself through folly and intolerance, and its association with political oppression. The price it paid was two hundred years of exclusion and a reputation gravely damaged.

Not until the end of the eighteenth century did Catholic strategy begin to change. Meanwhile, a number of attempts were made to re-establish work by various Franciscan missions. Martyrs were produced more than once, but no new foothold was gained.[2] Few

---

A New History of Ethiopia Being a Full and Accurate Description of the Kingdom of Abessinia Vulgarly, though Erroneously called the Empire of the Prester John (London, 1682); and J. Bruce, *Travels to Discover the Source of the Nile in the Years 1768, 1769, 1770, 1771, 1772, and 1773* (Edinburgh, 5 vols., 1790), ii. See also Girmah Beshah and Merid Wolde Aregay, *The Question of the Union of the Churches in Luso-Ethiopian Relations (1500–1632)* (Lisbon, 1964); C. F. Beckingham and G. W. B. Huntingford, *Some Records of Ethiopia Being Extracts From The History of High Ethiopia or Abassia by Manoel de Almeida* ... (London: Hakluyt Society, 1954); and Merid Wolde Aregay, 'Southern Ethiopia and the Christian Kingdom 1508–1708, with special Reference to the Galla Migrations and their Consequences', unpublished Ph.D. thesis (University of London, 1971), Chaps. V and VI, *passim*.

[1] See below, Chapter II.
[2] For a useful summary, see J.-B. Coulbeaux, *Histoire politique et religieuse*

expeditions made contact with the Court, and fewer still survived.[1] The principal exception was Fr. Remedius Prutky of Bohemia and his two colleagues, whose nine months' residence at the court of Iyyāsu II in 1752 is as neglected as it is important.[2] The records of their activities do not suggest, however, that the fundamental questions of approach had been rethought. Their mission arose from an invitation by the Emperor for the Franciscans in Palestine to send him 'maestri d'arte'.[3] From March to December 1752 the three missionaries resided in Gondar, where they formed a close connection with the royal family, especially enjoying the favour of Iyyāsu's mother and co-ruler, *Itēgē* Mentewwāb, a powerful figure indeed. No sooner had they decided to press the King for an open declaration than the Orthodox bishop raised the people and clergy against them. Despite royal advice, and continuing popular agitation, the Franciscans persisted, threatening 'eternal damnation if they did not yield obedience to the truths of the Gospel'. Finally, in December they were dismissed: '. . . in leaving . . ., we shook the dust off from our feet, and publicly upbraided the Emperor and his people with their infidelity, exclaiming with a loud voice, "We are driven away by false Christians; let us fly then and seek refuge among the Gentiles."'[4] Quite apart

d'Abyssinie depuis les temps les plus reculés jusqu'à l'avènement de Ménélick II (Paris, 1928), ii.

[1] One mission, protected by the Emperor Yosṭos, was executed after his deposition by the succeeding Dāwit III, in 1716. See C. Othmer, 'P. Liberatus Weiss, O. F. M. Seine Missionstaetigkeit und sein Martyrium (3 März 1716)', *Archivum Franciscanum Historicum*, xx (Quaracchi, 1927), 336–55. See also R. Basset, *Études sur l'histoire de l'Éthiopie* (Paris, 1882), 184–5.

[2] Little from his extensive writings has been published. See the two articles by Teodosio Somigli, 'La Francescana Spedizione in Etiopia del 1751–54 e la sua Relazione del P. Remedio Prutky di Boemia O.F.M.', *Arch. Fran. Hist.*, vi (1913), 129–43; and 'L'Itinerarium del P. Remedio Prutky, Viaggiatore e Missionario Francescano (Alto Egitto), e il suo viaggio in Abissinia—21 Febbraio 1752–22 Aprile 1753', *Studi Francescani*, N.S. xxii (Florence, 1925), 425–60. Extracts from his major work have been published in *La Missione Francescana in Palestina ed in Altre Regione della Terra*, vi (1895), and vii (1896). H. Salt, *A Voyage to Abyssinia and Travels into the Interior of that Country* . . . (London, 1814), Appendix III, is an English translation of the Italian document published by Fr. Teodosio in *Arch. Fran. Hist.* C. Beccari, *Notizia e Saggi di Opere e Documenti inediti Riguardanti la Storia di Etiopia durante i Secoli XVI, XVII, e XVIII* . . . (Rome, 1903), 64–5, lists the documents in the Archives of the Propaganda Fide in the *Scritture Riferite nei Congressi* series.

[3] Somigli, 'Francescana Spedizione', 131. A copy of the original Greek letter dated Gonder, 18 Oct. 1750, is found in APF, *Scritture Originali Riferite nelle Congregazioni Generali*, 749, 112ᵛ–13ʳ.

[4] Salt, *Voyage*, Appendix III, xxxv.

from their extreme intransigence and an almost provocative search for martyrdom,[1] Remedius and his colleagues perpetuated two aspects of the discredited Jesuit approach: a fixation upon the court; and a refusal to utilize any indigenous forms. Given the origins of their position, and the sympathy which the royal family expressed, the first was understandable. But the second was inexcusable. Remedius could see no value at all in Ethiopian Christianity, rather a host of abuses and irregularities: 'They have something in common', he remarked, 'with all people: Baptism with Christians; Sabbath with Hebrews; a multitude of wives, circumcision, and divorce with the Turks; many superstitions with the Gentiles. . . .'[2] His description of such festivals as Epiphany, and of the condition of the clergy, was wilful in its distortion. It was, then, a blessing, both for Ethiopia and Catholic aspirations there, that the mission was expelled.

A more novel attempt was made in the last decade of the eighteenth century. An Ethiopian convert to Catholicism, Fr. Tobias Gabra Egzi'abehēr, was consecrated bishop of Adulis and sent by the Propaganda to evangelize the peoples on the northern periphery of the Ethiopian State who were undergoing a process of paganization or Islamization.[3] It was to be a mission in which the Lazarists achieved notable success in the 1860s and 1870s. However, conditions at the end of the eighteenth century were exceedingly unsettled. Although he enjoyed some support from Ethiopian notables, Fr. Tobias was forced to spend most of his time from 1790 to 1797 in a monastery near Adwā, or wandering insecurely.[4] The consecration of an autochthon was the first clear foreshadowing of the conviction of Bishop Justin de Jacobis that the Ethiopian clergy were the proper point of departure for a missionary strategy. On the other hand,

---

[1] APF, *Scritture Riferite nei Congressi. Etiopia, Arabia . . .*, iii. 365–6; Fr. Remedius, 'Relatio Itineris in Æthiopiam', 15 Dec. 1756.

[2] APF, *SRC.AC*, iii. 374; Fr. Remedius, 'Brevis Relatio Status Æthiopie', 13 Jan. 1757.

[3] C. Beccari, *Rerum Aethiopicarum Scriptores Occidentales Inediti a Saeculo XVI ad XIX* (Rome, 1914), xiv. 416–17. See also M. Pacelli, *Viaggi in Etiopia del P. Michelangelo da Tricarico Minore Osservante Ne'quali si descrivono le cose più rimarchevoli ed osservabili incontrate in quella Regione sulle orme del Ludolf, De La Croix, ed altri Celebri Scrittori di quei luoghi* (Naples, 1797).

[4] See the principal published account by Fr. Tobias in Beccari, *Rerum*, xiv. 466–71; Fr. Tobias to Prop. Fide, Nagade, 23 July 1797. The Coptic Patriarch forewarned the Ethiopians of Tobias's identity and enjoined them to punish and expel him: C. Conti Rossini, *Documenta ad Illustrandam Historiam. 1. Liber Axumae* (Paris, 1909), 99–102.

whether through indolence or force of circumstance, Fr. Tobias singularly failed to produce results.[1] And the experiment was not repeated.

Protestant Precedents

Despite the long history of Catholic activity, pride of place in the nineteenth century was to go to the Protestants. Hitherto, the involvement of the Reformation Churches had been slight. Their first hundred years were marked by little missionary or ecumenical activity; even Constantinople was remote.[2] The first Protestant contact with Ethiopia came out of a growing interest in the eastern Churches and coincided precisely with the Jesuit expulsion.

Peter Heyling, a German Lutheran from Lübec, was the pioneer.[3] Making his way to Cairo, in 1633 he joined the party of the Orthodox bishop who was being sent to Ethiopia. At Suakin he had an encounter with the banished Catholic Patriarch Mendes, typical in its brevity and hostility of most such meetings in the period covered by this study. From his entrance into Ethiopia, however, Heyling's activities are shrouded in mystery and even his ultimate fate is uncertain. There is no evidence that he made any impact as a missionary, nor is there anything to suggest continuity with subsequent Protestant involvement.[4]

Far more important in capturing the interest of Reformation Europe were the scholarship of Ludolf and the activity of Bruce. Through contact with an emigrant Ethiopian, Ludolf in the mid-seventeenth century produced linguistic and historical studies of

[1] See Pacelli, *Viaggi in Etiopia*, and Beccari, *Rerum*, 434 f.; Fr. Michelangelo to Prop. Fide, Mocha, 30 Sept. 1789. Within twenty years even the memory of Fr. Tobias's presence had become distorted: N. Pearce, *The Life and Adventures of Nathaniel Pearce, Written by Himself, during a Residence in Abyssinia, from the years 1810 to 1819* ... (London, 2 vols., 1831), ii. 148–9. For the approach of Bishop de Jacobis, see below, Chapter IV.

[2] S. Runciman, *The Great Church in Captivity* (Cambridge: C.U.P., 1968), 238–320.

[3] Ludolf, *A New History of Ethiopia*, Book III, Chap. XIV; J. H. Michaelis, *Sonderbarer Lebens-Lauff Herrn Peter Heylings, aus Lübec, und dessen Reise nach Ethiopien: nebst Zulänglichen Berichte von der in selbigen Reiche zu Anfange des nächts-verwichenen Saeculi entstandenen Religions-Unruhe* ... (Halle, 1724). Michaelis is partially dependent upon Ludolf. See also O. F. A. Meinardus, 'Peter Heyling, History and Legend', *Ostkirchliche Studien*, cxli (1965), 305–26.

[4] Coulbeaux (*Histoire politique et religieuse*, ii. 250–2) believes that Heyling is remembered in the internal doctrinal disputes of the Ethiopian Church, but this is unlikely. See also W. Rüppell, *Reise in Abyssinien* (Frankfurt am Main, 1840), ii. 188, footnote, for a more cautious speculation on similar lines.

lasting worth.[1] It was probably through his account of the Jesuit activity that Protestants first became familiar with it. Still, Ethiopia remained a distant land for over a hundred years[2] until Bruce forcefully brought it back to attention. His primary impact, however, was that of a controversialist. His account was not published until 1790, and its reliability not established until yet later, by which time Protestant Europe had already begun its involvement. Nevertheless it was on Bruce that the first agent of the Church Missionary Society, Samuel Gobat, based his introduction to the country.[3]

Modern Evangelical involvement properly begins with the activities of Lord Valentia in the Red Sea in 1804–5; and, thus, from the beginning was connected with secular expansionism. Concerned at Napoleonic activities in Egypt, and convinced of the strategic and commercial value of the Red Sea area, Valentia sought contact with Gondar. Henry Salt was sent on a mission of friendship into the country, but he got no further than the court of Rās Walda Sellāsē of Tegrē.[4] British interest, however, was sufficiently stimulated for the Government to repeat Salt's errand in 1809.[5] Once more he failed to penetrate beyond the northern provinces. Nothing of political or diplomatic importance emerged, but the attention of the British and Foreign Bible Society had been caught and Valentia became president of its Abyssinian sub-committee. When Salt returned to Britain in 1810 he too joined the Society which then set about finding a text of the Holy Scriptures to be printed in Ge'ez.[6] Only a Psalter proved obtainable. Copies were printed and distribution was arranged through Salt's friend Pearce who had remained in Tegrē.[7] The religious preconceptions which underlay

[1] E. Ullendorff, *The Ethiopians. An Introduction to Country and People* (London: O.U.P., 1960), 9–11.

[2] David Mathew has pointed out the fanciful image held by eighteenth-century Britain as revealed in the *Rasselas* of Dr. Samuel Johnson: *Ethiopia. The Study of a Polity 1540–1935* (London, 1947), 103–4.

[3] In preference to the Jesuits, Poncet and Ludolf. Basel Mission Archives, B.V. 31; Gobat to Blumhardt, London, 20 Aug. 1825.

[4] G. Annesley, *Voyages and Travels to India, Ceylon, the Red Sea, Abyssinia, and Egypt, in the Years 1802, 1803, 1804, 1805, and 1806* (London, 3 vols., 1809), iii. See also I. E. Marston, *Britain's Imperial Role in the Red Sea Area, 1800–1878* (Hamden, Conn., 1961).

[5] Salt, *Voyage*; Mathew, *Study of a Polity*, Chap. XVI.

[6] J. J. Halls, *The Life and Correspondence of Henry Salt, Esq., F.R.S., etc. His Britannic Majesty's Late Consul General in Egypt* (London, 2 vols., 1834), i. 321–3; Salt to Murray, 17 Mar. 1812. There is a close connection with Bruce as Murray, Salt's correspondent, was the editor of the second edition of Bruce's *Travels* (1805). [7] Halls, op. cit. i. 444, 479–80.

the Bible Society's activities are implicit in the sombre picture which
Salt painted of the Ethiopian Church. Although it was basically
orthodox and had not lost all vestiges of genuine piety, nevertheless,
he commented,

At the present moment, . . . the nation, with its religion, is fast verging to
ruin; the Galla and Mussulmaun tribes around are daily becoming more
powerful; and there is reason to fear that, in a short time, the very name of
Christ may be lost among them.[1]

Meanwhile, another, more substantial, move was underway to
connect Ethiopia and Protestant Europe. A leading interest of the
recently founded Church Missionary Society was the Orthodox
world. To this end the Revd. William Jowett was stationed at
Malta with a commission to study the condition of 'religion on the
shores of the Mediterranean' and to recommend a strategy for 'pro-
pagating Christian Knowledge'.[2] The CMS had two objectives: the
reawakening of the Eastern Churches *per se*; and through their
revitalization the conversion of the neighbouring Muslims and
'Heathens'.[3] Proselytism of eastern Christians was not considered
desirable.

Although Jowett's only contact with Ethiopians was in Egypt, he
managed to collect considerable information and the much-sought
Amharic translation of the Scriptures.[4] From 1825 the CMS in the
Mediterranean concentrated on the Coptic Church and its daughter.
In many ways their Ethiopian mission was remarkably well prepared, beginning, as it did, with the Scriptures printed in the vernacular. None the less, there were inadequacies. Not a great deal was
known of the Jesuits, and Jowett's judgement on their mission was
shallow and naïve:

Had the Portuguese Missionaries, instead of attempting to torture the
Abyssinians into Popery, presented them with the Holy Scriptures in their
vernacular languages, may we not justly entertain the belief, that Chris-

[1] Annesley, *Voyages and Travels*, iii. 256.
[2] E. Stock, *The History of the Church Missionary Society. Its Environment, its
Men and its Work* (London, 4 vols., 1899–1916), i. 224.
[3] Ibid. See also *The Missionary Career of Dr. Krapf, Missionary of the Church
Missionary Society in Abyssinia and East Africa, and Pioneer of Central African
Exploration*, 5; reprinted from the *Church Missionary Intelligencer* of Feb. and
Mar. 1882.
[4] Wm. Jowett, *Christian Researches in the Mediterranean, from MDCCCXV to
MDCCCXX in Furtherance of the Objects of the Church Missionary Society . . .*
(London, 1822), 198–203. See also Ullendorff, *Ethiopia and the Bible*, 62 ff.

tianity would, long ere this, have penetrated, by the way of Abyssinia, into the very heart of Africa?[1]

Nor was there much reliable information, despite Salt and Pearce, on recent developments.

It was on religious questions that preparation was weakest. Bruce had merely confirmed Protestant anticlericalism. Although Jowett rightly stressed that respect for the Ethiopian ecclesiastics was a *sine qua non* of success, his view that 'they could demolish him [the Protestant missionary] by a single anathema',[2] owed more to Reformation propaganda than to an analysis of reality. As for indigenous doctrinal controversies, a recent pastoral letter of the Alexandrian Patriarch had been obtained.[3] Some of the issues were thus known, but the context was misleading, for the authority of the Patriarch was then slight in Ethiopia. On the practical side, the CMS had yet to accumulate a fund of experience on the eastern churches. Its missionaries in Ethiopia were real pioneers.

Despite his excessive gloominess, Salt had struck the proper note. Ethiopia was in a state of profound crisis. Institutional disintegration had reduced the country to a congeries of warring princedoms. National crisis was at once an opportunity for, and threat to, successful missionary enterprise.

[1] Jowett, op. cit. 228. See also R. Slade, *English-speaking Missions in the Congo Independent State (1878–1908)* (Brussels, 1959), 12–13 ff., for a similar judgement by Protestants of earlier Catholic work.

[2] Op. cit. 219.

[3] Ibid. 180–95. This document had been given by *Rās* Walda Sellāsē to Salt, who, in turn, gave it to the British and Foreign Bible Society: Salt, *Voyage*, 364–5; Halls, *Life and Correspondence*, i. 321–3, 334–5.

CHAPTER II

Doctrines and Divisions

THE second quarter of the nineteenth century saw deep divisions within Christian Ethiopia. Politically, all semblance of unity had disappeared; even the coherence of a 'geographical expression' was lost. National institutions had crumbled, to be replaced by conflicts of the provincial nobility. Three areas had emerged with particular prominence: the northern territories inhabited by the Tegreññā speakers; Bagēmder (the districts north and east of Lake Ṭānā); and Shawā (the mountainous regions of Manz and Marhabētē, extending down towards Dabra Berhān, and Bulgā). In the latter two, dynasties had arisen which imparted stability to the state structure; in the first, the prize was fought for anew on the death of each major prince. Elsewhere, Gojjām and Wallo were important. The former ambitious, but regularly the prey of Bagēmder domination; the latter separatist through its linguistic (Gāllā) and religious (Muslim) peculiarities. Finally the fringes of the Amharic-speaking areas in Semēn and Qwārā occasionally rose to brief prominence. Of the old imperial structure there remained only a name and a memory.[1]

The Church too was in a state of perilous fragmentation. No single authority was recognized throughout the old national territory. The Patriarch of Alexandria, who had never enjoyed an active influence, saw his missives rejected out of hand. The bishops whom he sent were abused and isolated. The monastic orders were at loggerheads and internally divided. Even the ancient faith stemming from the Syrian-Alexandrian tradition had been *de facto* repudiated by the most influential of the indigenous clergy. It has been suggested that the Church was 'the great unifying agent' during this period.[2] Occasionally, one even meets with the idea that it provided the

[1] A good survey of the period is M. Abir, *Ethiopia. The Era of the Princes. The Challenge of Islam and the Re-unification of the Christian Empire 1769–1855* (London: Longmans, 1968).

[2] Ullendorff, *The Ethiopians*, 82–3. See also Mathew, *Ethiopia. The Study of a Polity*, 106–7; and Taddesse Tamrat, 'Persecution and Religious Controversies', in Sergew Hable Sellassie (ed.), *The Church of Ethiopia. A Panorama of History and Spiritual Life* (Addis Ababa: The Ethiopian Orthodox Church, 1970), 29–30.

impetus to national renewal and reunification along the lines of the Greek Church slightly earlier.[1] The former view is misleading, the latter false. While Orthodox Christianity was a vital component of such national identity as existed, no organization corresponded to this community of feeling. The apostolic faith survived in a common liturgy, and yet more strongly as a folk religion. But the national Church, in any structural sense meaningful to a westerner or Greek, had virtually ceased to exist. How had this situation come about?

The Classical Position

The development of indigenous Christianity reached its peak in the reign of Aṣē Zarʿa Yāʿqob (1434–68). Doctrinally the Church reaffirmed its Alexandrian basis. Its teaching was the 'monophysite' faith of the minority party at Chalcedon. Led by the Patriarchs of Syria and Alexandria, this school opposed the western formula of two natures and one person in Christ. To the easterners, this distinction rested on entirely inadequate philosophical grounds. To reach the same essential faith received from the three earlier ecumenical councils, the minority group denied the *continuing* distinction between the Divine and human natures in Christ. They held, rather, that Christ was *from* two natures which effected a perfect *union* (= Geʿez, *Tawāhedo*).[2] They held that only one nature continued, a unique Divine-Human one. They did not necessarily, as is so often alleged, absorb the human into the Divine.[3] Thus, while their position was not far from the one established at Chalcedon, it was distinct. This faith was not significantly challenged in Ethiopia until the arrival of Catholic missionaries in the mid-sixteenth century.

[1] C. A. Frazee, *The Orthodox Church and Independent Greece 1821–1852* (Cambridge: C.U.P., 1969), Chap. III.

[2] I. Guidi, *Vocabolario Amarico-Italiano* (Rome: Istituto per l'Oriente, 1953), 553 (*wahada).

[3] In addition to the references in Chap. I, p. 6, footnote 1, see also A. F. Matthew, *The Teaching of the Abyssinian Church as set forth by the Doctors of the Same* (London, 1936); T. Poladian, *The Doctrinal Position of the Monophysite Churches* (Addis Ababa, 1963), 11, 14–15; Aymro Wondmagegnehu and J. Motovu (eds.), *The Ethiopian Orthodox Church* (Addis Ababa: Ethiopian Orthodox Mission, 1970), 95–100; V. C. Samuel, 'The Faith of the Church', in Sergew H. Sellassie, *Church of Ethiopia*, 43–54; and the Statement of Faith made at his investiture by His Holiness *Abuna* Tēwoflos, *Ethiopian Herald*, 11 May 1971. An important, and highly controversial, Catholic statement is put forward by Mario da Abiy-Addiʿ (Ayyala Takla Hāymānot), *La Dottrina della Chiesa Etiopica Dissidente sull'Unione Ipostatica* (Rome: Pont. Istitutum Orientalium Studiorum, 1956).

Although the reign of Zarʿa Yāʿqob had reaffirmed doctrinal ties with Alexandria, it also saw the definitive establishment of customs distinct from those of the mother church. This was particularly so with observation of the Sabbath. A custom known to the early Church,[1] it had never, till the fifteenth century, been universally accepted in Ethiopia. The authority of the Coptic bishops had hitherto prevented this. However, the religious statesmanship of Zarʿa Yāʿqob succeeded in reconciling the opposing factions and making the practice normal.[2]

Institutionally, his reign was no less important. Both the monastic orders and the episcopacy were brought under state domination and drawn into its structure. Two loose schools had emerged from the great monastic revival of the thirteenth and fourteenth centuries: that of Takla Hāymānot, centring round the monastery of Dabra Libānos in Shawā, enjoying great prestige throughout the area settled by the Amharic speakers; and that of Ēwosṭātēwos (Eustathius), originally a northern foundation, but subsequently also important in Gojjām.[3] In general, the former followed a strict Alexandrian line in both doctrine and practice; while the latter was much more radical and innovating. It was especially associated with observance of the Sabbath. In its early days, the monastic tradition had been extremely loose, resting more on charisma than discipline. Sharp clashes with the State occurred, most notably in the reign of Amda Ṣeyon (1314–44).[4] Royal patronage, however, converted a radical movement of hermits into a conservative establishment through lavish land grants. The acceptance of Sabbath observation was a decisive concession to the followers of Ēwosṭātēwos. Hereafter, both the bishops, whose authority was greatly rivalled by that of the monastic orders, and the monks themselves, were brought under very strong state influence. The decline of the State, and the rise of Christological controversies, destroyed for ever this classical settlement.

One final area is worthy of note: the life of the secular priests and the parishes under their leadership. By the medieval period, again, a lasting arrangement seems to have been reached. As in other peasant societies, the Church had established itself over a tenacious sub-

[1] E. Hammerschmidt, *Äthiopien. Christliches Reich zwischen Gestern und Morgen* (Wiesbaden: Harrassowitz, 1967), 132–3.

[2] Taddesse Tamrat, 'Church and State in Ethiopia', 431 ff.

[3] Ibid., Chaps. IV and V *passim*.

[4] Ibid. 222–6; and G. W. B. Huntingford, *The Glorious Victories of ʿAmda Ṣeyon King of Ethiopia* (Oxford: Clarendon Press, 1965), 5–8.

stratum of pagan beliefs, superstitions, and practices, the tendency of which was to assimilate the new religion into the old framework. The strong assaults launched by Zar'a Yā'qob on paganism revealed how thinly the Christian veneer had been spread in many places.[1] The saints of the Church partially replaced the numerous spirits with which the world had hitherto been populated.[2] Practice, too, was affected. Despite persistent attempts at reform, the Church was forced to admit failure. Social life, and above all marriage, remained beyond its control. Lightly disguised polygamy persisted amongst the upper classes, while peasant marital life was characterized by extreme laxity and impermanence. The principal ecclesiastical weapon was excommunication, withdrawal of the sacraments. It was ineffective and led to an unusual *modus vivendi*: the permanent excommunication of the bulk of the adult population.[3] Religious fervour, however, was not diminished. Infants and the aged communicated, while the remainder of the population channelled its devotion into fasting, which finally reached almost the status of a sacrament. Hence the very great importance of this practice in Ethiopia. Again, the observance of the Sabbath and other feast days fulfilled a similar surrogate function. Thus, through its schedule of feasts and fasts, the Church moulded the cycle of life throughout the Christian highlands. Through feast days, the saints and the Blessed Virgin became real; through fasts, atonement and repentance were expressed.

The clergy, too, were imbedded in popular society. Their life was indistinguishable from that of their parishioners. Only their marital habits were exceptional. The priest was expected to have but one wife. His children were married to the offspring of other clergy. Sons were expected to adopt the vocation of their fathers. Little formal training existed for the secular clergy: a primitive knowledge of reading, which was often, in fact, rote.[4] A wealthier parish might support one or two teachers. For the rest, a boy would have to

[1] Taddesse Tamrat, op. cit. 493–507.

[2] D. N. Levine, *Wax & Gold. Tradition and Innovation in Ethiopian Culture* (Chicago: University of Chicago Press, 1965), 67–71.

[3] Note here the extraordinary parallel with the Anglican Church of Buganda. J. V. Taylor, *The Growth of the Church in Buganda* (London: SCM Press, 1958), 182: 'A church in which the majority of adult members are permanently excommunicated is a monstrosity. . . .'

[4] See Haile Gabriel Dagne, 'The Ethiopian Orthodox Church School System', in Sergew H. Sellassie (ed.), *Church of Ethiopia*, 81–97. Compare the Greek Church following the war of independence. Possibly 1 per cent of priests had minimal literacy. Frazee, *Orthodox Church and Independent Greece*, 101.

travel to a monastic centre. Examination for ordination was extremely perfunctory; inevitably so with a rudimentary episcopacy and rugged terrain. No institutions existed for a continuing supervision of the clergy. If a priest lapsed from the expected morality, it was often his own people who barred him, not his superiors. He was then, a peasant amongst peasants. Learning was confined to the monasteries and the schools of Gondar.[1]

Economically the Church was in an ambivalent position. Individual monasteries and churches were often very rich, but they were largely independent of the hierarchy. The bishop held fiefs in several parts of the country, received ordination and consecration fees, and certain special levies.[2] But he never acquired sufficient wealth for action independent of the secular powers. The parishes had little. Some lands were set aside for the physical support of the church: candles, incense, thatching, might be bought with the proceeds. Few priests were salaried or enjoyed much support, outside the major churches in Gondar and Aksum, or places of royal benefaction. These churches were basically assimilated to the monastic pattern. In the majority of parishes, however, the clergy either inherited land in their capacity as peasants, or had special lands set aside for them. This was a small privilege for the number of clergy fluctuated according to the availability of land in the lay and clerical sections. Thus, structurally the Church was weak. Its roots lay in the parishes and the hierarchy enjoyed little control over them. Nationally, it flowered in the court, and under royal patronage. As the court weakened, the regional nobility replaced it. The parishes continued unaffected.

Controversial Origins

The Jesuit missionaries played a decisive role in shattering the classical, national pattern.[3] Their arrival in 1555-7 saw Ethiopia emerging from one crisis into another. The *Jihad* of Ahmad Grāñ had shaken the old order to its foundations by loosening the adherence of many Christians and by strengthening the provincial nobility. Restoration was made extremely difficult by the sudden emergence of the Gāllā peoples whose migrations over the next half-century were to roll back the frontiers of the state and drain its energies and resources in ceaseless conflict. The Jesuits did not enjoy

[1] Levine, *Wax & Gold*, 21–8.
[2] A. Pollera, *Lo Stato Etiopico e La Sua Chiesa* (Rome, 1926), Chap. XV.
[3] See above, Chap. I, p. 6, footnote 2.

PLATE I

a. King, abbot, and bishop. Detail from a canvas mural in the Māryām Church, Darasgē

b. The *Eçhagē Bēt*, Gondar

much influence until the early seventeenth century when a succession crisis raised them to national prominence. Since the death of *Aṣē* Galāwdēwos in 1559 the power and prestige of the monarchy had declined drastically through the reigns of Minās and Sarṣa Dengel.[1] By the death of the latter in 1596 the nobility had gained administrative and military control of their provinces, and the succeeding decade saw a prolonged attempt by them to entrench their position through a permanent weakening of the monarchy. Several puppets were put forward. The immediate struggle was resolved only by the emergence of the strong-man Susenyos in 1607. To escape from the clutches of the aristocratic cabal, the kings Zadengel (1603–4) and Ya'qob (1596–1603; 1604–7) had turned to the Jesuit missionary Paez. Armed intervention from Portuguese India, and constitutional advice along contemporary European absolutist lines, were the principal contributions anticipated. Their tentative beginnings were rigorously followed by Susenyos.

The cure, however, was worse than the disease. Catholicism was adopted without external military assistance, and served only further to discredit the monarchy and strengthen the disparate forces in opposition to it by giving them the ideological unity of fighting for the restoration of Alexandrian Orthodoxy. A period of intense violence ensued, culminating in the political defeat of Susenyos in 1632. But return to the medieval model, however avidly pursued, proved impossible. A general desire for peace, and revived nationalism sustained the State for only seventy years. On the death of Iyyāsu the Great in 1706 it began its long decline into disintegration. The monarchy had regained only a partial prestige by embracing the restoration of Orthodoxy. No lasting contribution had been made to resolving structural problems, and the nobility, with its provincial bases, remained a centrifugal force. Moreover, Jesuit influence survived in a legacy of Christological controversy.

The doctrinal debates of the seventeenth to nineteenth centuries have long been known and discussed.[2] Although no wholly satis-

---

[1] A fundamental reassessment of the political history of this period is contained in Merid Wolde Aregay, *Southern Ethiopia and the Christian Kingdom*, Chaps. III and IV. For the reign of Susenyos see ibid., Chap. VI.

[2] The best account remains I. Guidi, 'La Chiesa Abissina', *Oriente Moderno*, ii (1922–3), 123–8, 186–90, 252–6. The most comprehensive review of the evidence is contained in Mario da Abiy-Addi, *La Dottrina*. Pollera, *Lo Stato Etiopico*, while a useful compendium, has few original contributions. Its introductory value has largely been superseded by Hammerschmidt, *Äthiopien*.

factory account exists, the basic pattern seems simple: reaction to Catholic teaching was diverse, some Ethiopian scholars adopting modifications of received *Tawāhedo* doctrine which were a distinct move towards the western position. One of these new schools succeeded in establishing itself. A long period of resistance by traditionalists was followed by the rise of a second 'heresy' which claimed the larger portion of those who had remained faithful to Alexandrian teaching. By the early nineteenth century, adherence to received Orthodoxy was confined to a small party clustering around the discredited bishops. Moreover, the various doctrinal heresies rapidly assumed a regional character and came into intimate dialectical relations with the forces pulling the country apart. A solution was not reached until the forceful restoration of monophysite Orthodoxy by Tēwodros in 1854, subsequently confirmed by Yohannes IV in the Council of Boru Mēdā (1878).

Unction and Union

The emergence of the Christological controversies can be dated with some precision to 1620–2, the period immediately preceding Susenyos's reception into the Catholic Church, but following his attempts to impose western teaching.[1] Faced with the strong Jesuit challenge, and armed only with scattered writings of the Fathers, the Ethiopians were hard pressed. A number of solid defences of tradition were produced,[2] but many were thrown into confusion, and despite a firm determination to remain Alexandrian continually produced new formulations often moving in the direction of Catholicism. Amongst these 'heresies', from a monophysite standpoint, was the remarkably persistent *Qebāt*.[3] From its origins this doctrine was particularly associated with the Ēwostātian monks in Gojjām. That province, under the rule of the Catholic zealot, *Rās* Sela Krestos, saw very intensive Jesuit activity. With their daring ten-

---

[1] E. Cerulli, *Scritti Teologici Etiopici dei Secoli XVI–XVII*. ii. *La Storia dei Quattro Concili ed altri opuscoli monofisiti* (Città del Vaticano: Biblioteca Apostolica Vaticana, 1960), xiii–xiv, 164, 179–86; Mario da Abiy-Addi', *La Dottrina*, 96–7, referring to Paez and Mendez; Guidi, 'Uno squarcio di storia ecclesiastica di Abissinia', *Bessarione*, viii (1900), 11–13; Tellez, *Travels*, 242, for a slightly later date. Although Christological issues had played a small part in the medieval controversies, they had appeared in Ethiopia before the seventeenth century. No continuity can at present be established with the earlier period, however.

[2] Both volumes of Cerulli's *Scritti Teologici Etiopici* consist of works whose concern is the refutation of western teaching as presented by the Jesuits.

[3] Guidi, *Vocabolario*, 273–4: (*qabā*).

dencies the Ēwosṭātians may have been prone to the cogency with which the missionaries pressed their doctrine. Yet fervent adherence to observance of the Sabbath made them most resistant to Latin Christianity. From the mid-sixteenth century, the Jesuits seem to have opposed this practice.[1] The followers of Ēwosṭātēwos were caught. They seem to have resolved their difficulty by a partial acceptance of Chalcedonian doctrine and a total rejection of Latin practice. Their developed doctrine of *Qebāt* argued that the two natures of Christ had been fully united by the Unction (= *Qebāt*) of the Holy Spirit, whereby also He had fully assumed His office of Son.[2] Their central proof text was Acts 10: 38: 'You know about Jesus of Nazareth, how God anointed him with the Holy Spirit and with power.' Strict monophysites objected that the new teaching produced a degree of subordination in the persons of the Holy Trinity, and, moreover, tended to open the way for a continuing distinction between the Divine and human natures in Christ.[3] They countered by reaffirming the doctrine of *Tawāhedo* (= Union). There was no need, the Unionists argued, for separate action by the Holy Spirit; the Son Himself, co-eternal with the Father, had, by His act of uniting Divine and human natures, ennobled the flesh received from the Blessed Virgin. Their slogan was: 'The Son Himself the Anointer; the Son Himself Anointed; the Son Himself the Ointment.'[4]

While we may assume that all the followers of Ēwosṭātēwos did

[1] Girmah Beshah, *Union of the Churches*, 72, 85–6; and 107–10 for the so-called 'Confession of Galāwdēwos' which defends this practice, amongst others. The text is also available in E. A. W. Budge, *A History of Ethiopia Nubia & Abyssinia* (London, 1928) (reprinted Oosterhout N.B., The Netherlands: Anthropological Publications, 1966), 353–6.

[2] F. Béguinot, *La Cronaca Abbreviata d'Abissinia Nuova Versione e Commento* (Rome, 1901), 74, 87. This is the best-translated, most complete, version of the general chronicle first published, in a slightly different recension by R. Basset, *Études sur l'histoire d'Éthiopie* (Paris, 1882); for the basic passages in Basset, see pp. 140, 142–3, 160, 172. Yet another, independent Ethiopian account can be found in Guidi, 'Uno Squarcio', 15 ff. See also Paris, Bibliothèque Nationale *Fond Éthiopien-Abbadie*, no. 186; *Hāymānot Lamārqos*. None of these documents was written from an Unctionist standpoint. The only published one, of which I am aware, is I. Guidi, *Annales Regum Iyāsu II et Iyo'as* (Rome, 1912). Through out, I refer to the translations of the published documents. See also Merid Wolde Aregay, *Southern Ethiopia and the Christian Kingdom*, 549–55.

[3] Cerulli, *Scritti Teologici*, ii. 184–6; Guidi, 'Uno Squarcio', 15, n. 7. But see Mario da Abiy-Addi', *La Dottrina*, 112–17; for an interpretation of *Qebāt* as strict monophysitism, and *Tawāhedo* as innovating crypto-Catholicism.

[4] BN, *Éth.-Abb.*, no. 186; folio 1: G. Y. Hailu, 'Un Manoscritto Amarico Sulle Verità della Fede', *Atti del Convegno Internazionale di Studi Etiopici* (Rome: Accademia Nazionale dei Lincei, 1960), 349: Guidi, 'La Chiesa Abissina', 189.

not adopt the new heresy, it seems that most did. Their monasteries in Gojjām remained bastions of the new sect into the twentieth century and their northern relatives formed a base for the doctrine's extension into that region. The bishops were in a weak position, possessing no more power than the court allowed. Thus, defence of tradition was left to the followers of Takla Hāymānot, who, already in the reign of Susenyos, had emerged as the leading champions of the Alexandrian faith. It was but a continuation of their original orientation and persisted well through the seventeenth century. The monks of Dabra Libānos were becoming one of the pillars of the kingdom. Their abbots, the *eçhagēs*, were recognized as the most influential of Ethiopian clerics. Following the Gāllā migrations the mother monastery in Shawā had become sharply isolated and the order's centre moved to Azazo, just south of Gondar, where it took over lands of the expelled Jesuits.

In a series of councils lasting throughout the second half of the seventeenth century the Unctionist-Unionist debate was carried on.[1] Yohannes I (1668–82) encouraged the Gojjāmē sectarians. His son, Iyyāsu the Great (1682–1706), was a firm supporter of the Alexandrian faith and directed much energy and attention to a satisfactory resolution of the problem. He greatly favoured the followers of Takla Hāymānot, yet his power, and with it the last revival of medieval Ethiopia, was constantly being eroded. Conspiracies were common, and the *Qebāt* heretics retained the loyalty of the people of Gojjām. By the early eighteenth century the King was fading in his powers, and a sudden *coup d'état* staged by Gojjāmē notables, assisted by Empress Malakotāwit, resulted first in deposition, then sordid murder.[2] Sectarianism played a crucial role, and its divisive tendencies quickly became apparent. It was not long before a Gondar king openly espoused heresy. Tēwoflos (1708–11), and following him Dāwit III (1716–21), both favoured *Qebāt*. Tēwoflos's action drew fire from the monks of Dabra Libānos: 'Why', they said, 'do you change the faith by means of a proclamation, like an inheritance, or a fief, without a sinod?'; and the King replied: 'It's not because I hate you, but so that Gojjām will be subject to me.'[3] The *eçhagē's*

    [1] In addition to Béguinot, *Abbreviata*, Basset, *Études*, and Guidi, 'Uno Squarcio', see also Guidi, *Annales Iohannis I, Iyāsu I, Bakāffā* (Paris, 1903), 23–5, 41–3, 48–9, 55–6, 61–2, 80–99, 110–16, 121–5, 161–3, 199–200, 214–17.
    [2] Béguinot, *Abbreviata*, 82 f.; Basset, *Études*, 168–9; Bruce, *Travels*, ii. 513; Merid W. Aregay, *Southern Ethiopia and the Christian Kingdom*, 595–9.
    [3] Béguinot, op. cit. 90–1; Basset, op. cit. 176.

party continued to resist, but, though Orthodoxy was still dominant among them, they no longer presented a united front. In 1704/5, shortly before Iyyāsu's death, internal quarrels amongst the Dabra Libānos clergy had resulted in the temporary exile of *Abbā* Niqolāwos, who, since the 1670s, had been the leading champion of received monophysitism. Moreover, violence was brought into play, deeply embittering the controversy. Under Dāwit the orthodox *Tawāhedo* clergy were suppressed by force in Gondar, a number being killed by the Gāllā palace guards.[1] All the elements of decline were manifested in the incident: sectarian quarrels, a Praetorian guard, ethnic rivalries, and regionalism.

Three Births and the Knife

From the ecclesiastical angle the decisive event of the eighteenth century was the rise of a fresh heresy, more radical than *Qebāt*, which won over the last institutional basis of *Tawāhedo*—the Dabra Libānos clergy. The formula of this party was *Yaṣagā Lej* (= Son by Grace).[2] The rise to prominence of this dogma is, for the time being, impossible to date with precision. It seems to have first emerged at the time of Susenyos.[3] During the Unctionist-Unionist debate of the seventeenth century, both parties several times closed ranks to meet challenges from the left,[4] although this specific doctrine does not appear in the documents. The new teaching may have lain behind the internal Dabra Libānos quarrel of 1705. It emerges clearly only in 1763. In a major council at Kāylā Mēdā, Gondar, the two main monastic parties joined forces to reject a doctrinal letter of the Alexandrian Patriarch, and to depose the orthodox *Eçhagē* Hēnok. The victorious slogan was *Yaṣagā Lej*.[5] This council was of the

---

[1] Béguinot, op. cit. 101–2; Basset, op. cit. 187–90; Guidi, 'Uno Squarcio', 19–20; G. Y. Hailu, 'Un Manoscritto Amarico', 351. Basset's chronicle puts the number killed at over 100; Hailu's at a more realistic, but possibly still exaggerated, 24.

[2] J. Baeteman, *Dictionnaire amarigna-français suivi d'un vocabulaire français-amarigna* (Dire Daoua: Imprimerie Saint Lazare, 1929), 1144: (*ṣagā*).

[3] Cerulli, *Scritti Teologici*, ii. 164; Tellez, *Travels*, 242.

[4] For example, Guidi, 'Uno Squarcio', 19.

[5] Guidi, 'Uno Squarcio', 20–2; Guidi, *Annales Regum Iyāsu II*, 208–12. The Iyyāsu II chronicle, as published, contains two separate accounts of this council, from different standpoints, the second being contained in two footnotes on pp. 208 and 210. The patriarchal letter was probably similar to those published by Murad Kamil: 'Letters to Ethiopia from the Coptic Patriarchs, Yoʿannas XVIII (1770–1796) and Morqos VIII (1796–1809)', *Bulletin de la Société d'Archéologie Copte*, viii (1942), 89–143.

greatest moment for after it the bulk of the educated Ethiopian clergy, the only sector of any consequence in the matter, was separated from its traditional *Tawāhedo* faith as received from the see of St. Mark. Not until 1854 was the situation rectified. Yet a new unity was not achieved. *Qebāt* continued alongside *Yaṣagā Lej*, and the two parties were distinctly hostile, both to each other and to the tiny orthodox sect, now known by the derogatory name of *Kārrā* (= Knife).[1] And the politicians soon moved in to exploit the doctrinal situation.

Yaṣagā Lej was a radical heresy. It moved well beyond *Qebāt* towards Chalcedon. Indeed, it may well have moved beyond Chalcedon. Cardinal Massaja, the distinguished Capuchin missionary believed that this new heresy was only a thinly veiled Catholicism. But a more acute observer, the Lazarist Biancheri, saw distinct Adoptionist tendencies within the sect's teaching.[2] He was probably right. *Yaṣagā Lej* as propagated amongst the Dabra Libānos clergy of Azazo (but not, it seems, of the mother monastery in Shawā),[3] taught that Christ had become Son and Redeemer through the Grace of the Holy Spirit. A sharp degree of subordination and separation within the Trinity was thus effected. The radical nature of this sect's teaching was still more clearly seen in its extension to the doctrine of *Sost Ledat* (= Three Births).[4] Christ, it argued, was thrice born: once from the Father from all time; once in the Incarnation in the womb of the Blessed Virgin; once through the subsequent action of the Holy Spirit (either still in the womb, or, yet more radically, in the River Jordan; opinion was divided). Here the

---

[1] Fr. Mario denies at great length, but unsuccessfully, that there were three doctrinal parties: *La Dottrina*, 117–29. See Hailu, 'Un Manoscritto Amarico', 349–51, for a counter-analysis from the *Tawāhedo* school; and Aymro Wondmagegnehu, *The Ethiopian Orthodox Church*, 132–3.

[2] G. Massaja, *I Miei Trentacinque Anni Nell'Alta Etiopia. Memorie Storiche di Fra Guglielmo Massaja* (Rome, 12 vols., 1885–95), i. 116–17: *Annales de la Congrégation de la Mission* (*Lazariste*), xv (1850), 304–6; Biancheri to Sturchi, Rome, 24 Feb. 1850: Hailu, 'Un Manoscritto Amarico', 349, 351, also uses the term Adoptionist.

[3] Hailu's document, 'Un Manoscritto Amarico', stems from *Tawāhedo* circles in Dabra Libānos. Heresy was not established in Shawā until 1841. See below, Chap. III, pp. 50–1.

[4] This slogan does not appear until the nineteenth century in the doctrinal letter of the Alexandrian Patriarch, published in Wm. Jowett, *Christian Researches in the Mediterranean, from MDCCCXV. to MDCCCXX. in Furtherance of the Objects of the Church Missionary Society* (London, 1822), 181–94: and in the subsequent, sympathetic Ge'ez-Amharic commentary on it, BN, *Éth.-Abb.*, no. 186.

tendency towards Adoptionism was clear, and it was only the very open, sympathetic attitude which this sect revealed towards western missionaries (Catholic and Protestant),[1] which could have led Massaja into believing that their doctrine had anything to do with Roman Catholicism.

The bitter divisiveness of these quarrels is very widely documented. Many instances, particularly concerning the bishop, *Abuna* Salāmā (1841–67), will be discussed below. Gojjām remained strongly *Qebāt*. A political power, although declining, throughout the eighteenth century, its opponents readily adopted the other sects. Bagēmder went over to *Yaṣagā Lej*; central Tegrē to *Kārrā*, other parts of the north to *Qebāt*. Shawā remained remote till the 1840s. In 1803 *Rās* Gugsā, of the Yajju dynasty of Bagēmder, joined *Eçhagē* Walda Yonā in expelling the Unctionist clergy from his domain. In reprisal, the *Sost Ledat* were forced out of Gojjām and Tegrē. At the same time outright abuse of the bishops began. On the death of *Abuna* Yosāb, the last to enjoy authority, Gugsā plundered the episcopal property. He turned doctrinal propaganda against his principal rival, *Rās* Walda Sellāsē of Tegrē. In 1809–10 the Englishman Henry Salt reached Tegrē in an attempt to establish contact between England and the (non-existent) central government of Ethiopia. He returned with a letter from Walda Sellāsē which complained:

Hinorai Sawlt did not go to the king, for there is not at present a king orthodox in the Faith; and I have carried on hostilities with him who does not agree with us in the faith, who is called Gougousâ [*sic*]—and he has made a king who is not orthodox in the faith; and therefore I have gone to war with him. . . .

'And my faith is as thy faith. My faith affirms that the *Son* has two nativities. . . . They call me a deserter of the faith, but I have not abandoned my religion. All of them say 'Be as us, and profess a third nativity.'[2]

To the Dabra Libānos Three Births, the other parties opposed two. This has occasioned some confusion.[3] Both *Kārrā* and *Qebāt* argued that the births of Christ were confined to one from the Father from all time, and one in the womb of the Blessed Virgin. The disagreement of these two parties was confined to the role of the

---

[1] See below, Chap. III, pp. 32–3; and Chap. IV, pp. 74–5. But see also pp. 50–1.
[2] Public Record Office, FO I/1, 155–6; Râs Walda Selâssé to George III, n.d. See also Salt, *Voyage to Abyssinia*, 328, 363–5.
[3] See Fr. Mario, *La Dottrina*, 117–29, for a good example.

Holy Spirit in anointing Christ to His mission and in effecting the union of the two natures. The *Kārrā*, holding to the teaching of Alexandria, admitted no distinctions within the Trinity nor any derogation of the Son, and thus repudiated any significant action by the Holy Spirit, thereby gaining their 'Knife' label (either by cutting off the Holy Spirit, or the third birth).

Politically, then, doctrine was exploited. No doubt it also worked the other way, dogmatic differences accelerating the triumph of provincialism. That the clergy were bitterly divided is incontestable. They are known to have refused to take the Sacrament together, although how frequently is uncertain.[1] A church restored in the 1840s saw two altars consecrated, one for each of the heretical parties.[2] A dissident might be refused burial, even if very highly born.[3] The fate of *Abuna* Qērelos (1815–28?) reveals the situation clearly. He arrived after an interregnum of twelve years, yet very quickly fell into doctrinal controversy. His authority was first repudiated in Tegrē, by both Walda Sellāsē and the succeeding Sabagādis. Then in Gondar he was abused and expelled, again for doctrinal reasons.[4] His fate, even the circumstances of his death, are mysterious. Moreover, the traditional tie with Alexandria was also being questioned. Early in the nineteenth century an Armenian impostor seems to have acted as bishop in Shawā, while *Dajjāch* Sabagādis, late in the 1820s, made a brief attempt to contact the Armenian Patriarch for a legitimate bishop.[5]

The situation was perilous. Doctrinally the Church had lapsed into heresy; structurally, it had disintegrated. At the national level no institutions continued to function. The monks were divided into the two contending parties, or fell outside any organization at all. The secular clergy, as we have seen, had never been subject to a developed

---

[1] S. Gobat, *Journal of a Three Years' Residence in Abyssinia in Furtherance of the Objects of the Church Missionary Society* (London, 1834), 342–3.

[2] C. Conti Rossini, 'Nuovi documenti per la storia d'Abissinia nel secolo XIX', *RRAL*, S8, ii (1947), 384.

[3] N. Pearce, *The Life and Adventures of Nathaniel Pearce, Written by Himself, during a Residence in Abyssinia from the years 1810 to 1819* (London, 2 vols., 1831), i. 196–7; ii. 168–9.

[4] C. Conti Rossini, 'La Cronaca Reale Abissina dall' anno 1800 all'anno 1840', *RRAL*, S5, xxv (1916), 891–3; Conti Rossini, 'Nuovi Documenti', 364–5; Pearce, *Adventures*, ii. 66–7; I. Guidi, 'Le liste dei Metropoliti d'Abissinia', *Bessarione*, vi (1899), 13–14.

[5] Abir, *Era of the Princes*, 157: Basel Mission Archives, B. V31; Gobat, Cairo, 2 Jan. 1827; Gobat, Cairo, 29 Jan. 1827. Compare much earlier the presence of a Syrian prelate in Shawā. Taddesse Tamrat, 'Church and State', 130–3.

structure. Between bishop and parish there existed only loose and changing offices, dependent upon the feudal nobility. When the bishop's authority disappeared with that of the royal court, the bulk of the Ethiopian Church was delivered into the hands of the regionalists. In the first half of the nineteenth century the Ethiopian Church was as divided as the State. The restoration of unity came from above, and from without. Unification of the State was the pre-condition for unification of the Church.

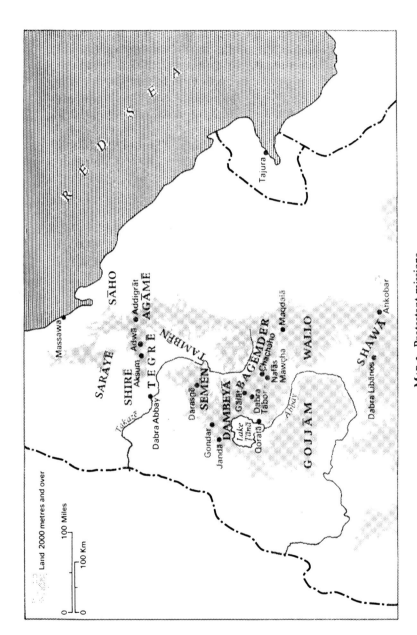

MAP 2. Protestant missions.

CHAPTER III

Dialogue

IN the 1820s a precarious stability prevailed in Ethiopian politics. The Yajju rulers of Bagēmder enjoyed a clear pre-eminence. In the north *Rās* Walda Sellāsē had died in 1816. Confusion reigned for five years until *Dajāzmāch* Sabagādis, a Sāho from Agāmē, succeeded in establishing his rule. He then sought an opening at Massawa to tap the first stirrings of fresh foreign influence in the Red Sea. Salt's visits had made only a slight impact, although two companions Coffin and Pearce stayed on. The first Europeans to establish a firm and continuous link with Ethiopia were the Church Missionary Society agents Gobat and Kugler. They arrived at the court of Sabagādis in February 1830.

In founding its Mediterranean activities the CMS drew heavily on graduates of the Basel Mission training school. The majority received Lutheran orders, although two were ordained in London. In 1825 Samuel Gobat and Christian Kugler were singled out for Ethiopia and received further training at the Society's institute in Islington, then a northern suburb of London. In 1826 they joined their colleagues already established in Egypt and applied themselves to making contact with Ethiopians. Their initial discoveries greatly stimulated missionary fervour; but reports of the disturbed conditions prevailing in the highlands following the death of the Yajju ruler *Rās* Gugsā in 1825 caused them continually to postpone their departure. Moreover, they came quickly to understand that the prince who controlled the north perforce dominated foreign relations. In 1827 they met an embassy from Sabagādis to the English King.[1] It was Ethiopia's first initiative in foreign affairs for many decades, and the missionaries capitalized on it. Kugler accompanied the emissary Coffin to England, while Gobat attended the sickness of one of the Ethiopian delegates who remained in Cairo.[2] The

---

[1] Abir, *Era of the Princes*, 34–5: Basel Mission Archives, B.V39, 27; Kugler to Blumhardt, Alexandria, 30 Oct. 1827: Church Missionary Society Archives, C.M/o46, 8; Kugler to Coates, London, 21 June 1828.

[2] *Samuel Gobat. Bishop of Jerusalem. His Life and Work* (London, 1884), 88–9.

services thus rendered, and the friendships won, proved to be the necessary contact. Late in 1829 Gobat and Kugler left Cairo accompanied by several pilgrims. The following February they were received by Sabagādis in Addigrāt. Modern missions began.

Preliminary strategy was simple: the distribution of vernacular Scriptures and exploration. Kugler was to hold the base in Tegrē while Gobat passed on to Gondar. The latter's approach, as we shall see, was to engage the clergy in religious dialogue, thus creating a relationship of mutual trust and confidence. Only in this way could the CMS hope to achieve its objective of stimulating to renewal without proselytism. Gobat was strikingly successful. However, his colleagues, excepting only Krapf, proved inadequate and their shortcomings destroyed the mission. Initially Gobat and Kugler owed their position to Sabagādis, whose interest arose from the value of the missionaries as agents of his foreign policy. To support his ambitions against the Yajju, he needed fire-arms which could only be obtained with European assistance through Massawa. Moreover, he was interested in foreign skills.[1] Nevertheless, his religious curiosity was quickly roused. His first question to the missionaries concerned their value as artisans.[2] They rather side-stepped and presented their mission in terms of the general welfare of Ethiopia and the propagation of 'useful knowledge'. In theological discussion the missionaries declared for a two-birth definition, at which Sabagādis 'rejoiced exceedingly'. Indeed, they seem quickly to have established a spiritual *rapport*, which led the prince to declare:

I am about to build a new church, & I will give this new church to you without any other condition, but, that you do not marry; . . . if you can comply with this demand, you have then full liberty to teach & to preach in that church according to your wishes.[3]

Although the offer was never put to the test, the friendship expressed in it remained firm until the *dajāzmāch's* death the following year.

Probing

Meanwhile Gobat convinced Sabagādis of his earnest intention to proceed to Gondar. Benefiting from a temporary *rapprochement*

[1] W. Rüppell, *Reise in Abyssinien* (Frankfurt am Main, 1838), i. 339–41: PRO, FO 1/II; 1–2, Suporguadis [*sic*] to George IV, Adwan, 24 Apr. 1827; 112–13, Palmerston to Suporguadis [*sic*], 6 Feb. 1832.

[2] *Der evangelische Heidenbote*, iv (Basel, 1831), 25; Kugler, Quila, 10 Aug. 1830.

[3] CMS, C.M/o28,8; Gobat and Kugler to Coates, Adigrate, 19 Feb. 1830.

between Sabagādis and Webē, *dajāzmāch* of Semēn, he reached his destination on 26 March 1830. Conditions were extremely insecure. The death of Gugsā, and of Webē's father, Hayla Māryām, the following year, had set in motion renewed competition which was to culminate in the Battle of Dabra Abbāy in 1831.[1] Webē held a pivotal position, as the most powerful Amharā subordinate of the Yajju. The day following his entry into Gondar Gobat met this prince who was to determine the fate of missions in Ethiopia for the next twenty-five years.

Webē was eager to entertain Gobat, and favourably impressed the missionary with his religious attitudes:

He is less superstitious, and consequently less under the influence of the priests than Sebagadis; although in all his conduct (in which pride is not predominant) he gives indubitable marks of his fear of God, and of his philanthropy.[2]

It was a fair judgement. Webē proved himself both traditionally pious and resistant to Orthodox opposition to missions. But it was some years before he was sufficiently established to act freely. In the meanwhile Gobat turned to Gondar and the Ethiopian Church.

Security in Gondar depended largely on the sanctity of the *eçhagē*'s quarter as a place of asylum. The *roi fainéant* Gigār was without power or influence. As Gobat described him, '. . . he has neither temporal grandeur, nor spirit, nor heart.'[3] The *eçhagē* was then both the source of Gobat's physical safety and the object of his spiritual concern. The Lenten fast delayed an encounter but, in the interim, he found the clergy friendly (99). When finally they met on 17 April *Eçhagē* Filpos persuaded Gobat of his friendship and concern. Despite the disturbed times a life of dialogue and discussion proved possible and the missionary came to know the *eçhagē* well. Their conversations covered the main points in dispute between the Eastern and Western Churches, and within the Ethiopian Church itself. Gobat felt free to speak with the utmost frankness:

I do not know [he wrote] how far travellers may have reason for saying, that the opinion entertained by the Abyssinians, concerning the Virgin and

---

[1] Conti Rossini, 'La Cronaca Reale Abissina dall'anno 1800 all'anno 1840', *RRAL*, S5, xxv (1916), 900 ff.; 'Nuovi Documenti per la storia d'Abissinia nel secolo XIX' (I), *RRAL*, S8, ii (1947), 370 ff.

[2] CMS, C.M/o28, 113; Gobat's Journal, 25 Feb. 1830–16 Feb. 1833, p. 23.

[3] *Journal of a Three Years' Residence in Abyssinia in Furtherance of the Objects of the Church Missionary Society* (London, 1834), 89–90. Where convenient, references are incorporated into the text.

the saints, cannot be spoken against without risk of danger; but I know that I every day clash with their opinions, and I have not yet seen any one lose his temper with me. The more bluntly I reprove the priests and others, the more those who hear it respect me. . . . (215: see also 64-5, 109-10)

The first extended dialogue was typical. At question were the two Natures of Christ and their relationship. Gobat sought an explanation of received differences which would not place them in irreconcilable positions. Blaming 'the confusion of languages' he turned to essentials: '*Missionary*: "Do you believe Jesus Christ to be perfect God and perfect Man?" *The Etchegua*: "Yes, with all my heart!" *Missionary*: "Well, we are brothers in this respect, although we express ourselves differently." ' And he drew a practical moral: 'As for us, we believe we ought not to anathematize any but those who love not our Lord Jesus Christ' (125-6). The same pattern was constantly repeated, a frank exposition of differences, and the linking of Evangelical convictions to a common body of Christian doctrine.

Gobat's concern with Regeneration and Justification led them to the Incarnation and the role of the Blessed Virgin:

'. . . I conclude [he told the *eçhagé*] that it is a great error to call Mary, "the Mother of God", with all the respect I have for her, the *highly favoured among women*. I think we ought to content ourselves with calling Mary "the Mother of Jesus" as the Apostles did.' The *Etchegua*: 'It is true! it is true! I had already had that thought' (130-1).

Agreement was more a tribute to the spirit of dialogue than to any power of persuasion; but in view of the subsequent difficulties into which the Protestants fell on this very point it was impressive enough. On yet another occasion the two Natures were referred to the Bible with the judgement that as Scripture was silent, and as it was a source of controversy and division, one ought to 'avoid saying "one or two natures" '. The *eçhagé* replied: 'It is impossible for us better to express ourselves. Let this be also our belief' (189-90).

So far as the Ethiopian sectarian controversies were concerned, Gobat lamented that theology had become so fixed on 'inessentials', and the source of such bitter divisions. He deeply regretted that the parties no longer took the Holy Sacrament together (342-3).[1] Although he believed that the *Sagā Lej* was fundamentally at error, none the less he found it the most 'tolerant'; this being perhaps a

[1] For Gobat's discussions of this central point of Ethiopian theology, see his *Journal*, pp. 73-4, 93-5, 169-71, 226-8, 242-3, 249-50, 254-5.

reflection both of its strength in Gondar and its uneasiness in heterodoxy. With it he established his greatest *rapport*. A willingness to engage in dialogue and the refusal to further doctrinal divisions impressed more than clear objections to cherished beliefs and practices. A fellowship of mutual respect and inquiry was thus created.[1] Many of Gobat's points were traditional Reformation claims: that the practices of Confession and Absolution were the source of 'tyrannical authority' for the clergy (204–5); that fasting was a denial of the doctrine of Justification by Faith (52–3, 55–6); that veneration of the Virgin and invocation of saints were unscriptural practices (226–8, 131, 199–201); and that the Scriptures were the sole judge of faith and doctrine. Despite disagreements, Gobat became accepted as an authority (201). Especially appreciated was his reliance upon and knowledge of Scripture (236). Indeed *Eçhagē* Filpos was sufficiently impressed by an exposition of the burning question of Christ's anointing publicly to refer to the missionary for a decision (242).

None the less, acceptance was not unqualified. Filpos was sensitive to the dangers of political imperialism, and too quick an embracing of foreign teaching (208). Wounds inflicted by the Portuguese-Jesuit alliance could still smart. And theological differences were sometimes too great to be bridged. Ethiopian sensitivity was deeply offended by Protestant views on the Blessed Virgin: '. . . when I began to prove to him that she was a sinner,' Gobat recounted, 'he kindled with an indignation which he wished to hide . . .' (227–8).

Gobat also struck up an intimate acquaintance with a young man, Habta Sellāsē, relative of Sāhela Sellāsē, *negus* of Shawā. This friend soon rose in the service of Webē, where he became closely involved with foreign missions. In his humbler station he often discussed doctrine, and was attracted by Gobat's willingness to express ignorance (179–80). Still, even he begged the missionary to restrain his anti-Marian views, lest he make many enemies for himself (132). Habta Sellāsē was much taken by accounts of the work of Evangelical Missions (97–8), and proposed that they evangelize the Gāllā in his native Shawā. This idea had already occurred to Gobat.[2] Especially appealing was the suggestion that '. . . we should

---

[1] But see also A. d'Abbadie, *L'Abyssinie et le roi Théodore* (Paris, 1868), 28–9; G. Lejean, *Théodore II le nouvel empire d'Abyssinie et les intérêts français dans le sud de la Mer Rouge* (Paris, n.d.), 37–8; for unfavourable views of Gobat's technique.

[2] *Missions-Magazin*, xi (Basel, 1826), 471–2.

not have to pull down, before building' (158–9, see also 123 and 195). A plan of action was devised: 'When I shall return to Gondar with a greater number of copies of the Gospel, he will conduct me to Schoa, introduce me to the king, his friend, & then go with me to establish a Mission among the Galla.'[1]

In the meanwhile the missionary was both flattered and appalled to hear that he was being discussed as a possible bishop. Yet it was not without precedent. Various travellers observed an avid desire for a new metropolitan, and several were embarrassed to be received as such.[2] The episcopacy of Qērelos had been turbulent,[3] and, as we have seen, partially discredited the Coptic connection. Thus Gobat's ability to cut through the doctrinal controversies towards reconciliation undoubtedly made him popular (249, 255). Still, one should not take his candidacy for Ethiopian metropolitan too seriously. Ten days before he left Gondar he recorded in his journal:

There is a general cry among the people that I ought to be asked to become their Abuna: but I reply, that a man who fears God, and who keeps his word, cannot be Abuna in Abyssinia, unless the people would submit to a general reform of their religion. . . . The more I speak to them against their superstition and wickedness, the more I gain the respect of every body (259–60).

Bishops of impeccable legitimacy had a difficult enough time. But even more important than popular rejection was the political instability, which, on all sides, compromised ecclesiastical authority. Gobat soon received an object lesson through the downfall of his most weighty friend.

Echagē Filpos was deposed. The rule of *Rās* Māryē, successor to Gugsā as governor of Bagēmder, had been characterized by extreme violence in Dambeyā leading to the plundering of the *echagē*'s quarter. The ecclesiastic responded by excommunicating the prince, who, at the first opportunity, replaced him. On 3 October 1830, *Echagē* Gabra Sellāsē was enthroned.[4] Gobat visited his old friend:

---

[1] CMS, C.M/o28, 9; Gobat to Sister, Gondar, 24 June 1830.

[2] Rüppell, *Reise*: E. Combes and M. Tamisier, *Voyage en Abyssinie, dans le pays des Galla, de Choa et d'Ifat* (Paris, 4 vols., 1838): *Missions-Magazin*, xxii (1837), 378.

[3] Guidi, 'Le Liste dei Metropoliti d'Abissinia', loc. cit. See also above, Chap. II, p. 26.

[4] 'Nuovi Documenti I', 372–3, 375; for Filpos see also the extremely interesting 'Il libro delle leggende e tradizioni abissine dell'ecciaghe Filpos', *RRAL*, S5, xxvi (1917), 699–718, published by Conti Rossini.

... and instead of complimenting him with complaints, as all the rest did, I congratulated him that God had withdrawn him from the situation in which he was before immersed; so wearying, and so dangerous to his soul. ... Since then, he repeats my words to all who come to see him; adding that I am the only man that knows the truth, and speaks in sincerity of heart (260–1).

The eclipse of Filpos was a fitting accompaniment to Gobat's departure. More than anything else, their friendship had convinced the missionary that it was possible to make contact with Ethiopian piety and that sufficient common ground existed for the dialogue to be resumed at the first opportunity. Moreover, it had become obvious how important princely favour was to the success of religious enterprise. Gobat was able to win it; his successors were not.

He left Gondar on 4 October, greatly encouraged: 'If I may judge of Abyssinia from its capital,' he noted in his diary, 'our Mission may expect happy results from its labours . . .' (262). Before his departure the missionary put forward a plan for the reformation of the Orthodox Church.[1] Some of his suggestions were perceptive and far-seeing, others merely reflected Protestant preconceptions. Considering 'the ignorance and corruption of the priests' a root cause of much trouble, he urged more stringent control of ordinands and the establishment of rigorous theological training. Although the condition of the clergy, in fact, had little to do with national decline, it was an apt proposal. So too were his recommendations for the expansion and indigenization of the episcopacy, the spread of popular literacy, and vernacular Scriptures. Less realistic was the abolition of images and the cult of the Virgin. Yet Gobat's suggestions have a facile ring, for both the strength and the weakness of the Ethiopian Church came from its profound embedding in popular culture. Almost a century passed before the implementation of the more reasonable ones. Yet when they came they followed his pattern. First the episcopacy was expanded; then theological education began; finally the Church's superstructure was indigenized. Nevertheless there is still little control of ordinands, and illiteracy remains staggering. Perhaps the pace could have been quickened, although the experience of *Abuna* Salāmā and Tēwodros proved how resistant the Church was to change.

On 17 October Gobat reached Adwā. Three days later he was reunited with Kugler. Meanwhile the time was passed with Sabagādis

[1] *Samuel Gobat*, 129 ff.

who was preparing for his final fatal campaign. They conversed
much and Gobat was deeply moved: '. . . he manifested so much
friendship toward me, that I cannot doubt his sincerity' (266). The
prince paid tribute to the missionary's piety: 'I love you,' he said,

'not because you are a great man, not because you are a white man; but
because you love the Lord whom I wish to love with all my heart. I pray
you to be my brother and to consider me as your brother.' No said I, I will
be your son and you shall be my father. At this he kissed my hand crying
and said: 'I am not worthy to be called your father; but I will be a faithful
brother to you.'[1]

Remarkable in any circumstances, the bond was more striking for
the brevity of their acquaintance. Sabagādis's attitude towards the
mission had been formed by Kugler.

Kugler had not proved adept at dialogue. Early on he spoke
vigorously against the veneration of the Virgin, so shocking the
prince that, 'this single conversation was quite enough for him,
[and] he took good care of avoiding every thing in our conversations which might lead to such like arguments'.[2] Their relationship
had a strong secular dimension. Medical knowledge was in much
demand and the source of considerable prestige.[3] Yet more important
were the skills of Kugler's carpenter companion Aichinger. Convinced
that religious and secular progress were linked, the missionaries had
brought this craftsman, who was quickly employed on a church
near Addigrāt.[4] Kugler wrote: '. . . Aichinger is truly the favourite
of Sebagadis who shows his love and regard for him on every occasion.'[5] Kugler, of course, was not wholly dependent on his cam-
panion. The prince undoubtedly respected the missionary and anticipated benefiting from his presence. The Europeans received full
princely support, notably in housing and food, although they were
not thereby forced into constant attendance at court. A common
enough pattern, it was to be repeated by the Protestants in Shawā
and under Tēwodros.[6] It is noteworthy, however, that in Ethiopia

---

[1] *Church Missionary Record*, iii (1832), 26–7. Cf. *Journal*.

[2] CMS, C.M/046, 24; Kugler's Journal, 25 Feb. 1830–24 Apr. 1830, entry for
11 March.

[3] Ibid. 25 Feb. and 8 Mar. See also Gobat, *Journal*, 149–55, 194.

[4] *Record*, ii (1831), 129; Kugler to Coates, Quila, 10 July 1830. See also C. W.
Isenberg and J. L. Krapf, *Journals of the Rev. Messrs. Isenberg and Krapf . . .
Detailing their Proceedings in the Kingdom of Shoa, and Journeys in Other Parts of
Abyssinia* (London, 1843), 512–13.

[5] CMS, C.M/046, 23; Kugler to Coates, Quila, 2 Oct. 1830.

[6] CMS, C.M/046, 21; Kugler to Coates, Quila (?), 10 July 1830. Other examples

the only successful missions, *qua* missions, were those free of such political dependence: the Catholics and the Falāshā mission.

Kugler's principal preoccupation was the normal, pioneering Evangelical one of language study and translation. Although Amharic and Ge'ez were known to European scholars, this was not the case with Tegreññā and Kugler bent himself to compiling a dictionary and rendering one of the Gospels into the northern vernacular. He also attempted to establish a school, with little success.[1] In October Kugler felt sufficiently established to seek a more permanent centre. Sabagādis was approached with the suggestion of Adwā. The missionary assured him that nothing was wanted but 'his friendship and protection' and 'that we were ready and able to afford the necessary assistance for their improvement in every respect'. Sabagādis, whose pleasure with Aichinger was increased by the information that yet finer work could be expected, readily concurred.[2] Adwā appeared a sensible choice in that it was Tegrē's principal town, providing rich opportunities for contacts both with the clergy and a network of traders. Only experience could reveal it as the very core of Orthodox resistance to foreign religion. Gobat and the Catholic de Jacobis quickly realized this; but clerical hostility merely fed the fervour of Isenberg, upon whom the CMS leadership devolved in 1834. The consequences were disastrous.

Yet the moment appeared propitious. The mission was moving towards acceptance and a still warmer relationship with its protector. Suddenly, threatening news arrived.[3] *Rās* Māryē of Bagēmder had secured an alliance with Webē and was preparing a massive northern campaign. Sabagādis moved on Adwā to meet the threat. Kugler followed, joining Gobat, and together they awaited the outcome.

They had but a brief stay together. On 10 December Kugler suffered a hunting accident which led to his death on the 29th. This in turn provoked the mission's first crisis with the Orthodox establishment. The clergy of Madhānē Ālam Church refused Gobat's request for burial in a consecrated plot, on the grounds that his colleague had neither confessed, nor received absolution (277).

---

are the Plymouth Brethren in Katanga, and Buganda under Mutesa: R. Oliver, *The Missionary Factor in East Africa*, 73 ff.; R. Rotberg, 'Plymouth Brethren and the occupation of Katanga, 1886–1907', *Journal of African History*, v (1964), 285–97.

[1] CMS, C.M/046, 22; Kugler to Coates, Quila, 6 Aug. 1830. Gobat held a low opinion of Kugler's linguistic work; C.M/028, 11.

[2] CMS, C.M/046, 23; 2 Oct. 1830.   [3] Gobat, *Journal*, xiv.

More deeply, this church under its *alaqā*, Kidāna Māryām, was implacably opposed to Protestantism, as the future proved. For the time being the shock of Sabagādis at this shoddy treatment of his friend produced a blast which caused the opposition to crumble:

'What, wretch that you are! [he fulminated with a messenger from the church] you refuse a sepulchre to a stranger, who is a better Christian than all the priests of my country? Do you not know that Kugler was my brother? yes, my son? and you refuse him a sepulchre in the church that I have built?' (282).

However much a personal loss to Gobat, Kugler's death little affected the mission. But the demise of Sabagādis, a few weeks later, did. In the short run, it plunged Tegrē into years of civil war; in the long run it removed Protestantism's best-disposed friend. On 14 February 1831, the Māryē–Webē alliance prevailed having forced the Takazē ford. On the 15th Sabagādis was executed as a reprisal for Māryē who had fallen in the battle.[1] Before he died the prince designated his eldest son Walda Mikā'ēl as successor and enjoined him to 'deal well with his English friends' (289). Nevertheless Gobat was stunned, as he wrote to his parents: '. . . my best friend and second father, Saba Gadis, is no more.'[2]

In the company of Walda Mikā'ēl Gobat fled from the invaders, taking shelter in the Sāho country beyond Addigrāt. The victors advanced to Aksum where Dori, who had succeeded as *rās*, fell ill. The Gāllā withdrew. Dori soon died and the office of *rās* was passed to his young nephew, Ali. Meanwhile in the north Webē had secured Gāllā support for his Tegrē ambitions and set about realizing them. The result was near-chaos as Tegrē resistance fractured before the Amharā onslaught. On the advice of Walda Mikā'ēl, Gobat established himself at Addigrāt in May 1831, but he was unhappy with his position. He missed the fellowship and dialogue of Gondar: '. . . the character of the people [he wrote] appears quite contrary to mine . . .'; and he had no knowledge of Tegreññā.[3] A year later he was visited by the German traveller, Rüppell, who disparaged the missionary's relation with the local people.[4]

---

[1] *Samuel Gobat*, 142. See also *Journal*, 286–91, 298–302; 'Cronaca Reale', 908 ff.; 'Nuovi Documenti I', 375 ff.; and Abir, *Era of the Princes*, 35–6.

[2] Basel Mission Archives, B.V31; Behâte, 25 Feb. 1831: copy at CMS, C.M/028, 13.

[3] Ibid. His Amharic had served him well in Gondar, but was less useful north of the Takazē.

[4] *Reise*, i. 342–4.

PLATE II

b. Samuel Gobat, Bishop of Jerusalem

a. Johann Ludwig Krapf as a young man

Few people came to dialogue and Gobat was forced to busy himself with small tasks (302). His final months, however, were consoled by the companionship of two boys of respectable backgrounds, Hadāra and Kidāna Māryām. The treachery of an old acquaintance of Gobat had tried to exploit their desire for a pilgrimage to Jerusalem to sell them into slavery at Massawa. They escaped and joined the missionary at Addigrāt. They were probably the only Ethiopians fully to adopt Evangelical views under CMS stimulus.[1] It was small refreshment in Gobat's spiritual desert. He sought to return to Europe: for fellowship, medical attention, and the restoration of his impoverished material resources.[2]

By mid-1832 Gobat's protector was in decline. In March and June Webē had advanced on Addigrāt (310–13), where his ascendancy permitted him to pass the rains. On 12 November Walda Mikā'ēl and his brothers capitulated (325). Webē now dominated the north although he did not yet control it. Order was again possible, and Gobat made good his escape. Before departing he again met the prince, who once more proved receptive to a conciliatory approach: 'I thought it my duty', Gobat noted, 'to avoid wounding their feelings; and I endeavoured to tell them what there was positive in religion, rather than contradict them where it was not absolutely necessary' (328). On 12 December 1832, he left Massawa; two months later, he arrived in Cairo. Despite the barrenness of his Tegrē sojourn he consoled himself with Gondar and the conviction '. . . that all the great people of Abyssinia, who know me, consider themselves as my friends' (330).

On reaching London he plotted the mission's development. His approach was orthodox, foreshadowing the general African pattern. A school staffed by lay converts was to be the centre of a 'christian colony' where neophytes might be 'removed from the manifold and almost unsurmountable difficulties to which they would else be exposed every where except in the missionary houses'. He hoped that the community would be self-supporting, through cultivating the land. From the station preachers would go forth 'in the company of such of the natives as would be the best help to them'.[3] Such

---

[1] CMS, C.M/o28, 113; Gobat's journal Feb. 1830–Feb. 1833, 190–3. See also *A Short Biography of the Abyssinian Hadara* (C.M/o28, 34a). They both died very young, and had little effect on the mission's development.

[2] CMS, C.M/o28; 15, Gobat to Jowett, Cairo, 9 Mar. 1833; 16, Gobat to Coates, Cairo, 27 Mar. 1833.

[3] CMS, C.M/o28, 18; Gobat to Coates, *Report on Reasons for Visit to London,*

separatism, of course, was a grave compromise in the search for fellowship with the Orthodox Chuch, and a repudiation of the disavowal of proselytism. Yet with this scheme in mind he returned to Cairo, in August 1834 joining C. W. Isenberg.[1]

Gobat noted a sharp difference of approach with his new colleague; a disagreement which throws further light on the former's methods, and explains much of the latter's subsequent activity. Isenberg believed in an intransigent maintenance of European standards, both secular and religious; while Gobat, despite exclusivist tendencies, advocated identification with indigenous customs. He reported to London:

> I hope Brother Isenberg and myself shall do very well together though we are not quite of the same opinion with respect to our outward manner of living at home and abroad; that is, I think we can better get access into the heart of the Abyssinians and influence them by removing as much as possible, whatever might draw their attention on our outward appearance, for example, eating, clothing, etc. like themselves, which I believe was the practice of our Lord when on earth whilst Brother Isenberg hopes to have more influence upon them by keeping at a distance. I think we may prove both and hope it shall never be a cause of mutual coldness.[2]

The concluding optimism was to receive cruel disillusioning. Strategy was also at issue. Gobat held out for Gondar, Isenberg for Tegrē. Despite the former's experience, and in the face of his objections, the latter prevailed, and they settled at Adwā. Gobat's health collapsed before their arrival, and he had little influence on subsequent developments.[3]

Protestantism in Adwā

Tegrē was again unsettled by the challenge to Webē from a younger son of Sabagādis, Kāsā, Shum of Tambēn. In league with the Yajju Gāllā, the shum held out until Easter 1835, when the prince of Semēn gained a temporary victory. Tegrē demanded his constant presence, but he was already distracted with the wider ambition of

---

n.d. (summer 1833). For the pattern elsewhere see Oliver, Missionary Factor, Chap. II; Ajayi, Christian Missions in Nigeria, Chap. V; Slade, English-Speaking Missions, Chap. III.

[1] H. Gundert, Biography of the Rev. Charles Isenberg Missionary of the Church Missionary Society to Abyssinia and Western India from 1832 to 1864 (London, 1885).

[2] CMS, C.M/o28, 24; Cairo, 15 Oct. 1834.

[3] CMS, C.M/o28; 113, p. 24; 18, para. 4; 30, Gobat to Coates, Benygen, 6 Jan. 1838: Record, viii (1837), 16; Isenberg to Coates, Adowah, 6 Feb. 1836.

supplanting *Rās* Ali. The prospect of peace and security had sharply receded.[1] In June Webē visited Adwā. Isenberg had no conception of the importance of princely support, and it took Gobat's rise from his sick bed, producing collapse, to press home the lesson. The *dajāzmāch* acceded to a request for protection, but neither physical support nor personal affection were forthcoming.

Both hope and discouragement were produced by the discovery that Gobat's Gondar friend, Habta Sellāsē, was now high in the councils of Webē. With the title of *alaqā*, he had jurisdiction over the clergy of Tegrē, an office of potential benefit to the mission. However, Habta Sellāsē's new responsibilities made him much less free to engage in conversation, and he appeared remote. Isenberg was frankly disappointed. Habta Sellāsē had come, he believed, to 'the same superestimation of human traditions as other Abessinian priests'. And his 'fall' was attributed to 'his natural timidity and fear to displease any man'.[2] An extremely unfortunate conclusion was drawn. The case in hand, Isenberg held, demonstrated the futility of 'mere conversational preaching', and thus invalidated the technique of dialogue. What was needed, he claimed, was systematic teaching and preaching, particularly by sermons. Underlying this dogmatism was a deep pessimism at their situation. 'The people's minds', he lamented, 'are closely attached to superstition and ignorance.' Incapable of, and opposed to, conversational *rapport* with the clergy, Isenberg withdrew into linguistic studies.[3] With Gobat incapacitated, the mission turned in on itself.

Tensions developed between the two missionaries.[4] Externally, they became increasingly dependent upon their carpenter Aichinger, who placated the clergy of Madhānē Ālam by his services to them. But they fell out with him, wasting time and energy on fruitless quarrels, and dissipating precious good will. They took some comfort from the progress of their converts Hadāra and Kidāna Māryām, but Isenberg was unable to prevent their zeal from taking unfortunate expression:

Some of our people had disputed with them [he wrote of the priests], and shewn their disgust at the superstition of the Abessinian Church, declaring

---

[1] CMS, C.M/o35; 7, Isenberg to Coates, Massowah, 29 Dec. 1834; 8, ibid., Adowa, 13 June 1835; Combes and Tamisier, *Voyage*, i. 239–40, 264–6.

[2] *Record*, vii (1836), 13; Isenberg to Coates, Adowa, 13 June 1835. Whether Gobat shared this view, as implied by Isenberg, is open to doubt.

[3] Ibid. See also Ullendorff, *Ethiopia and the Bible*, 67–70.

[4] CMS, C.M/o35, 11; Isenberg to Coates, Adowah, 6 Feb. 1836.

their better views of the Gospel doctrine as they had received it from us. This gave offence. [!] Among other things, Kiddane Mariam had called the Abessinian Churches tempels of idols &c.[1]

The clergy protested to Webē, who was unmoved for the time being. Yet the charges against him reflected Isenberg's alienation. The Protestants were accused of '. . . having religious services of our own, ourselves performing baptism, the Lord's supper, marriage, burial; not attending their churches, not observing their fasts, not worshipping Virgin Mary and the Saints . . .'. Nor was the mission strengthened by an appeal to their protector, Webē: '. . . he answered: that in the same manner as they exercised their religious services at their choice, and the Musselmen at theirs, so we should be at liberty to do also as we pleased, because we did nobody any harm.'[2] The final confrontation had been foreshadowed.

In mid-1836 Dr. Wolff, an agent for the London Society for Promoting Christianity Amongst the Jews (which was subsequently to support work in Ethiopia), arrived in Adwā. He brought news of reinforcements, and provided the opportunity for Gobat's departure. The latter had remained only out of a sense of duty, and the fear that his health was unequal to the journey.[3] He left under a cloud. He informed Jowett that there was no news from Ethiopia: 'for we have been doing nothing for its inhabitants . . .', and judged that the mission 'had not yet really begun'.[4] Isenberg, he implied, was largely to blame. This view was reflected by Wolff who had intended a gift for the mission: 'But', he announced, 'as Mr Gobat told me that he entirely disapproved of a Missionary establishment at Adowah . . . I have withdrawn the Donation. . . .'[5]

For a while things were quiet. In September 1836 Webē visited Adwā and Isenberg paid his respects.[6] Progress was reported and the favourable political development that Webē and Kāsā had reconciled their differences and cemented an alliance with dynastic

---

[1] *Record*, viii (1837), 12; Isenberg to Coates, Adowah, 11 July 1836.

[2] Ibid. The terms were remarkably similar to those in which Webē was to defend the Catholic mission, ten years later. See Chap. IV, p. 90.

[3] *Samuel Gobat*, 178; CMS, C.M/o28, 25; Gobat to Jowett, Cairo, 22 Nov. 1836. See also Combes and Tamisier, *Voyage*, iv. 136.

[4] CMS, C.M/o28, 25; and Basel Mission Archives, B.V 31; Gobat to Blumhardt, Cairo, 30 Nov. 1836.

[5] CMS, C.M/o8, 32; Wolff to Jowett, Jiddah, 6 Oct. 1836. See also Basel Mission Archives, loc. cit.

[6] *Record*, ix (1838), 11; Isenberg to Coates, Adowah, 28 Sept. 1836.

marriage.[1] Three months later Blumhardt arrived. He took over the mission's correspondence which became a dreary record of clerical opposition and increasing isolation. They concentrated on language and almost a year after his arrival, Blumhardt wrote that: '. . . we are as yet chiefly confined to the persons belonging to our household, and to those who visit us.'[2] How different was their approach from Gobat's. They had no shortage of visitors, but they were unable, probably unwilling, really to engage with them:

. . . many priests and other people [he wrote] are dayly visiting me, partly in order to enter in disputes or in order to spy out our views in doctrinal points where we differ from them and afterwards to stir up the people against us.[3]

The reaction of the missionaries to clerical hostility was not to attempt reconciliation, but to affirm their conviction of the effectiveness of remaining at a distance: they built a wall round their prospective house.[3]

The only encouragement to the CMS came from Shawā. Webē, although consistent in protection, was growing cooler, while his uneasy ally Kāsā made no response to overtures.[4] However, in September 1836, the mission received from Sāhela Sellāsē an invitation to visit his Kingdom. The *negus*, Isenberg reported, 'particularly mentioned Aichinger as having heard of his skill'.[5] A treatise was drawn up explaining the nature of Evangelical missions, and if, after the receipt of the treatise, the King should still wish them to come, Blumhardt was ready.[6]

Events quickened with the arrival of J. L. Krapf in December 1837. Krapf's trip up from Massawa was attended by unusual difficulties, and the Adwā clergy reacted with alarm at the mission's increase of strength.[7] A month later Webē made his annual incursion into Tegrē. Blumhardt and Isenberg took their colleague to meet

[1] CMS, C.M/o48, 17; Lieder to Coates, Cairo, 22 Apr. 1837, quoting Isenberg. See also A. von Katte, *Reise in Abyssinien im Jahre 1836* (Stuttgart u. Tübingen, 1838), 78–9.

[2] CMS, C.M/o13, 12; Blumhardt to CMS, Adowa, 13 Nov. 1837. See also von Katte, op. cit., for a comment on Isenberg's isolation.

[3] CMS, C.M/o13, 8; Blumhardt to Coates, Adowah, 8 May 1837.

[4] CMS, C.M/o13, 10; Blumhardt to Coates, Adowah, 22 July 1837; 12, ibid.. 13 Nov. 1837.

[5] CMS, C.M/o35, 17; to Coates, Adowah, 3 Oct. 1837.

[6] CMS, C.M/o13, 10. See below, pp. 46 ff., for the follow-up.

[7] CMS, C.M/o18, 42a; Blumhardt to Blumhardt, Adowah, 20 Feb. 1838.

the prince at Aksum. He was well received. However, the mission's enemies also moved to exploit the prince's presence, and two days after his arrival on 7 January 1838 Webē was faced with the excommunication of the two members of his court most favourably disposed to the foreigners, Habta Sellāsē and Takla Giyorgis.[1] It was the beginning of the final confrontation, postponed only by a brief about face. The previous year there had been a heavy clash between Ethiopian and Egyptian troops near Matammā and the highlanders were in deep fear of retaliation for the victory they had achieved.[2] Webē approached the powers. His natural line to Britain was the mission, and on 15 January its members were summoned to court:

> . . . he wished us to write to our Government [Isenberg recounted] saying that he would write himself and send messengers bearing our letters to our country to establish a treaty of friendship between the two nations and to ask for assistance against the Turks.

As a *quid pro quo*: '. . . we urged to him the necessity of his protecting us, which he promised to us in the strongest terms.'[3] Panic, however, was scarcely a substitute for confidence. Moreover, as the Egyptian scare receded, a more pressing concern arose in a fresh challenge to Webē from Kāsā. By the time it had been dealt with the missionaries had lost their last chance. A prolonged campaign kept the *dajāzmāch* from Adwā till the end of February. On his return no further mention was made of the embassy.

In the meanwhile a valuable chance of reconciliation with *Alaqā* Kidāna Māryām was foolishly thrown aside. Through the influence of Habta Sellāsē the *alaqā* initially agreed to open the churches to worship and the administration of the sacraments after the Anglican liturgy. This extraordinary concession was quickly retracted in favour of toleration on the condition of a public acknowledgement of the Ethiopians as Christians, through attendance at and association with the Epiphany celebrations. At first, the missionaries felt obliged to accept, for, as they put it, '. . . we must still consider the Abessinian Church as a Christian body, although in error.' However, their alienation was too profound to permit them to associate with the Orthodox against the local Muslims unless 'we [had] been

---

[1] CMS, C.M/o35, 19; Isenberg to Coates, Cairo, 23 July 1838.
[2] 'Cronaca Reale', 913; Abir, *Era of the Princes*, 100–5; Hill, *Egypt in the Sudan 1820–1881* (London, 1959), 33–4. See also Combes and Tamisier, *Voyage*, iii. 346–7; and CMS, C.M/o35, 17; Isenberg to Coates, Adowah, 3 Oct. 1837.
[3] CMS, C.M/o35, 19; C.M/o18, 42a.

allowed to declare our disapproval of their errors at the same time'. The breach was irreparable.[1]

The CMS mission to the Eastern Churches had eschewed proselytization. Committed to intercourse with the existing structures, they hoped gradually to foster renewal and reform. The policy was attended with extraordinary practical difficulties and required great tact and patience. Repudiation of the invitation to an unequivocal acceptance of indigenous Christianity signified the end of the mission. Expulsion was as irrelevant as inevitable.

On 2 March 1838 two strange Europeans reached Adwā: Arnauld d'Abbadie, a private French traveller; and Fr. Giuseppe Sapeto, the Lazarist priest.[2] Their arrival filled Adwā with rumour and alarm.[3] Webē was suspicious; and on his behalf Takla Giyorgis wrote asking 'what the object of the Franks was in increasing so much in Abessinia'. Isenberg, with consummate tactlessness, expressed disapproval of the Ethiopians' 'ill behaviour' and 'folly'.[4] The Catholics successfully dissociated themselves from the Protestants.[5] Clamour arose for expulsion and there was no shortage of witnesses testifying to the latter's blasphemies.[6]

On 9 March summoned to a council under the local governor, the missionaries received Webē's order of expulsion. The charge 'was brief, comprehending the points of difference of religion which had often been mentioned'. Indignation from Isenberg produced the plausible explanation '. . . that we had been tolerated only, because they and [Webē] had expected us to repent of our heresies and practices; but the time of patience having fruitlessly elapsed, matters had necessarily arrived to this result.'[7]

Ostentatious aloofness produced foreseeable results.[8] The coinci-

[1] CMS, C.M/o18, 42a.

[2] Arnauld d'Abbadie, *Douze ans dans la Haute-Éthiopie (Abyssinie)* (Paris, 1868); G. Sapeto, *Viaggio e Missione*, and *Etiopia. Notizie Raccolto dal Prof. Giuseppe Sapeto. Ordinate e Riassunte dal Comando del Corpo di Stato Maggiore* (Rome, 1890). See also *Voyage en Abyssinie. Communication faite à la Société de Géographie, par M. Antoine D'Abbadie* (Paris, 1839), and below, Chap. IV.

[3] CMS, C.M/o13, 13; Blumhardt to Blumhardt, Jidda, 26 Apr. 1834; d'Abbadie, *Douze ans*, 14–15.   [4] CMS, C.M/o35, 19.

[5] *Douze ans*, 18–19; Sapeto, *Viaggio e Missione*, 103–6.

[6] CMS, C.M/o13, 13. See also Congrégation de la Mission (Paris), *Lettres manuscrites de Mgr. de Jacobis*, ii, no. 161; de Jacobis, Adoua, 2 Dec. 1839.

[7] *Record*, x (1839), 66–7; Isenberg to Coates, Jiddah, 26 Apr. 1838.

[8] J. L. Krapf, *Travels, Researches, and Missionary Labours during an eighteen years' residence in Eastern Africa . . .* (London, 1860), 18–19; d'Abbadie, *Douze ans*, 17–18, 551.

dence of Sapeto's arrival produced that myth that 'Romanist intrigues
. . . ultimately put an end to the Mission'.[1] This fabrication merely
hindered a proper assimilation of the lessons to be learned. On 12
March Isenberg, Blumhardt, and Krapf withdrew.

Shawā and the Gāllā

Repudiation in Tegrē produced a subtle shift in the mission's
objective. The 'heathens' of southern Ethiopia replaced the Orthodox church. Gobat's interest in the Gāllā was shared by Krapf,[2]
and a favourable response having been received from Sāhela Sellāsē,
Isenberg and Krapf set out for Shawā.[3] Chastened by bitter experience
they resolved to cultivate the clergy avoiding all controversy, thus
securing a base for southward penetration. An ominous urgency
arose from the 'need' to forestall Catholic influence. The alleged
intention of d'Abbadie and Sapeto 'to bring Abbessinia over to the
Church of Rome' rendered it 'necessary for us to hasten to that
country to counteract them'.[4] This ulterior motive led to further
disasters.

On 29 May 1839 over a year after their expulsion from Tegrē the
two missionaries entered Shawā. Their relations with Sāhela Sellāsē
were dominated by his interest in European technology. Some four
years earlier Combes and Tamisier had been impressed by the negus's
cultivation of artisans.[5] Following an introductory meeting on 7
June the Shawān made himself clear: 'He wishes to make use of us
as physicians, architects, artists, &c.' Little time was wasted on
religion.[6] Four months produced no quickening of royal interest
in Evangelical Christianity: 'In the King we cannot put our confidence, [wrote Isenberg] for he does not seem to feel the necessity of a
reformation of their Church, and endeavours to preserve all things
in their old state. . . .'[7] Still, curiosity and material interest overcame

---

[1] Stock, History of the CMS, i. 350–3.
[2] Basel Mission Archives, B.V. 110, ii. 2; Krapf to Blumhardt, Cairo, 18 Aug.
1837.
[3] CMS, C.M/035, 21; Isenberg to Coates, Cairo, 20 Dec. 1838.
[4] CMS, C.M/035, 21. His italics.
[5] Voyage, ii. 347–50.
[6] Journals of the Rev. Messrs. Isenberg and Krapf . . . (London, 1843), 62.
Subsequent references are incorporated into the text.
[7] CMS, C.M/035, 33; Isenberg's Journal 13 Oct. 1839 to 1 Sept. 1840, 22–3.
See also Gabra Sellāsē, Chronique du règne de Ménélik II roi des rois d'Ethiopie
(Paris, 2 vols., 1930–1), trans. Tasfā Sellāsē, ed. M. de Coppet, pp. 70–7, for confirmation of the King's traditional piety.

any scruples; and the *negus*'s favourable disposition was a sufficient base, provided the clergy were not antagonized.[1]

Isenberg remained but four months and left to arrange the publication of his linguistic work and other books for the mission's use. His parting was amiable,[2] but preceded by an event greatly to influence subsequent developments. The French traveller Rochet d'Héricourt arrived. Between him and Krapf a serious rivalry developed, and the tenacity with which Krapf pursued it led to compromising political activity. The missionary alleged that the King's interest was captured by a scheme wherein the application of European military discipline would gain him national ascendancy. Rochet, whose ideas these were, would represent them to his government.[3] Whatever the Frenchman's real interests and proposals, he certainly convinced English observers that he harboured these hare-brained ambitions.[4]

On 1 March 1840, Rochet left bearing a letter to Louis Philippe. No written mention was made of any wider intention than friendly intercourse. Nevertheless Krapf took very seriously the Frenchman's talk which foreshadowed the Dakar to Obock schemes hatched fifty years later. He feared the establishment in eastern Africa of an empire rivalling British India, the Shawān King becoming a French puppet. Patience would surely have seen the dissipation of this private project. But Krapf convinced himself of the necessity for counteraction. In his justification altruism and self-interest were happily married:

Knowing that the King of Shoa has some real desire of making some reforms in his country, and being afraid, that the way might be obstructed to all Europeans on account of Mr. Rochet's revolutionary play, I thought I might venture to make use of the friendly sentiments the King entertains towards me, and to rouse up on a prudent manner in his mind the desire of coming in some nearer connexion with the English government, thinking that if he would join in friendship with the English, he might be reduced

[1] CMS, C.M/035, 25; Isenberg to Coates, Angollala, 9 June 1839; Rochet d'Héricourt, *Voyage sur la côte orientale de la Mer Rouge. Dans le pays d'Adel et le royaume de Choa* (Paris, 1841), 141–2.

[2] CMS, C.M./035, 33; 50–1: Rochet, *Voyage*, 148–9. But see below, p. 55, for Harris's view.

[3] CMS, C.M/044, 27; Krapf's Journal, 13 Oct. 1839 to 1 Sept. 1840, 27. See also Rochet, *Voyage*, 314–18: and Ministère des Affaires Etrangères, *Mémoires et documents. Afrique*, xiii. 287; Sāhela Sellāsē to Louis Philippe, n.d.

[4] Krapf is supported by Johnston, *Travels in Southern Abyssinia, Through the Country of Adal to the Kingdom of Shoa* (London, 2 vols., 1844), ii. 318–19. Rochet's own account does not illuminate the question.

from many narrow and selfish ideas, and the plans of Mr. Rochet might be prevented.[1]

It was an imperialist piece of reasoning, and issued in a letter from Sāhela Sellāsē to British India.

The missionary sought support from the consul in Cairo. He used the carrot of British duty to spread civilization and suppress the slave trade, and the stick of increasing French influence. Intervention would bring order to the distracted state of Ethiopia, and radiate out to central Africa the blessings of commerce and civilization. Swift action was required.[2]

Krapf's letter to Cairo resulted in a recommendation from the Foreign Office that the India Government '. . . encourage the Disposition of the King of Shoa to seek a British Connection'.[3] Aden had only recently been secured and the prospect of an extension of influence to the African shore was attractive. The upshot was a lavish embassy under Captain William Cornwallis Harris, as pompous a person as appeared in our period. Krapf was pleased that Indian experience of 'native and uncivilized princes' was brought into play for: 'They know also to teach them consistency, if they change their minds having formed an alliance.'[4]

Meanwhile, however, the mission had enjoyed considerable freedom for religious activities. Its first step was towards the creation of a school. A request to the King for boys met little response (63, 75–6). Clerical visitors grew in number, and from them youths were gradually obtained. Almost a year transpired before a nucleus of three was formed. Great caution was taken not to offend 'in order that these people cannot say with justice that we endeavour to overthrow their order',[5] although Krapf tried a flanking attack on devotion to the saints by lampooning Greek and Roman mythology,

---

[1] CMS, C.M/o44, 14; Krapf to Coates, Ankobar, 4 July 1840. See also E. Ullendorff and C. Beckingham, 'The First Anglo-Ethiopian Treaty', *Journal of Semitic Studies*, ix (1964), 187–200; and the unpublished Ph.D. thesis (London, 1966) of K. Darkwah, 'The Rise of the Kingdom of Shoa 1813–1889', 48–54, for a similar judgement of Krapf's hastiness.

[2] PRO, FO 1/III, 53–6; Krapf to Campbell, Ankobar, 3 July 1840. The CMS tacitly supported Krapf: ibid. 51; Coates to Palmerston, 1 Dec. 1840.

[3] PRO, FO 1/III, 65–6; and Marston, *Britain's Imperial Role in the Red Sea Area*, 128 ff.

[4] India Office, *Bombay Secret Proceedings* (*BSP*), 166, no. 2473; Haines to Bombay, 24 July 1841; containing Krapf to Haines, Ankobar, 8 June 1841. See also ibid. 170, no. 3080; Harris to Bombay, Allia Amba, 19 Dec. 1841; and Krapf to Harris, Ankobar, 21 June 1841.

[5] CMS, C.M/o35, 33; 90–1.

leaving parallels to be drawn by the students.[1] Numbers finally reached ten, but it is impossible to discern any lasting influence made upon them.

A leading preoccupation was southward expansion into pagan territory. Evangelizing the heathen Gāllā, Isenberg believed, was now their *raison d'être*.[2] Contrary to expectation, however, the Ethiopians did not welcome the proposal. Sāhela Sellāsē protested that the Gāllā would never relinquish 'their savage state' and that he had tried, by word and force, without success.[3] Krapf persisted realizing that royal support was essential. Evangelical arguments were buttressed by: '. . . the great advantage arising to the King himself from the christianization of the Gallas, who would then be good subjects to him, considering him a King united to them by the bond of the same faith . . .' (210). Forced conversions as practised by the Shawāns were simply, Krapf believed, a reflection of the low spiritual state of the Ethiopian Church; and he came to the conviction that '. . . the light of the Gospel and Science will be kindled first among the Gallas, and thence proceed to the Abyssinians, who have nothing but the name of Christ'.[4] On one occasion he went so far as to hope that the Gāllā 'in time might become for Africa, what our Germany became for Europe'.[5] By the end of 1840 the new strategy was formalized in the proposal that operations in Shawā be reduced to a holding operation, while concentration moved southward.[6] Shawā was too precarious.

Uneasiness at his present situation arose out of a sense of hostility in clerical circles and the *negus*'s continuing ambivalence. Yet a real attempt at *rapprochement* with the clergy had been made. Both Isenberg and Krapf attended church services (71–2, 155–7) and conversed with the clergy. Light was discovered in the darkness of indigenous Christianity. While many priests remained sceptical and suspicious, real friendships were established, and common ground struck: 'our doctrine and lives were blameless,' their visitors maintained, 'only they would like us to fast, and receive

---

[1] *Heidenbote*, xiv (1841), 97; Krapf of 6 June 1841; and *Record*, xiii (1842), 97; Krapf to Coates, Ankobar, 1 Feb. 1841.

[2] Krapf, *An Imperfect Outline of the Elements of the Galla Language Preceded by a Few Remarks Concerning the Nation of the Gallas and an Evangelical Mission Among Them by the Rev. C. W. Isenberg* (London, 1840), xii.

[3] CMS, C.M/o35, 33; 21.   [4] *Imperfect Outline*, 2.

[5] *Heidenbote*, xiv (1841), 44; letter of 1 Oct. 1840.

[6] CMS, C.M/o44, 16; Krapf to Coates, Ankobar, 1 Dec. 1840.

with them the blessed sacrament' (138). Here was a step forward indeed. The missionaries made a qualified agreement to fast and honestly expressed their tactical reasons for doing so (139). Pressed for participation in the Eucharist, Krapf felt obliged to decline: 'because they had mixed up so many things with the Communion which did not agree with Scriptures, and because by doing so a unity was to be expressed between us and them which did not exist.'[1]

It was a misfortune that their warm reception came from the party which was both a minority, and in decline. Of the five churches of Ankobar two adhered to received *Tawāhedo* orthodoxy, while the remainder followed *Yaṣagā Lej*. Theologically Krapf and Isenberg found traditional Alexandrian teaching too 'Pelagian' and 'mono-physitic', the *Sost Ledat* heresy being more congenial to their western minds. None the less, it was the traditionalists who welcomed and befriended them.[2] One *alaqā* of this group warmly recommended Isenberg's translation of the Heidelberg Catechism to his clergy. Regrettably, the days of *Tawāhedo* were numbered. The doctrine of the three births, which had reached Shawā in the reign of Sāhela Sellāsē's grandfather, Asfa Wasan,[3] was now on the way to estab-lishment. And its methods were distinctly unpleasant and intolerant. Some time during 1840–1 its adherents secured a ban on public profession of Alexandrian teaching. Other points, however, remained at issue and heated debate continued. Strange views were put for-ward on the veneration of the Blessed Virgin. For a time acrimony surrounded the question of whether the human soul has pre-natal knowledge and moral responsibility.[4] The suggestion that it did became a source of friction between the Gondar and Shawān pro-ponents of *Ṣagā Lej*, the former resisting the affirmative proposition.

Sāhela Sellāsē, no theologian, attempted to balance the two factions. An aggressive and monolithic Church could compromise royal authority. Moreover, despite official support for the three births, Isenberg reported that 'he is said personally to incline more to the opinions of the contrary party'.[5] In February 1840 a *Tawāhedo*

[1] CMS, C.M/o35, 33; 56.   [2] CMS, C.M/o35, 33; 14–15.

[3] Gabra Sellāsē, op. cit. 61–2; Rochet d'Héricourt, *Second voyage sur les deux rives de la Mer Rouge dans le pays des Adels et le royaume de Choa* (Paris, 1846), 226–7; W. C. Harris, *The Highlands of Ethiopia* (London, 2nd ed., 3 vols., 1844), iii. 189–90.

[4] CMS, C.M/o35, 33; 7–8, 12–13, 71: Rochet, *Second voyage*, 225–7; Harris, *Highlands*, iii. 190.

[5] CMS, C.M/o35, 33; 12–13.

dabtarā was elevated to the post of chief *alaqā* in Shawā. This produced a blast from Gondar,[1] and became the chief bone of contention. An appeal to *Rās* Ali to mediate with the *eçhagē* was rejected. Sāhela Sellāsē then attempted to wash his hands of the affair by throwing all responsibility onto the *rās*. According to Harris:

... the Negus, after fruitless efforts to satisfy the disputants, or to determine the point at issue, has at length adopted the alternative of commanding both parties to proceed to Gondar in order that the matter may be decided before Ras Ali.[2]

However, this dodge was sabotaged by Zanaba Warq, the Queen Mother, who thereby forced the argument back into the local arena.[3] On 24 November 1841, the King capitulated and a purge of the traditionalists began. Deposition, excommunication, banishment, and expropriation was their lot. Krapf was deeply distressed and feared, rightly, for the cause of Evangelical missions:

... all the ecclesiastics of a larger and better mind, and all friends of mine, were dismissed with one blow, and banished [from] Ankober whilst a monkish and fanatick party prevails now in the Shoan Church and plunges it into a still greater abyss of darkness, than in which it was already before.[4]

The support which he had so ably built was undercut. He was forced to fall back on Anglo-Shawān relations.

The Harris embassy had arrived in July 1841, and Krapf became very closely identified with it. He was in the anomalous position of being chief interpreter and adviser to both Sāhela Sellāsē and the English, although he was wholly committed to the latter. In his opinion only the diplomatic success of a treaty enforceable by British might might guarantee his continuance in Shawā. 'My own existence', he wrote, 'is in question at present. Our spiritual Embassy to these countries will be according to the success of the British

[1] IO, *BSP*, 159, no. 1486B; Haines to Bombay, Aden, 4 Mar. 1841; enclosing Krapf to Haines, Ankobar, 5 and 17 Dec. 1840.
[2] Ibid. 189, no. 2060A; Harris to Willoughby, Ankober, 14 Oct. 1842—a mistake for 1841.
[3] Harris, *Highlands*, iii. 191. The account in *Highlands* is based on *BSP*, 189, 2060D; Harris to Willoughby, Ankober, 27 Nov. 1841. Harris must have leaned heavily on Krapf for events taking place so soon after his arrival. For Krapf see *Record*, xiv (1843), 28; Krapf to Coates, Ankober, 14 Dec. 1841. Neither is entirely coherent for Krapf seems to have telescoped the events of the whole year to the end of 1841. See also Abir, *Era of the Princes*, 157–9, for a good account.
[4] *Record*, xiv (1843), 28.

Mission, with them we fall, and them we stand.'[1] The prospects were not good. Powerful court factions were opposed to all dealings with foreigners, and they had considerable popular support. The King dallied. He had hoped to exploit the British occupation of Aden to increase his autonomy from Gondar, but the size and ostentation of the embassy were frightening, even to him. Harris seems to have been inept. He tried to placate the clergy who led the opposition, but his contempt for them could scarely have been concealed.[2] As the negotiations dragged on, Krapf became worried, and anxiety led him to uncharacteristically violent views. 'The cause in Shoa is proceeding', he announced, 'If the King will not, they will teach him, as they taught the Pasha.—The strongest will be the master.'[3]

Eight days before the doctrinal *coup*, the treaty was concluded, on 16 November 1841.[4] It was, from its inception, a dead letter. The King had signed only to put Harris off, freeing himself for the impending ecclesiastical crisis. The ascendancy of the Three Births in no way lessened clerical hostility to the British presence. Rather the reverse. Doctrine and politics were thus intimately linked, and Harris and Krapf resorted to faith in the influence of the newly arrived Egyptian bishop *Abuna* Salāmā, hoping that he would both alleviate the attack from the Church, and actively further British interest. Initially they were not disappointed, the bishop tried to help. In February 1842 he threatened Sāhela Sellāsē with excommunication if he did not reverse his theological policy.[5] In April he instructed that Harris be informed of 'the very high predilection of the Archbishop towards the English nation' and assured him that 'I shall be most happy to render you any service in my power in this country'.[6] The ambassador was invited to Gondar.

---

[1] CMS, C.M/051, 4; Mühleisen to Coates, Aden, 4 Nov. 1841; quoting Krapf to Mühleisen, Ankobar, 25 July 1841.

[2] Harris, *Highlands*, ii. 20. Johnston, a private traveller who fell out with the embassy, was highly critical of Harris: *Travels*, ii. 70–1.

[3] CMS, C.M/044, 22; Krapf to Kruse, Ankobar, 4 Sept. 1841.

[4] Ullendorff and Beckingham, 'The First Anglo-Ethiopian Treaty', loc. cit. Of the 16 articles, numbers XIII and XIV deal with the rights of British subjects in Shawā, and were of concern to Krapf.

[5] CMS, C.A5/016, 2; Krapf to Coates, Ankobar, 28 Feb. 1842: IO, *BSP*, 189, no. 1060K; Harris to Willoughby, Ankober, 28 Feb. 1842: BN, *Éth.-Abb.*, 267, 135. For a further discussion of Salāmā, see below, Chap. IV, pp. 85–91.

[6] IO, *BSP*; 196, no. 3489, Harris to Willoughby, Ankober, 4 July 1842: 193, no. 2919, Salāmā to Harris, Gondar, 12 Apr. 1842: and ibid., Harris to Salāmā, Ankober, 13 May 1842. Antoine d'Abbadie wrote Salāmā's letter to Harris: BN, *Éth.-Abb.*, 267, 135.

Nevertheless, the real effect of these initiatives was the opposite of that anticipated. The metropolitan soon came to an open breach with the Shawān court; and his Anglophile stance merely brought upon English influence the discredit which he himself shortly suffered.

With the signing of the treaty, Krapf felt secure enough to leave Shawā. Harris remained to defend and protect him. Long absence from European society had placed him under a great strain. On his way to Egypt he hoped to reconnoitre the northern situation and pay his respects to Salāmā. He also intended to hasten the reinforcement of his mission. His parting with Sāhela Sellāsē was warm and affectionate, as Harris described it: 'His Majesty appeared to be deeply affected, and in faltering accents repeated his sorrow at the long separation in prospect—entreating the speedy return to Shoa of the worthy missionary, whom he invariably styled his Father.'[1] On 12 March 1842 Krapf left Shawā, never to return.

His trip from Shawā to Massawa was disastrous. He was plundered in Wallo, and had to proceed directly to the coast. He arrived destitute. He then crossed to Aden where, still under the influence of his harrowing experience, he wrote a long letter advising the India Government on how to deal with Ethiopian princes. His forthright personality was not susceptible to diplomatic finesse. He recommended military aggression and subjugation. To become civilized Ethiopia must have English tutelage: '. . . the British must become the guardians of Abyssinia whatever measures must be applied whether they are of a forceable or peaceable nature.' He cynically suggested that a pretext might be found in some minor violation of the Anglo-Ethiopian Treaty. Apart from appeals to the 'civilizing mission', the only justification offered was his fear of French imperialism, and this was largely a projection arising from his background. A contradiction of the broader ends he sought, his policy was brutal: its rejection a blessing.[2] The India Government reacted laconically: 'I confess Mr. Kraapf's [sic] description gives me but small hope of our being able to form a beneficial connection with Abyssinia, except by means which we can never dream of resorting to, namely by compulsion.'[3]

In 1841 there had been a fundamental shift in the CMS's emphasis. Out of a Mediterranean extension, the East African Mission was

[1] IO, BSP, 191, no. 2602; Harris to Willoughby, Ankober, 28 Mar. 1842.
[2] Ibid. 190, no. 2404; Krapf to Bombay, Aden, 6 June 1842.
[3] Ibid., no. 2405; Minute by the Honourable the Governor . . ., n.d.

created, directed to the southern Gāllā.[1] New instructions stressed
the need to divide attention between cultivating the bishop, and
expanding work among the Gāllā.[2] They met with protest. Isenberg
and Krapf quite rightly maintained that control of the Shawān
clergy lay not with Salāmā, but Sāhela Sellāsē. Of his support they
expressed no doubt, while Krapf anticipated the difficulties which
the metropolitan was to have even to assert himself in Gondar.
Together they were convinced that support from the British Government would bring unimpeded progress. It therefore came as a deep
shock when they were forbidden re-entry to Shawā.

On their arrival at Tajura in November 1842, a letter from Sāhela
Sellāsē to the Sultan awaited them. It strictly forbade the passage of
all Europeans but Rochet: '... when you find any "fringi" approaching, besides Roschet hinder him and if necessary kill him and hear
ye people of Tedjoura I do not wish you to send any European
besides Roschet . . .'[3] It was equally a surprise to Harris still in
Shawā. When the ambassador confronted the *negus*, he received a
simple and plausible explanation. Popular opinion, he was told,
was against the missionaries' return; an explanation supported by
Harris's observation that the clergy's reaction had been immediate
and hostile. Shawā was undergoing a deep internal crisis, largely
brought about by religion. The *negus* was perfectly frank:

> I am pressed sufficiently at present; half my people are adopting a new
> creed, the people of mans [*sic*] and the people of Morabeitie. The Abuna
> is also threatening me with his displeasure and Krapf and Isenberg wish to
> introduce another business. They shall not come. I have written to
> Mahommed to stop them, and the Chiefs of the road will take their
> property, and perhaps kill them if they attempt the journey—my son, my
> brother, mention this subject no more.[4]

His ban, then, arose out of a natural desire to keep the situation as
simple as possible. Moreover, what personal ties the King may have
had to Krapf had been severely strained. The missionary believed
that the *negus* had had a hand in his despoliation in Wallo, and had
been impetuous and intemperate enough to express this view

    [1] Stock, *History of the CMS*, i. 353.
    [2] CMS, C.A5/o16, 8; Krapf to Coates, Cairo, 3 Oct. 1842: C.A5/o13, 4;
Isenberg to Venn, Barmen, 3 Aug. 1842.
    [3] IO, *BSP*, 200, no. 104; Sahala Selassi to the Sultan of Tadjoura, n.d. (trans-
lated by Isenberg). 'Fringi' (*Franj*) is a corruption of Frank. Traditionally a term
for western Christians, it is now generally extended to all Europeans.
    [4] Ibid. 204, no. 1144; Harris to Willoughby, Ankober, 30 Jan. 1843.

directly in a letter to him. Sāhela Sellāsē had reacted with hurt surprise.[1] Moreover, Harris suggests that during his brief stay Isenberg's outspoken views had given offence and 'that a very strong and natural prejudice had risen against him amongst all classes throughout the kingdom'.[2] Although this view may well have been coloured by news of what had happened in Tegrē, it was entirely in keeping with Isenberg's previous and subsequent behaviour.

The Shawā mission had failed. But its collapse was due to reasons partly beyond control. Krapf had carefully tried to make clerical friends, and their dismissal was tragic. The traveller Johnston several times records gratuitous expressions of warmth towards the missionary.[3] However, he had unwisely offended the King. Moreover, the measures which Krapf took to guarantee his position were also partially responsible. The Harris embassy had given great offence, and compromised their friends.[4] Finally one returns to Shawā's internal crisis which was too profound to allow of much foreign involvement, particularly religious. Harris shortly left Shawā, a wreck of a treaty in hand. Neither diplomat nor missionary, under British protection, entered Shawā for many years. The only upshot was Krapf's celebrated search for an Evangelical El Dorado amongst the Gāllā of East Africa.

Tegrē Again

Although they had little hope, the missionaries were not quite prepared to quit. They fell back on the last resort of reaching Gondar through Massawa to receive the bishop's protection. It was a broken reed, as they had themselves foreseen. Isenberg and his new colleague Mühleisen went directly to Massawa, while Krapf contemplated reaching the Gāllā directly from the south. Krapf was too late, after changing his mind, to join the brethren in Tegrē. Given Isenberg's record, the absence was fatal. Moreover, the political climate was again confused. Motivated by ambition, in 1841 Webē had elaborated a grand campaign to unseat and replace Rās Ali. In

---

[1] Ibid. 193, no. 2918A; Harris to Willoughby, Ankober, 8 May 1842. See also India Office, *Political and Secret Records. (Secret Letters Received) (Aden)*, 27, no. 2, 320–1; Christopher to Haines, Massowah, 28 June 1843.

[2] IO, *BSP*, 204, no. 1144; Harris to Willoughby, Ankober, 30 Jan. 1843.

[3] Johnston, *Travels*, ii. 64; and 'Six Months in Southern Abyssinia . . .', *Hunt's London Journal*, 1844, 323.

[4] Johnston, *Travels*, ii. 84.

January 1842, he marched on Dabra Tābor and the following month, after a bizarre sequence of events, he was defeated.[1] On the missionaries' arrival, Webē's hands were still full clearing up the aftermath of his setback. The Protestants wisely tried to avoid him altogether, by passing through Sarāyē and Shirē. On their way distressing news arrived that the clergy of Madhānē Ālam, Adwā, awaited them. Although it was now the more imperative to avoid Adwā, their bearers refused to co-operate. They appealed to the prince. Again Isenberg blundered. He tactlessly reminded Webē of his sinfulness in being party to the mission's earlier expulsion, and scarcely redeemed himself with the high-minded assurance that the missionaries had never ceased to pray God for his forgiveness.[2]

Webē temporized in the interests of gaining foreign support. He directed them to Adwā and enjoined them to live quietly, attending church. A monumental bungle ensued. Isenberg sent directly to *Alaqā* Kidāna Māryām, requesting the restoration of the mission's property.[3] Gathering his clergy, the *alaqā* confronted the missionaries on the market-place, bearing provocative symbols of Orthodoxy. Kidāna Māryām challenged them to comply with their instructions from Webē, by venerating the cross and the Virgin. Isenberg was incapable of conciliation. Although he claimed pity and forgiveness for those who hated and calumniated him, he would yield no point of faith, and repudiated the challenge.[4]

Isenberg was neither a bad man nor without friends, but his inflexibility rendered them powerless. A further appeal was made by both parties to Webē, and the missionary followed through with a personal visit.[5] On 22 June 1843, he was turned out. Complaining both of Isenberg's personal hostility and the offence he had given

---

[1] 'Nuovi Documenti II', *RRAL*, S8, ii (1947), 380 f. See also Chap. IV, p. 67; and Abir, *Era of the Princes*, Chap. VI.

[2] CMS, C.A5/013, 30; Isenberg's Journal, May 1842 to Dec. 1843, entry for 2 May 1843. These journals were published in German: *Abessinien und die Evangelische Mission. . . . Tagebuch meiner dritten Missionsreise vom Mai 1842 bis December 1843 . . .* (Bonn, 1844). Their original language is uncertain, but it may have been English.

[3] CMS, C.A5/013, 20; Isenberg to Coates, Adoa, 5 June 1843.

[4] Ibid. See also two other first hand accounts by H. Lefebvre, *Voyage en Abyssinie exécuté pendant les années 1839, 1840, 1841, 1842, 1843* (Paris, 1845–8), ii. 325–7; and *Abbā* Takla Hāymānot in C. Conti Rossini, 'Vicende dell'Etiopia e delle missioni cattoliche ai tempi di Ras Ali, Deggiac Ubie e Re Teodoro, secondo un documento abissino', *RRAL*, S5, xxv (1916), 466–8.

[5] CMS, C.A5/013, 21; Isenberg, Krapf, and Mühleisen to Coates, Massowa, 28 Aug. 1843. See also C.A5/013, 30.

to Ethiopian susceptibilities, the prince refused passage to Gondar and ordered an expulsion.[1]

A week later the missionaries gathered in Sarāyē to await a reply from Salāmā. It was barren. Although stressing his sympathy, he dwelt on his own difficulties. The Ethiopians, Salāmā said, were reluctant to receive foreign education and resisted all efforts to correct their erroneous theological views. Bitterly, the Protestants were forced to withdraw.

There is little doubt that Isenberg bore a large degree of responsibility. Only to the extent that it was a foregone conclusion can he be absolved. This was clear to his CMS contemporaries. Lieder, a missionary in Egypt in close touch with Salāmā, charged that:

Mr. Isenberg . . . fully knowing the feelings of the priests and influential men of Tigre towards him *personally*, should not have gone there again, for the failure was a certainty to all in Cairo, beforehand, who were acquainted with the circumstances. . . .[2]

Confirmation comes from informed French sources. Some years later the Jidda consul wrote:

I am convinced that the preaching of the Rev. Samuel Gobat was neither violent nor blundering and that it was his successor, Mr. Isenberg, who ruined Protestant hopes in Abyssinia. . . . The apostolate of Mr. Gobat was always perfectly conciliatory. Mr. Isenberg's rejected all concession.[3]

The mission *qua* mission had come to nought. Although a great deal of intelligence was accumulated, it could not be turned to any purpose. Apart from the production of valuable language studies and Ethiopia's introduction to the missionary constituency, few lasting consequences are discernible. Political exclusion did not prevent dialogue: it was a sign that it had ceased to exist. Yet Gobat, and to a lesser extent Krapf, retained some credit. Twelve years later a fresh Protestant approach was attempted.

[1] CMS, C.A5/013, 21.
[2] CMS, C.M/048, 58; Lieder to Secretaries, Cairo, 20 Jan. 1844.
[3] MAE, *Corr. pol. Ég. Mass.* i. 201; Fresnel to Bastide, Djeddah, 3 Jan. 1849.

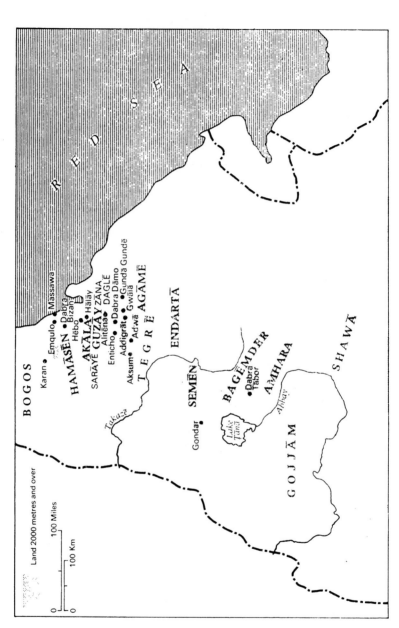

RED SEA

Karan●
Emqulo● ●Massawa
●Dabra
HAMĀSĒN   Bizan
Hēbo● ●Halāy
AKĀLA●   ZĀNA
SARĀYĒ GUZĀY DAGLĒ
Enticho● ●Dabra Dāmo
Aditēna●
Addigrāt● ●Gundā Gundē
Aksum● Gwāla● ●Gwāla
Adwā● AGĀMĒ
TEGRĒ

ENDARTĀ

Takazē

SEMĒN

Gondar●

BAGĒMDER
●Dabrā
Tābor
AMHARA
Lake
Tānā

Abbay

GOJJĀM

SHAWĀ

Land 2000 metres and over

100 Miles

100 Km

Map 3. Catholic missions.

CHAPTER IV

Towards an Ethiopian Catholicism?

CATHOLIC missionary enterprise took two forms. In the area with which we are concerned, Lazarists worked amongst Orthodox Christians, while, in south-western Ethiopia, Capuchins led a mission to the Gällä. Although the latter is peripheral to our study, it serves as an important point of reference. The circumstances surrounding Rome's resumption of interest were arbitrary. Since the departure of Fr. Tobias in 1797 Ethiopian affairs were held in abeyance, despite an abortive suggestion in 1832 by the Vice-Prefect of the Holy Land that CMS activities ought to be countered.[1]

The *deus ex machina* was Fr. Giuseppe Sapeto, a young Lazarist stationed in Syria, who, in 1837, volunteered to scout the situation.[2] The *fait accompli* was accepted by Propaganda, despite some surprise and distress to Sapeto's superiors.[3] His restlessness and impatience with discipline disqualified him from establishing a mission; but eminently suited him to his pioneering role. In Cairo, he joined Antoine and Arnauld d'Abbadie with whom he reached Massawa.[4] By March 1838 he and Arnauld were in Adwā to witness the CMS expulsion; a lesson in the dangers of religious enthusiasm. Fr. Giuseppe quickly ingratiated himself with the Adwā clergy, inducing *Qedus* Gabre'ēl Church to send a declaration of submission

---

[1] For all questions dealing with the origin and early development of the Lazarist mission the writings of Fr. L. Betta are extremely useful. See 'L'Inizio della Missione Lazzarista in Abissinia (1838–1842)', unpublished thesis (Rome: Pontificium Institutum Orientalium Studiorum, 1950), copy at the Lazarist Curia Generalizia, Rome. And on this point, pp. 196–202 ff. The more important sections of the thesis were published as 'Il B. Giustino de Jacobis Prefetto Apostolico dell'Etiopia', *Annali della Missione*, lxvii (1960), 288–313, 350–73; lxviii (1961), 154–206. See also Archives of the Propaganda Fide, *Scritture Riferite nei Congressi. Etiopia . . .*, iii. 528–9; Memorandum on Ethiopia, 23 Sept. 1832.

[2] See S. Pane, *Il Beato Giustino de Jacobis* (Naples, 1949), 131–2; Sapeto to Cardinal Mai, 24 Feb. 1837. See also Betta, 'Inizio', 233 ff.

[3] APF, *SRC.AC*, iii. 629ʳ–30ᵛ: Durando to Guarini, Turin, 19 Sept. 1838.

[4] For Sapeto's activities see his *Viaggio e Missione Cattolica fra i Mensâ i Bogos e gli Habab con un Cenno Geografico e Storico dell'Abissinia* (Rome, 1857); and G. Giacchero and G. Bisogni, *Vita di Giuseppe Sapeto. L'ignota Storia degli Esordi Coloniale Italiani rivelata da Documenti Inediti* (Florence, 1942).

to Rome.[1] Encouraged by Sapeto's reports, and doubtlessly considering the increasing involvement of both France and the Lazarists in the Levant, Propaganda asked the Congregation of the Mission to undertake the work.[2] Again, on the initiative of Propaganda, Fr. Justin de Jacobis of the Province of Naples was appointed Prefect Apostolic of Ethiopia and neighbouring regions.[3] By October 1839 he was in Adwā. Thus, of a double *fait accompli*—Sapeto's on Rome, Propaganda's on the Lazarists—was born an exemplary career.

The subsequent origin of the Capuchin mission was linked to the same events. For some time European attention had been directed to southern Ethiopia.[4] Travellers and missionaries announced the existence of a densely populated area, dominantly pagan, yet containing islands of Christian traces. Sapeto reported the exciting potential of the Gāllā.[5] The Belgian diplomat and Catholic layman, Blondeel, noted from Gojjām the great promise to missions held out by the southern Gāllā.[6] Finally, in 1843 Sapeto's earlier companion, Antoine d'Abbadie, became the first modern European to penetrate to the Gibē River region, heart of the cluster of Gāllā states in south-west Ethiopia. Basing his belief both on the widespread Christian remnants, and on pagan receptivity, he wrote to the Propaganda 'of the possibility of an imminent conversion of the Galla peoples'.[7] Strengthening the more second-hand reports of Blondeel and Sapeto, his intelligence was well received. The Capuchins accepted the mission, established by Papal Decree on 30 April 1846. By the end of the year Bishop Guglielmo Massaja with four Piedmontese confrères had landed at Massawa. The duality of Catholic purpose represented by his presence persists to this day, for, while

---

[1] APF, *SRC.AC*, iii. 618ʳ.

[2] Ibid. 603–4; Sapeto report of July 1838: and ibid. 642; Étienne to Mai, Paris, 30 Nov. 1838.

[3] Betta, 'Inizio', 259 ff. See also P. Gimalac, 'Le Vicariat apostolique d'Abyssinie (1830–1931)', *Revue d'histoire des missions*, ix (1932), 129.

[4] Lack of space prevents detailed treatment. See my thesis, 'European Religious Missions in Ethiopia 1830–1868' (London, 1967), Chap. V; and Abir, *Era of the Princes*, Chap. IV.

[5] Congrégation de la Mission (Paris), *Lettres manuscrites de Mgr. de Jacobis*, ii, no. 423; Sapeto to Étienne, Adwa, 10 Dec. 1839.

[6] P. Roeykens, 'Les Préoccupations missionaires du consul belge Ed. Blondeel van Cuelenbroeck en Abyssinie (1840–1843)', *Bulletin de l'Académie Royale des Sciences Coloniales*, N.S., v (1959), 1149–50.

[7] G. Massaja, *I Miei Trentacinque Anni di Missione Nell'Alta Etiopia* (Rome, 12 vols., 1885–95), i, Appendice, 199–203 for the several documents.

de Jacobis was to work within the Ge'ez rite, Massaja working 'in partibus infidelium' was to impart the Latin.[1]

Both missions had an extraordinary reception. Two centuries of bitter anti-Catholicism had been dissipated by Ethiopia's internal disintegration and its accompanying growth of sectarianism. Apocalyptic condemnations were now the preserve of the backwoodsmen; in the urban centres, and larger monasteries, foreigners met with coolness, but tolerance. In short there had been a revolution. For almost a century and a half all Europeans had been viewed as potential religious agents: now it was the reverse; the missionaries were seen, above all, as representatives of Europe and her technological triumphs. The coals of the old fires still smouldered, but the religious neutrality of many early modern travellers had helped damp them further. Only the wind of outspoken provocation, as in the case of Isenberg, or the threat of Latin imperialism, could again fan them to flames. Catholics had almost ten years of peace before the arrival of a Roman bishop, Massaja, sparked the first outbreaks of serious persecution. By then the groundwork had been laid. Subsequent attacks on Catholicism are to be seen, not so much as expressions of ancient religious animosity, but of renascent nationalism.

Still, much credit for the establishment of Catholicism in Ethiopia must go to its principal representative. In any new situation, personality plays an important role in the definition of policy. Broad directives, laid down over long distances, need translation and application. The events of the early seventeenth century are inseparable from Paez and Mendez who helped form them. So, too, in the nineteenth, it was Justin de Jacobis (1800–60) who determined the main lines of Catholic development.

He was clearly an impressive man,[2] whose reputation has withered too long under the shadow of his celebrated contemporary, Massaja.[3]

[1] Despite the evident intentions of Propaganda to the contrary, see below pp. 80 ff.

[2] See, in particular, the biography by his disciple, Fr. Takla Hāymānot, *Episodi della vita Apostolica di Abuna Jacob ossia il venerabile Padre Giustino De Jacobis* . . . (Asmara, 1915). See also Pane, *Il Beato Giustino de Jacobis*; and S. Arata, *Abuna Yakob Apostolo dell'Abissinia (Mons. Giustino de Jacobis C.M.) 1800–1860* (Rome, 2nd ed., 1934).

[3] For whom see the autobiography, *35 Anni*; and the two collections of letters: G. Farina, *Le Lettere del Cardinale Massaia dal 1846 al 1886* . . . (Turin, 1936); and E. Martire, *Massaia da Vicino* . . . (Rome, 1937), of which Farina's is the more basic. Of the innumerable biographies see E. Cozzani, *Vita di Guglielmo Massaia* (Florence, 2 vols., 1943), and F. Valori, *Guglielmo Massaia* (Turin, 1957).

Fellow Europeans and Ethiopian disciples witness to a deep piety and devotedness, contained within a conservative framework of deference to religious and civil hierarchy. Although humbly born, he had adopted Neapolitan aristocratic culture; yet, through its time-bound and decadent forms shines an original and profound virtue—apostolic humility. This was the strongest source of attraction to his disciples, and won him Massaja's homage. It was also the basis of his remarkable identification with Ethiopia and with the life of his disciples. As Pane says: 'Probably no Catholic missionary has so penetrated into the Abyssinian soul as he did; none knew it so much as he did; none so conformed himself to it as he did.'[1] Indeed, his humility, and the apostolic fervour to which it was intrinsic, made him the only missionary of our period whose living memory survives.[2] Witnesses thirty-five years after his death were still profoundly moved; and his person is cherished today by the older adherents of the Ge'ez rite. Devotion to Ethiopia and to his clerical converts dominated his apostolate.

Yet even in the life of this saint, Adam manifested himself. Peasant guile and aristocratic finesse did not eradicate optimism or political *naïveté*. After four years in Ethiopia, he wrote to the French government: 'I limit myself to the following proposition: *Abyssinia in its entirety is preparing to become Catholic in the very near future.*'[3] These characteristics could lead to a clouding of critical judgement. Normally, his approach was one of respect for political authority, but remoteness from it. Thus, while he successfully guided his mission through the cockpit of Tegrē politics, he refused too close an attachment to his protector. Nevertheless, the opposition of Tēwodros caused him to turn to men of straw. The results were unfortunate, but not disastrous.

By contrast, Massaja appears almost worldly. While the Lazarist adopted the style of an itinerant Ethiopian *mamher* (teacher), eating and living with his pupils, the Capuchin was familiar with the

---

[1] Pane, *Il Beato*, 293–4.

[2] Various conversations have confirmed this. Amongst the clergy, literacy has helped, but a semi-literate informant, largely ignorant of European sources also concurred, despite a number of miraculous accretions. By contrast, the memory of Massaja in the south-west has vanished, while J. M. Flad, the distinguished missionary to the Falāshā, whose career is discussed in Chap. VI, has lost all personal attributes, and signifies merely an epoch. See also the extremely interesting source I have labelled 'Testimonies', Archivio della Procura Generale della Congregazione della Missione presso la S. Sede, *passim*.

[3] *Revue d'histoire des missions*, ix (1932), 552; Adoua, 4 Oct. 1843.

centres of power from Shawā to Rome, Turin, and Paris. Of course different ministries are valid, and the cardinal did have his humility, even if it had ostentatious overtones. Massaja is to be distinguished for his vigour, and the multiplicity of his interests, which make him the larger figure. Yet both, compared with contemporaries in African missions, are of great importance for their creative flexibility. In their ability to respect indigenous usage, and their formation of a national priesthood, they were far ahead of their time. If precedence here goes to de Jacobis, credit must still be shared.

Both Catholic representatives, like Krapf, had recourse to European imperialism. It would be unfair to portray de Jacobis as an aggressive herald of foreign domination; but he was, none the less, a proponent of French influence. He was more important than the consuls at Massawa, and probably had a hand in every communication between Tegrē and Paris from 1840 to 1860. He protested the reluctance of his political involvement with some reason; still, it was real, and not limited to diplomatic formalities. Massaja has suffered from attempts to make him a national hero. He was not responsible for Italy's interest in the Horn of Africa, yet he did cultivate it. During our period his theatre was too remote to permit much collaboration with traders or consuls, yet, in 1858, he responded warmly to a Sardinian request for co-operation and intelligence;[1] while, for some years in Shawā, he was to act almost as Menilek's diplomatic tutor.[2] Neither man saw his political activity as an end in itself, although Massaja is more open to the charge of ambiguity. Certainly, for de Jacobis, diplomacy was largely used to maintain his mission in a difficult environment. For, while his intentions and personality shaped the growth of an Ethiopian Catholic Church, the context of that development was set by the Ethiopian state.

The World of Man

The confusion following the death of Sabagādis had lessened by the late 1830s, but not disappeared. Some stability emerged as the political succession in Amharā settled on Rās Ali, and in Tegrē on Dajāzmāch Webē. Yet, both men were vulnerable. Ali was a boy, dominated by Manan his mother and various uncles. Suspicious and

[1] Farina, Lettere, 212–29.
[2] R. A. Caulk, 'The Origins and Development of the Foreign Policy of Menilek II, 1865–1896', unpublished Ph.D. thesis (University of London, 1966), Chap. I.

indecisive, the *rās* was aggravated by restless flanks in Gojjām, Semēn, and the eastern Gāllā territories. Yet, compared with Webē, he still benefited from the mantle of primacy inherited from Ali I. Webē's strength was also his weakness. A foreigner to Tegrē, he was removed from that province's petty regional and dynastic rivalries, yet he could never arouse popular support. Control of Tegrē demanded his constant presence there. Thus, the great strategic advantage of an opening to the sea at Massawa was largely offset by the challenges of local chieftains, and the rivalry of his brother Marso.

From 1839 to 1855 Webē was the dominating figure in Lazarist politics. Partly a result of his control of the northern approaches, it was equally a matter of policy. Just as Webē had shown himself tolerant of the Protestant presence, so too he welcomed the Catholics. The greater political and diplomatic skill of de Jacobis soon turned this northern warlord into a constant friend and protector.

Apart, perhaps, from a warm regard for de Jacobis's piety, Webē showed little interest in Catholicism. He rarely discussed religion with the Lazarists. On one occasion he is said to have declared publicly: 'I will have no other belief than that of Rome',[1] but it seems to have been an aberration. His pro-missionary policy was a political one, above all an expression of foreign policy. Webē's external relations were dominated by Ali, to the south, and the Islamic powers on his northern and western frontiers. Ambition was at work, for he sought to dislodge the *rās* from his control over the vestiges of the imperial heritage.[2] Equally, in the north he wanted to re-establish the rule of the medieval Emperors along the Red Sea coast,[3] thus challenging the long-standing Turkish-Egyptian establishment at Massawa and the more recent Egyptian expansion into the Sudanese borderlands. To support his hopes, and to protect himself from the consequences of their repeated frustration, Webē turned to the European powers.

Faute de mieux, it was France. The CMS banishment had been erroneously taken by the British as a sign of Webē's hostility to them. The weakness of their secular representation in the early 1840s prevented the correction of this impression. The Catholic missionaries were the only residents of the area with close ties to Europe, and

---

[1] Ministère des Affaires Etrangères, *Corr. pol. Ég. Mass.*, i. 98ʳ; de Jacobis to MAE, Adowa, 4 Oct. 1843: Archivio della Procura Generale Cong. Miss. presso la S. Sede, *Giornale B. Giustino de Jacobis*, iii. 59.

[2] Th. Lefebvre, *Voyage en Abyssinie exécuté pendant les années 1839, 1840, 1841, 1842, 1843* (Paris, 6 vols., 1845–8), i. 292–3.

[3] 'Nuovi Documenti III', 397–8; Abir, *Era of the Princes*, 119 ff.

so he turned to them. The willingness of the mission to serve Webē's desire for a foreign connection was made the more valuable by the hostility of De Goutin, the French consul, towards the Tegrē prince.[1] Nevertheless, Webē's protection arose from more than expediency, as its constancy testified. Fraught with difficulties, religious and political,[2] he was forced to banish the missionaries on several occasions; but his reluctance always carried conviction. Indeed, the Lazarist faith in Webē suggests personal involvement and attraction on both sides, which is none the less real for being largely undocumented.[3] It is to the mission's political involvement that we must now turn.

Sapeto's arrival in Adwā, in March 1838, preceded by six months the consolidation of Tegrē, which followed Webē's victory over Kāsā Sabagādis; yet the *dajāzmāch* quickly took up the question of a mission to France. Sapeto was receptive, seeing greater security in an increase of French influence.[4] Negotiations were eased by the presence of Lieutenant Lefebvre, then on a semi-official voyage of scientific discovery. Webē's objectives, as stated to Sapeto, were friendship and the acquisition of artisans, in return for which he would cede coastal lands (outside his control), protect French citizens, and channel his trade to the new French possession.[5] Behind the nonsense of 'protection', to which Sapeto refers, lay the abortive diplomatic overture to Britain in early 1838, and the fear of Egypt which had occasioned it. The operation, of course, was premature, given the outlook of Europe's chancelleries; and, despite Lefebvre's sponsorship of a small embassy, few tangible benefits ensued. Yet the presents brought back,[6] and the subsequent establishment of the Massawa consulate were, to Webē, a stimulus to further activity, and a sign of European interest.

De Jacobis arrived at the end of October 1839, accompanied by Fr. Luigi Montuori. Too late to be involved in the embassy's

---

[1] MAE, *Corr. pol. Ég. Mass.*, i. 191; De Goutin to de Lamartine, Massouah, 1 July 1848.

[2] *Annales de la congrégation de la mission*, xv (1850), 321–3; Rapport, Biancheri to Sturchi, Rome, 24 Feb. 1850.

[3] See, for instance, Biancheri's claim that Webē 'loves and venerates' de Jacobis, APF, *SRC.AC*, v. 293ᵛ–4ʳ; Biancheri to Prop. Fide, Massua, 10 Aug. 1850; or de Jacobis's glowing tribute to Webē's chivalric qualities, *Annales*, xviii (1853), 419–20.

[4] Giacchero and Bisogni, *Vita di Sapeto*, 36.

[5] *Lettres de Jacobis*, ii, no. 423; Sapeto to Étienne, Adwa, 10 Dec. 1839.

[6] Lefebvre, *Voyage*, i. 151–8, 229–31. They included fire-arms.

dispatch, the newcomers benefited from the optimism surrounding it. Having gained satisfaction that the Catholics would not offend Ethiopian veneration for the Blessed Virgin, as the Protestants had, and reserving freedom of worship, Webē extended his protection.[1]

The Catholics then implemented a strategy of dispersal. Sapeto left for Shawā, and Montuori for Gondar, while de Jacobis remained in Adwā. Their style of life followed that of the Evangelicals; a quiet withdrawal and invitation to conversation. Generally, there was optimism, soon tempered by reality. In April 1840 Webē broached to the mission a cherished project: obtaining a bishop from Alexandria. The benefits were obvious: acclaim from the Christian population, now without a spiritual leader for a decade; and ideological support for his challenge to *Rās* Ali, widely compromised by his Islamic associates. European protection was desirable. Earlier parties bringing bishops from Egypt had been held to extortion in the Red Sea, while the Egyptian cities and the Patriarch's court were centres of intrigue, and relations with Mehemet Ali continued strained. Moreover, Webē may have sought to lend weight to his rather uneasy claim. Although the Patriarch had expressed agreement, there was still the danger of equivocation. To secure his substantial investment, the *dajāzmāch* turned to the powers. This placed the Catholics, standing for France, in the extraordinary position of facilitating the emergence of a coherent, organized opposition. Webē had proposed that de Jacobis accompany the emissaries. The missionary was both reluctant and confused. At first he refused, but then, on the acceptance of conditions, agreed. He insisted to the prince that the Patriarch's permission should be solicited for the building of Catholic churches, and that the delegation continue to Rome. He even suggested obtaining a Coptic Catholic bishop, instead of a monophysite one.[2] To his great fortune, this hasty notion was ignored. However, little opposition was expressed to his intention of interviewing the Patriarch on reunification with Rome.[3] For Webē was playing a double game.

[1] APF, *SRC.AC*, iii. 709ᵛ ff.; de Jacobis to Card. P ef., Adua, 2 Nov. 1839.

[2] *Lettres de Jacobis*, ii, no. 169; to Étienne, Adova, 26 Apr. 1840: APF, *SRC.AC*, iv. 48; to Card. Pref., Cairo, 3 May 1841. Propaganda shared his unwisdom in this. Betta, 'Inizio', Chap. V, 348 ff.

[3] Pane, *Il Beato*, 328–30: *Lettres de Jacobis*, ii, no. 170; to Étienne, Ahalhe maireal (?), 27 Jan. 1841: APF, *SRC.AC*, iv. 48–9; to Card. Pref., Cairo, 3 May 1841: Lefebvre, *Voyage*, i. 297–8.

PLATE III

a. Abuna Salāmā, *c.* 1860   *b. Dajjāch* Webē in the early 1840s

c. Webē. A stylized portrait

Reluctant to commit himself solely to France, he approached the British. Aware of the India Government's overtures to Shawā, he was stimulated by jealousy and the renewed signs of interest. William Coffin was dispatched with a letter for the Cairo consul. The prince tried to exploit Anglo-French rivalry: 'And as I am now sending for an Aboon, I would entreat you to facilitate his way hither, that no disaster may happen to him. "With us is the power", say the French; but "the Englishman is strong" say we. . . .'[1] Expressing Webē's conviction that Protestantism and British interest were closely linked, Coffin informed the CMS that both he '. . . and his people have long ago expected a Missionary . . . and have expressed their surprise that hitherto none had come'.[2] The fish refused to bite. Neither the CMS, nor Harris, could be expected to recommend further involvement in Ethiopia when the next few months were so rudely to disillusion them. Only the immediate interest of British protection for his bishop was realized by Webē.[3]

Equally, both de Jacobis and the Tegrē lord were frustrated in the broader hopes which they entertained of the embassy to Cairo. Webē's attack on *Rās* Ali was defeated; while the Patriarch repudiated all Catholic influence. A young man educated in a CMS school was appointed, taking the name Abbā Salāmā. With his arrival the northerners marched on Ali's capital of Dabra Tābor. Success was turned by self-confidence to defeat; Webē's ambitions were foiled; and the control of the bishop passed into the hands of *Rās* Ali.[4]

In 1842, de Jacobis returned to an unsettled Tegrē. In Alexandria he had failed to influence the bishop's election, or to persuade the Patriarch to engage in closer relations with Rome. However, he had succeeded in taking part of the embassy to Rome. While there, the mission was strengthened by the addition of Fr. Biancheri. Yet, the situation was precarious. Central authority had collapsed in the north, while the existence of *Abuna* Salāmā threatened a united Orthodox opposition.

As Webē had moved south on Dabra Tābor, rebellion rose to the rear. His governor of Aksum, *Nabred* Walda Sellāsē, and *Bālgāda* Arāyā of Endartā, were the most prominent contestants. Moreover,

---

[1] PRO, FO I/III, 149; Oubié to Victoria, (1841). See also ibid. 123; Barnett to Blackhouse, Alexandria, 19 Sept. 1841.

[2] CMS, C.M/045, 104; Kruse to Coates, Cairo, 15 Sept. 1841.

[3] See below, p. 86, for an account of Salāmā's election.

[4] 'Nuovi Documenti II', 380–1; 'Vicende', 462–5. See also above, Chap. III, pp. 55–6; and below, pp. 87–8.

following his victory, Ali had appointed Webē's disgruntled brother Marso to the former's post.[1] Webē was soon rehabilitated, and, with Ali's support, prevailed over Marso. He then turned to Arāyā, a descendant of both *Rās* Walda Sellāsē and Sabagādis. De Jacobis had wisely repudiated the rebel's overtures, thus earning Webē's gratitude. Despite the attempts of the metropolitan to threaten the mission from Gondar, its position actually grew stronger as Tegrē again settled down, the old order prevailing. By 1845 some early reservations of de Jacobis towards Webē had passed; he was now 'nostro inalterabile amico'.[2]

Frustrated in the south, the *dajāzmāch* turned northwards, where Ethiopian ambitions were countered by Egyptian penetration.[3] European support was thus desirable, and he looked to the missionaries. Again the absence of Protestants brought dependence on France. In May 1845 Webē requested French protection. Having persuaded the chief to seek a protectorate such as 'France had established over Tahiti', de Jacobis wrote the letter.[4] After a passage extolling the virtue of Louis Philippe and his fame as protector of Christians, the letter went on:

It is, then, right that I claim today from Your Majesty both friendship and powerful protection against my enemies the Mohammedans, who are preparing (so it seems) war against the Christians of Ethiopia, at the same time, both from Sennaar and from the Red Sea, while they seek to create for themselves a party amongst the Mohammedan population of our country.[5]

The seed fell on stony ground. Partition lay a generation off, and the letter's reference to Algeria was hardly a happy one. The Foreign Office minuted 'Arrest the zeal of these men', and instructed consul De Goutin to express the Minister's disapproval and conviction that missionaries were best occupied with affairs of religion.[6] De Jacobis never forgot the rebuke. He had placed himself in an ambiguous position, as he declared in a letter to Étienne, his superior:

---

[1] De Jacobis, *Giornale*, ii. 78 ff.; Krapf and Isenberg, *Journals*, 359–61, 489 ff.
[2] APF, *SRC.AC*, iv. 483ʳ; de Jacobis to Prop. Fide, Guala, 21 Nov. 1845. But compare *Lettres de Jacobis*, ii, no. 201; to Étienne, 28 Oct. 1842.
[3] MAE, *Corr. pol. Ég. Mass.*, i. 130; De Goutin to Guizot, Massouah, 20 Feb. 1845. See also Hill, *Egypt in the Sudan*, 83–4; and Abir, *Era of the Princes*, 119 f.
[4] *Lettres de Jacobis*, ii, no. 226; to Étienne, Guala, 10 Dec. 1845.
[5] MAE, *Corr. pol. Ég. Mass.*, i. 141ʳ; Oubyé to Louis Philippe, Adoa, 24 May 1845.
[6] *Rev. his. miss.*, xv (1838), 603–5: De Goutin to Ministre, Massaouah, 1 July 1845; and Ministre to De Goutin, 15 Nov. 1845.

It is a very remarkable thing, most honoured Father, that I who do not at all like politics, I who always read the Rule of our Holy Father which forbids us to concern ourselves with politics, I finally who keep always on me the precious letter . . . reminding me of my duty to keep myself far from politics, that I should find myself by necessity mixed up in just such an affair![1]

Yet there seems to have been little 'necessity'. No immediate threat to the mission existed, only the imagined one of increased British influence. Catholic preconceptions had been imposed. Imperialism was foreshadowed in these mutual suspicions of the European sects, and, despite his sincere reluctance, de Jacobis accepted political involvement as inevitable to his situation. He took up the role again.

1845 saw the first peak in the mission's relations with Webē. The metropolitan's return to Tegrē in 1846 altered the situation drastically. The doctrinal conflicts in the central provinces, and the unwillingness of any prince to support him, had rendered *Abuna* Salāmā's position untenable. Driven from Gondar in disgraceful circumstances, he sought more congenial surroundings. The immediate effect of his arrival was to crystallize public hostility to the mission. It also drew Webē once more towards the south. At the end of 1846 war broke out with Ali.[2] Episcopal sanction was a powerful support for the northerner's ambitions against the Gāllā. Yet this campaign was more miserable than the last. The *rās* seized the initiative and penned Webē in the Semēn mountains, forcing him to yield.

Webē's defeat considerably increased Salāmā's scope for action. As was usual, a move to the south had stimulated the emergence of Tegrē dissidents; while the frontiers were again disturbed. Webē walked a knife's edge, drawing on both Orthodox and Catholic support. But the metropolitan was too influential and prevailed.[3] The arrival of Massaja, a Catholic bishop, played into his hands. Propaganda had instructed the Capuchin that, on his way to the south-west, he should aid the Lazarist mission by the Catholic ordination of some Ethiopians converted by de Jacobis. Word soon reached the authorities of Massaja's episcopal status. Tolerating missionaries and winking at a few proselytes was one thing, a rival hierarchy quite another. Webē acted decisively. Peace was concluded

[1] *Lettres de Jacobis*, ii, no. 226; Guala, 10 Dec. 1845.
[2] 'Vicende', 478–80; 'Nuovi Documenti II', 389–90. See also BN, *Éth.-Abb.*, no. 267, 'Journal de voyage', 135ᵛ; Gondar, 8 Dec. 1847. de Jacobis, *Giornale*, iv. 40.
[3] 'Nuovi Documenti III', 396.

with Ali in July 1847. The following November saw Massaja's expulsion.[1]

Yet privately the *dajāzmāch* was ambivalent. Genuinely afraid of a public Catholic bishop, he willingly aided Massaja when the latter returned incognito.[2] Moreover, no move was taken against the Lazarists. De Jacobis was convinced 'that nine years of constant protection for us in a Prince both heretical and Abyssinian, is a very portentous thing.'[3]

Nevertheless Webē's difficulties continued. The threat of an Egyptian invasion of Hamāsēn distracted attention from the ever-restless Tegrē nobility.[4] Salāmā exploited the situation from his aerie on Dabra Dāmo by appeals to the Orthodox chiefs, fortified with an extremely effective anathema. As de Jacobis noted in his journal: 'After having excommunicated Webē, Abuna Salāmā has posted such a severe interdict on the Church, and on all other Christian practices, that no one celebrates Mass, no one baptizes, and no one fasts.'[5] It was too much for the harassed prince: 'At that time the Dajāzmāch Ubié caused the metropolitan Salama to come down from Debra Dammo, concluding a brief peace, because abuna Salama had multiplied anathemas.'[6] Domestic harmony was more important than the insubstantial aid of France or personal loyalty. On 10 October 1848 de Jacobis was banished.

The exile did not last long. The *dajāzmāch* resorted to several devices to readmit the Lazarists. First, in a spurious fit of loyalty, he appealed for the help of *Rās* Ali.[7] Then, more realistically, perhaps, he sought the offices of Rolland, the French consul at Massawa, to reconcile the two ecclesiastics. This, too, failed.[8] The gradual restoration of Webē's authority eased the situation, and gave him more independence in his dealings with the metropolitan, whom he did not fear to defy on suitable occasions. Yet his actions were circumscribed by the latter's influence over the lesser political figures—

---

[1] Massaja, *35 Anni*, i. 76–7; Takla Hāymānot, *Abuna Jacob*, 116–17.

[2] Massaja, *35 Anni*, i. 106–7.

[3] APF, *SRC.AC*, v. 22ʳ; de Jacobis to Prop. Fide, Wojerat, 15 Feb. 1848.

[4] PRO, FO 401/I, 24; Plowden to Palmerston, Massowah, 16 Aug. 1848.

[5] De Jacobis, *Giornale*, iv. 90; 21 July 1848. So successful an interdict is extremely rare.

[6] 'Nuovi Documenti III', 397. See also 'Vicende', 486–7: and *Lettres de Jacobis*, ii, no. 267; Massauah, 27 Oct. 1848.

[7] *Annales*, xiv (1849), 669–70, 674–5; letters from Fr. Stella, Gondar, 10 Feb. and 20 Feb. 1849.

[8] *Rev. his. miss.*, xvi (1939), 437; Rolland to MAE, Massouah, 6 Nov. 1849.

both rivals and subordinates. Still Webē evoked the mission's grudging respect and affection:

This blessed sovereign is so mysterious in all his operations that no matter how much one studies it is impossible to discover what are his true sentiments. He hates the abbuna Salama, he has taken from him his lands and has practically reduced him to begging ... and for fear of him he keeps at a distance Monsig.r de Jacobis whom he loves, and venerates.[1]

De Jacobis soon returned, but the *status quo* from 1850 to 1855 was uneasy. During his first exile at Massawa, the Lazarist had been consecrated bishop by Massaja.[2] This placed an additional strain on his relations with Webē, but they soon eased. Occasional withdrawal to the coast proved a sufficient safety valve.

The political and religious insecurity of Tegrē caused the mission to turn northward. A voyage of exploration by Sapeto and Stella led, in 1852, to the founding of work in the Bogos country.[3] Gradually, the centre of the mission had shifted from its beginnings in Adwā via Agāmē to Akāla Guzāy. Here, in a string of converted parishes on the eastern rim of the plateau, was the nascent Ethiopian Catholic Church, largely beyond the effective control of Webē. Yet, without his support, it is unlikely that the seed could have been planted.

In the light of the seventeenth-century precedent, it was remarkable enough that one Ethiopian ruler should prove so benevolent towards Catholicism. Yet Webē was not alone. Without exception, all major political figures of the 1840s shared his approach, and the mission had real, if transitory, connections with them. By 1845 the principal question around which relations were formed was Fr. Montuori's project of persuading the Ethiopian princes to replace *Abuna* Salāmā with a Ge'ez rite Catholic bishop.[4] De Jacobis had come to realize the fruitlessness of such schemes, but, despite his opposition,[5] Montuori was not to be dissuaded. Interviews with Sāhela Sellāsē and *Rās* Ali increased his conviction that these princes were willing to turn to Rome.[6] Montuori left Ethiopia to press his case at the Vatican, where, however, wisdom prevailed.

---

[1] APF, *SRC.AC*, v. 293ᵛ-4ʳ; Biancheri to Prop. Fide, Massua, 10 Aug. 1850.
[2] The date of the consecration is uncertain. Pane (*Il Beato*, 635–6) locates it between 23 Dec. 1848 and 8 Jan. 1849.   [3] Sapeto, *Viaggio e Missione*.
[4] APF, *SRC.AC*, v. 156; Memorandum of Montuori, n.d.
[5] Ibid. iv. 551ʳ; de Jacobis to Card. Pref., Guala, 25 Mar. 1846. Ibid. v. 154ʳ-6ᵛ; Biancheri to Prop. Fide, Roma, 11 Nov. 1849. See also Betta, 'Inizio', Chap. V, 348 ff., for Propaganda's own schemes, now suspended; and Pane, *Il Beato*, 591–603, 645–7.   [6] 'Memorandum', loc. cit.

Mistaken as he was about the acceptance of a Catholic bishop, Montuori none the less reflected the desire of the princes for closer relations with the mission, and its sponsoring power. *Rās* Ali was well disposed, and, until the arrival of Salāmā in Gondar, he protected it. The presence of the metropolitan in the city, and the consequent outbreak of ecclesiastical turmoil, however, made the place insecure, and Montuori, who had been building up a small band of Catholics, fled to the Sudan. Nevertheless, Catholic presence was maintained through the *rās*'s support of a number of highly-placed sympathizers—principally *Aṣē* Yohannes III and *Eçhagē* Māhṣantu, whom we shall look at more closely below.[1]

With the bishop's exile in 1846, central Ethiopia enjoyed greater freedom in its relations with the mission. Two Lazarists, Stella and Biancheri, returned to Bagēmder where they enjoyed the *rās*'s active protection. Ali even toyed with Biancheri's project of having de Jacobis, now bishop, accepted as metropolitan;[2] and cordially received Massaja in 1850–1.[3] He convinced the Capuchin that only the support of France was wanting for a more pronounced promissionary policy. Moreover, Massaja's colleagues travelled in Ali's territories with some freedom, Fr. Giusto da Urbino remaining in the Ṭānā region until 1854.[4] While this activity remained slight, and the Catholic presence dispersed, the best measure of its quality is the hopes which it raised for the future. De Jacobis planned to expand into the central provinces, and, in 1854, set out for a tour of inspection. The rise of Tēwodros brought an abrupt end.

Only tenuous contacts were established with Shawā, but they were, nevertheless, revealing. Consistent with his early policy of encouraging European contact, in 1838 Sāhela Sellāsē wrote inviting Sapeto in much the same terms as Isenberg had previously received.[5] Illness prevented an acceptance. However, following Shawā's

---

[1] 'Vicende', 474; *Annales*, xi (1846), 65–6; de Jacobis to Étienne, Guala, 10 Dec. 1844.

[2] APF, *SRC.AC*, v. 633; Biancheri to Prop. Fide, Halai, 12 July 1853. See also ibid. 436; Biancheri to Fransoni, n.d. [but *c.* Jan. 1852].

[3] For Stella, see *Annales*, xiv (1849), 658–69, 674–8; xv (1850), 543–6. Also Massaja, *35 Anni*, i. 137–46.

[4] Massaja, *35 Anni*, i. 145. See also, Jaenen, 'Blondeel: The Belgian Attempt to Colonize Ethiopia', *African Affairs*, lv (1956), 217. For Massaja's colleagues, see *35 Anni*, i. 92–3, 144–5, 195; ii. 124–5: and F. Tarducci, *Il P. Giusto da Urbino Missionario in Abissinia e Le Esplorazioni Africane* (Faenze, 1899).

[5] APF, *SRC.AC*, iii: 607–9, Sapeto to Prop. Fide, Adoa, 26 July 1838; 682, ibid. 4 July 1839.

rupture with the Orthodox bishop, Montuori visited it in 1846, raising great hopes.[1] Again circumstances intervened with the death of Sāhela Sellāsē in 1847. His successor, Hāyla Malakot, professed welcome for the Capuchins, and actually entertained one for a period, but was unable or unwilling to reopen the Zeila route.[2] Since they were never put to the test, uncertainty clouds the *negus*'s intentions. Nevertheless it seems clear that they arose from broader considerations of resuming his predecessor's interest in the exploitation of foreign influence, for, at much the same time, an approach was made both to the British government and the CMS in Cairo, suggesting the return of Krapf.[3] Yet, with the Zeila route closed, Shawān policy was doomed to frustration. Not until Menilek reopened it in 1867 did European missionaries reappear.[4]

The most remarkable invitation to the Catholics came from Gojjām. However short-lived, the Gojjāmē flirtation demonstrated most convincingly the secularization in Ethiopian attitudes towards Rome. In 1841–2, a Belgian consular official, Blondeel, visited the province. The following year he wrote to the Propaganda of his dealings with the princes Goshu and Berru:

I sought to inspire in them the desire to have Catholic missionaries with them and I succeeded in concluding with each of them a convention, of which the letters which they sent me and which I have the honour to communicate to Your Eminence, form the contracts. From this it results that they have undertaken to receive and protect two or three missionary priests, and to give them some sacred land (guèdam) on which to establish their church, their school and their house. . . .[5]

He went on to describe the princes' avidity for European 'arts and crafts', and for assistance in converting newly conquered Gāllā peoples to Christianity, to render them more loyal. The two themes of European knowledge and internal political aggrandizement emerge clearly from the princes' letters: 'Send a Man to my Country, who

---

[1] For Montuori's account of his trip to Shawā, see Sapeto, *Viaggio*, 468–70.

[2] Massaja, *35 Anni*, i. 92–3, 104–5, 145; Farina, *Lettere*, 109–10.

[3] C.M/o48, 79; Lieder to Secretaries, Cairo, 5 June 1849. See also FO 401/I, 39; King of Shoa to Queen Victoria, n.d.

[4] For Catholic missions in Shawā, after this date, see Caulk, 'Foreign Policy of Menilek', Chap. I, and K. Darkwah, 'The Rise of the Kingdom of Shoa 1813–1889', unpublished Ph.D. thesis (University of London, 1966).

[5] APF, *SRC.AC*, iv. 334ʳ; Blondeel to Fransoni, Borgo S. Sepolcro, 20 June 1843. See also Roeykens, 'Les Préoccupations missionnaires du consul belge Ed. Blondeel . . .', 1141 ff.; and A. Duchesne, *À la recherche d'une colonie belge. Le Consul Blondeel en Abyssinie (1840–1842). Contribution à l'histoire précoloniale de la Belgique* (Brussels, 1953), Chap. V.

teaches. I will receive this Man as a Brother, and will cause him to stay in a monastery. If he wants to go to the Galla Country to make them Christians, I will send a Man with him.'[1]

Gojjām was never really a promising field for the Catholics.[2] One of the principal battlefields of the Jesuits, its Orthodox peasantry has maintained a reputation for resistance to foreign influence. Moreover, despite its allegiance to the heretical *Qebāt*, its princes pursued a policy of support for *Abuna* Salāmā, following his arrival in Gondar. Remote from any contact with the European powers, Berru and Goshu rightly saw the bishop as a more useful tool in their struggle to emerge from *Rās* Ali's predominance.[3] Still, they were one with their contemporaries in their attempts to exploit religion.

The World of God

An undue concentration on political issues, however, would be a serious distortion of the mission's life. Its early work revealed remarkable sympathy for Catholicism among the Ethiopian clergy. Some *preparatio Catholica* is required to explain the mission's support by a wide range of mature and recognized public figures, amongst them the *Eçhagē* Māhsantu, *Asē* Yohannes, and the clerics Habta Sellāsē and Kidāna Māryām. Both Takla Hāymānot and Gabra Mikā'ēl, the most famous converts, were from the clerical tradition; the latter enjoying a reputation as a teacher, and acceptance in court circles. Naturally, they looked to the mission to provide answers for problems arising from their own experience.

The first place to turn for an anticipation of Catholicism would be the sects. Despite some missionary ambivalence about the dogmatic status of *Qebāt* and *Sost Ledat*, it is clear that Catholics were better received by the latter. Although Massaja boldly proclaimed that Dabra Libānos was 'più vicina alla fede cattolica',[4] the Lazarists were more cautious. De Jacobis at first supported this view, but later retreated to neutrality, while Biancheri, perhaps the most perceptive, labelled it Adoptionist and Nestorian.[5] Lay Catholic views equally

---

[1] APF, *SRC.AC*, iv. 253ʳ; letter from Goshu, n.d.

[2] Ibid. 446–7; de Jacobis to Prop. Fide, Guala, 20 Feb. 1845.

[3] 'Nuovi Documenti II', 395; and Massaja, *35 Anni*, i. 143–4. But see also, APF, *SRC.AC*, iv. 693; d'Abbadie to Franzoni, Gola, 2 Sept. 1847.

[4] *35 Anni*, i. 116–17.

[5] De Jacobis, *Giornale*, ii. 95; iii. 52–3: APF, *SRC.AC*, v. 714; de Jacobis to Prop. Fide, Abissinia, 7 Jan. 1854: *Annales*, xv (1850), 304–6; Biancheri to Sturchi, Rome, 24 Feb. 1850.

differed. Blondeel strongly favoured the identification of *Qebāt* with Catholicism, while d'Abbadie seems to incline to Dabra Libānos.[1] Whatever the dogmatic position, the missions' early support came almost exclusively from the followers of Takla Hāymānot. However, just as important as sectarian allegiance was the rancour and frustration of the doctrinal controversies. Many sensitive clerics must have been disaffected from the whole business, and their alienation was still more fertile a field for the assurances of Rome, so tellingly manifested in de Jacobis's piety.

By the 1840s the clergy of Gondar had weathered many storms. At the head of the strongest sect, they enjoyed some reputation for liberality and openness, with a weakness for religious dialectic. Gobat had been impressed by their tolerance,[2] and Sapeto was well received in 1840-1, the first Catholic priest to enjoy the protection of *Eçhagē* Māhṣantu.[3] The Ethiopian records stress this clergyman's constant strife with Salāmā on doctrinal matters, and give him a prominent part in the latter's expulsion from Gondar.[4] Thus, while there was an element of closing the ranks with the other enemies of Alexandrian theology, the *eçhagē* gave positive signs of pro-Catholicism. His protection for the Catholics was often in the face of strong opposition. Moreover, on separate occasions he expressed to d'Abbadie and Blondeel his strong desire to make a pilgrimage to Jerusalem and Rome.[5] In early 1848 Māhṣantu was abducted to Gojjām in revenge for Salāmā's exile. Thereafter, he ceased to be of importance. Although he is much more to be noted for his favour to Catholicism than for any open espousal of it, Massaja suggests that he was converted.[6]

The now decadent Gondarine branch of the royal family also witnessed clear sympathy for Catholicism. Antoine d'Abbadie remarked: 'Paez had been successful above all with the members of the royal family who witness even today a great respect for Catholics.'[7] *Aṣē* Yohannes III, Emperor briefly in 1841, was the most notable,

[1] APF, *SRC.AC*, iv. 334–5; Blondeel to Fransoni, Borgo S. Sepolcro, 20 June 1843: Roeykens, 'Préoccupations missionaires', 1150: BN, *Éth.-Abb.*, 266, 39ʳ; and 267, 124.

[2] *Journal*, 343.   [3] Sapeto, *Viaggio*, 110–11.

[4] 'Nuovi Documenti II', 383–7; 'Vicende', 468–80 *passim*, 500. See also d'Abbadie, *Voyage en Abyssinie*, 14–15.

[5] APF, *SRC.AC*, iv. 179ᵛ; Blondeel to Fransoni, Gondar, 1 Mar. 1842: Roeykens, 'Préoccupations missionaires', 1144–7: BN, *Éth.-Abb.*, 266, 39ʳ: and de Jacobis, *Giornale*, iii. 233.

[6] Massaja, *35 Anni*, i. 143–4.   [7] BN, *Éth.-Abb.*, 267, 134ᵛ.

although his sister, *Wāyzaro* Hirut, the closer.[1] Yet references to these figures, although frequent, are not extended. Imperial patronage may have lent lustre, but it brought no weight.

The native Tegrē clergy was generally luke-warm. On one occasion, Catholic mass was performed in an Orthodox church,[2] but public reaction did not encourage repetition. For much of its stay in Adwā the mission had to be guarded in worship. Amongst the local clergy, adherence to the bishop's party was strong. De Jacobis's warmest associates in the area were Amharā followers of *Sost Ledat*, members of Webē's court. The most distinguished of these men were Habta Sellāsē and *Alaqā* Kidāna Māryām,[3] whose attitudes to foreign missions, in very different ways, had already been influenced by their contact with the CMS. Undoubtedly the *alaqā*'s experience with the Protestants contributed to his sympathy for Catholicism, a point made by contemporaries: '. . . the alaka Kidona Mariam, . . . sworn enemy of Protestant missions, found in the hate which he bore for them an additional motive for protecting with all his power, and it was great, Catholic missions.'[4] Yet this would hardly explain his constancy.[5] Rather, we must see him as typical of a new kind of Ethiopian churchman—tolerant to Rome, and sensitive to common devotional practices.

Habta Sellāsē, the friend of Gobat's Gondar days, represents a different approach. He is one of the few Ethiopians in lesser position to emerge as clearly dedicated to innovation and the promotion of European influence. Webē had appointed him *Liqa Kāhnāt*, supervisor of the Tegrē clergy,[6] a post of considerable influence; while in 1840 he became head of the delegation to Alexandria. The Catholic sources confirm Gobat's estimation of his person: 'un cuore ed un carattere magnifico'.[7] In 1841 Habta Sellāsē visited Rome, and returned an even firmer pro-European. As two French travellers

[1] De Jacobis, *Giornale*, ii. 112–13; iii. 284–5: *Annales*, x. 153; de Jacobis to Étienne, Adowa, 18 June 1843: *Lettres de Jacobis*, ii, no. 299; to Biancheri, Allitienà, 14 May 1851.

[2] APF, *SRC.AC*, iii. 607ᵛ; Sapeto to Prop. Fide, Adoa, 26 July 1838. This was repeated in Gondar, *Viaggio e Missione*, 106–7, 111.

[3] De Jacobis, *Giornale*, ii. 195; iii. 52–3. It is not certain that Kidāna Māryām was an Amharā, but he owed his position to Webē. See above, Chap. III, pp. 33–4, 38, 41, 44, 56.

[4] Lefebvre, *Voyage*, i. 108.

[5] De Jacobis, *Giornale*, ii. 195: APF, *SRC.AC*, v. 45ᵛ; Schimper to [Massaja?], Tecundi, 15 Jan. 1848.

[6] BN, *Éth.-Abb.*, 267, 134ʳ.

[7] *Lettres de Jacobis*, ii, no. 171; de Jacobis to Guarini, Alexandria, n.d.

reported: 'The Alaca Aptésellassi [*sic*] . . . told us in parting: The sun shines in your country, but Abyssinia is still in the shadows; let us hope in God.'[1] His enthusiasm inspired the *eçhagē*'s hopes of pilgrimage, and he became a powerful witness, who helped ease the mission's path by testifying against Ethiopian preconceptions of Rome.[2] Yet despite a constant use of his position to protect the mission, there were limits beyond which he would not go. He opposed Massaja's presence on the grounds that he infringed indigenous ecclesiastical sovereignty.[3] He was, then, the prototype of a creative nationalist, open to progressive influence, yet constantly reserving his own autonomy.[4]

Apart from the Dabra Libānos clergy, no clear pattern of sympathy emerges, except, perhaps, amongst the northern *Qebāt*. For some time, however, the mission enjoyed influence at the monastery of Gundā Gundē, a foundation of the medieval Stephanite heretics.[5] As yet, our information is too scarce to establish the doctrinal allegiance of the monks, a number of whom were converted, one receiving ordination from Massaja in 1846. *Mamher* Walda Giyorgis was openly pro-Catholic: '. . . the abbot', wrote de Jacobis, 'is asking urgently to return to the bosom of the Catholic Church, where already six of his colleagues have preceded him.'[6] Initially the missionaries had profited from the influence of Fr. Gabra Mikā'ēl who had been the *mamher*'s teacher. The sympathy of Gundā Gundē benefited the mission in two ways: it provided several clerical converts; and it allowed the establishment of the first modern Catholic parish at Gwālā, one of its fiefs.[7] With the election of a new abbot, around 1850, Catholic tendencies were suppressed.

[1] *Annales*, ix (1844), 286; Note of Galinier and Ferret to Bourville, Cairo, Sept. 1842.

[2] Takla Hāymānot, *Abuna Jacob*, 38.

[3] Ibid. 27-8, 116. See also APF, *SRC.AC*, iv. 338^r; de Jacobis to Fransoni, Adowa, 21 June 1843: and Coulbeaux, *Un Martyr abyssin. Ghebra-Michael de la congrégation de la mission (Lazariste)* (Paris, 1902), 123-5.

[4] His influence was eclipsed with Webē's fall in 1855. H. Stern, *Wanderings among the Falashas in Abyssinia Together with a Description of the Country and its Various Inhabitants* (London, 1862), 144-5.

[5] A. Mordini, 'Il Convento di Gunde Gundie', *Rassegna di Studi Etiopici*, xii (1953), 29-71; Taddesse Tamrat, 'Some Notes on the Fifteenth Century Stephanite "Heresy" in the Ethiopian Church', ibid. xxii (1966), 103-15; 'Cronaca Reale', 896-7.

[6] *Annales*, xii (1847), 317; de Jacobis to Spaccapietra, 20 Oct. 1845. See also Massaja, *35 Anni*, i. 70-1.

[7] APF, *SRC.AC*, iv. 608^r; de Jacobis to Prop. Fide, Massauah, 2 Dec. 1846. See also de Jacobis, *Giornale*, iv. 173.

Around 1848 *Abbā* Takla Alfā, a monk of Dabra Bizan and a *Qebāt* partisan, was converted. He seems to have enjoyed a national reputation amongst the Ēwosṭātians for his austerity and sanctity. He won the mission several parishes in Akāla Guzāy and proselytized amongst his fellow sectarians in Gojjām. However, the party as a whole remained recalcitrant. Takla Alfā himself survived an initial period of persecution, but eventually ceded under pressure. Ephemeral as his Catholicism, and that of the *Qebāt* monks, proved to be, it placed another stone in the foundations.[1] For the parishes, converted under his influence, held fast. Indeed, they seem scarcely to have noticed their transition from Orthodoxy to Catholicism. 'Many of these *Cabats*', wrote de Jacobis, 'are today Catholics. However, we have had to prohibit their calling themselves *Cabats* and now they know that they ought solely to call themselves Roman Catholics.'[2]

The foregoing has revealed that the early work of Catholic missions rested upon the sympathy of followers of the *Sost Ledat* doctrine, some *Qebāt* support, and an exploitation of Ethiopian tolerance. Yet it was the personality of Justin de Jacobis which won for Rome its most distinguished converts, Fr. Takla Hāymānot of Adwā and Fr. Gabra Mikā'ēl. Gabra Mikā'ēl, in part, came to Catholicism through disillusionment with, and disaffection from, the doctrinal debate. An opponent of the Three Births, he early decided that orthodoxy lay in a redefinition of the Two Births, but again parted company with the established parties over the question of the Holy Spirit, and the Unction of Christ.[3] He held responsible teaching posts and was appointed to the Alexandrian delegation in 1840.

The determining experiences of his life were the trip to Rome in 1841, and his meeting with de Jacobis. The grandeur and order of the Papal Court contrasted sharply with the confusion of the Ethiopian Church, and his favourable impression was nurtured by the Lazarist. On his return from Rome and Egypt, he first tried to resolve the sectarian question in Gondar. But the futility of this soon becoming apparent, he turned to the mission, and, after a period of considera-

---

[1] For *Abbā* Takla Alfā and the *Qebāt* see: 'Vicende', 488–9, 508: Massaja, *35 Anni*, i. 91–2: APF, *SRC.AC*, v. 172–3, *Abbā* Takla Alfā to de Jacobis, n.d.; and 547, de Jacobis, Halai, 11 Jan. 1852: de Jacobis, *Giornale*, iv. 67, 162, 164.

[2] APF, *SRC.AC*, v. 714ᵛ; to Prop. Fide, Abissinia, 7 Jan. 1854.

[3] J. B. Coulbeaux, *Un Martyr abyssin*. Coulbeaux seems dependent on Takla Hāymānot's two works 'Vicende' and *Abuna Jacob*, although he also had access to independent material. We have no writings of Gabra Mikā'ēl himself.

tion, entered the Catholic Church.[1] In 1851 he became the first priest ordained by Bishop de Jacobis. His influence on the mission's development was immense, for he won over both Aṣē Yohannes and a number of lesser men, who formed the backbone of the indigenous clergy.[2] Of the remaining converts, the most outstanding was Takla Hāymānot of Adwā. From a clerical family, he owed his conversion, at the age of about fifteen, directly to the personal influence of de Jacobis. Nowhere is the force of the latter's personality more convincingly portrayed than in the biography by his disciple. In the period covered by this study he emerged as one of the principal defenders of the tradition established by his mentor. Subsequently, he developed into a major figure in the formation of a proto-modern national literature, although his role is almost universally ignored.[3]

An investigation of the mission's converts and sympathizers thus reveals diversity. No tie of sectarianism, class, or office unites them. Two hundred years of insulation had dissipated the strongest Ethiopian objections to Catholicism. Feelings could still be raised against Rome, but the reaction was no longer immediate. Furthermore, the troubled condition of their country prepared Ethiopians to seek foreign answers to traditional concerns. A man of tact, understanding, and deep piety could exploit this readiness. Such was Justin de Jacobis, outstanding in his sympathy and respect for the integrity of Ethiopian experience. The successful implanting of Roman Catholicism in Ethiopian culture is largely attributable to him.

The Rites

From its beginnings in Adwā the mission grew northwards, although, until the rise of Tēwodros, it maintained a colony in Gondar. For several years de Jacobis and his small band of disciples had wandered the Tegrē plateau. Then, in 1844 Webē gave them the fief of Enticho east of Adwā, and approved their conversion of the parish church at Gwālā, just outside Addigrāt.[4] From there in the next few years they worked up through Zāna Daglē to Sarāyē and Hamāsēn; Alitēnā in 1845; Hēbo and Hālāy by 1852. In 1854 their

---

[1] Coulbeaux, *Un Martyr abyssin*, 95–100.

[2] Ibid. 53–4; Takla Hāymānot, *Abuna Jacob*, 87–8.

[3] In addition to *Abuna Jacob* and 'Vicende', see Maura da Leonessa, *Lettere di Abba Tecle Haymanot di Adua* . . . (Rome, 1939).

[4] De Jacobis, *Giornale*, iii. 146–7, 231; iv. 5, 37, 196: *Annales*, x (1845), 170, 185–6; xi (1846), 74 ff.; xvii (1852), 131–5; xviii (1853), 408–9.

nominal adherents may have numbered five thousand, although we have no solid statistical information.[1] In most cases, entire parishes were taken over following the conversion of one of their clerical sons. Success finally raised the basic problem of rites, and the attendant question of the status of Ethiopian orders.

In two fields, integral to contemporary missiology the Catholics were creative. Their attempts at indigenization and the formation of a national clergy were ahead of their time. Both were closely linked. Indigenization was primarily a question of rites. As noted Catholic attitudes had evolved drastically since the Jesuits. Continually Propaganda stressed the autonomy of local usage. Although many details were left unresolved, and despite the retention by both Lazarists and Capuchins of the Latin rite for themselves, Rome insisted that the Ethiopian Catholics be respected in their own practices. To this end, de Jacobis's consecration enabled him to work within the Ge'ez rite, although, for the want of authoritative texts on the latter, he rarely used the privilege.[2] Moreover, it was deemed 'more convenient' to extend Orthodox practice to the Abyssinian Gāllā 'as this system will contribute to maintain uniformity and peace'.[3] De Jacobis never questioned the decision, and, despite an absence of much theoretical discussion on his part, his entire career was a continuous identification with his neophytes. Truly did Massaja remark: '. . . he greatly loves the abyssinian rite and Abyssinia.'[3] The Capuchin, on the other hand, fervently resisted acceptance of indigenous tradition. Pius XI was to speak of 'being moved to a yet warmer love for the true Bride of Christ' by looking upon her 'entrancing beauty in the diversity of her various rites'. Far from this being the case, Massaja declaimed: 'The oriental rites are an eternal monument to the obstinacy of these peoples . . . the levantines will never be Catholics in their hearts until they are latins, and sons of latins born and educated in the latin rite.'[4] Missions must work to eliminate differences.

[1] *Annales*, xvii (1852), 137; Poussou to Salvayre, 12 Feb. 1852.

[2] Betta, 'Il B. Giustino de Jacobis Prefetto Apostolico d'Abissinia', *Annali della Missione*, lxvii (1960), 370–2, n. 77, has a very important discussion, based on the Propaganda's outgoing correspondence which I have not used.

[3] Betta, loc. cit.

[4] Archivum Generale, O. F. M. Cap., LA25, 2; 'Osservazioni sopra il decreto della S.C. di Propaganda Fide emanato il 20. Novembre 1838 relativamente al trassito degli orientali da un rito ad un'altro', 30 Jan. 1864. For Pius XI, see C. Korolevsky, *Living Languages in Catholic Worship. A Historical Inquiry* (London, 1957), 186, n. 5.

PLATE IV

b. The young Bishop Guglielmo Massaja

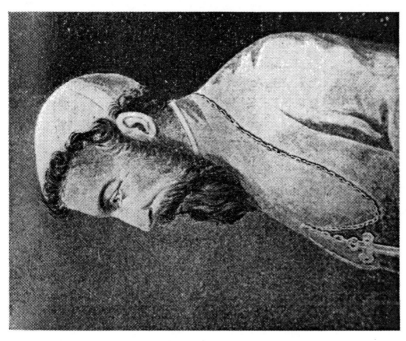

a. Bishop Justin de Jacobis

While in the north de Jacobis worked through a converted clergy and parish system, leaving intact traditional customs; in the south Massaja introduced Latin ones. He instructed his subordinates: 'As soon as you see some beginnings of Christianity, in the exercise of worship, you will do everything possible to introduce Roman Catholic practices. . . .'[1] This might be defended on the grounds that his mission was to pagans, but the argument is doubly fallacious. First, the Capuchins based themselves almost exclusively on the region's Christian elements: recent immigrants; survivals of earlier colonies; and the remarkably persistent Kafā Church.[2] Practically no religious contact was made with 'heathens'. Secondly, the area was culturally, historically, and economically linked to the Ethiopian state. The latter's contraction throughout the seventeenth and eighteenth centuries weakened only the political tie. Thus Massaja's approach was essentially imperialistic. Summing up his arguments, he proclaimed:

. . . the supreme advantages which implanting the latin rite and literature in these savage countries would produce, . . . are not small as everyone can see, these countries coming with the *european* rite and literature to attach themselves essentially to us, and to the mother Church with the vehicle of the language which can communicate to them infinite treasures of science and the spirit, things which, if it pleases God to bring it about, in time could become even for Abyssinia, a support and shield to maintain it in the catholic faith. . . .[3]

These views drew fire from two sides, within his own mission. On the one hand, his coadjutor Felicissimo Coccino is reported to have strongly favoured 'the absolute abolition of the latin rite';[4] while Fr. Léon des Avanchers viciously attacked the flexibility with which Massaja applied his strategy.[5] For the Capuchin proved extremely tolerant in practice. The Ethiopian calendar was preserved, as were

---

[1] Farina, *Lettere*, 96; 'Ricordi di Mons. Massaja ai Missionari Galla', Gualà, 24 Sept. 1847.

[2] See my thesis, 'European Religious Missions', Chap. V.

[3] APF, *SRC.AC*, vii. 109r; Massaja to Prop. Fide, Sciap-Kafa, 13 June 1861. My emphasis.

[4] AG, OFM, H44, 3; Gabriele da Rivolta, Massawah, 7 Oct. 1861. I have not observed these views in Coccino's correspondence, although his general disgruntlement is consistent with them. In any case, Fr. Gabriele, Massaja's procurator at Massawa, certainly held the views which he also attributes to Coccino.

[5] APF, *SRC.AC*, vi. 399v–400; des Avanchers to Card. Pref., Limou-Enarea, 26 Oct. 1859. See also AG, OFM, LA25, 5; Massaja to des Avanchers, Tetmara-Kafa, 22 Jan. 1860.

G

indigenous fasting and dietary practices. Circumcision was permitted, and distinct forms of devotion honoured,[1] the net result of which was the establishment in south-west Ethiopia of a Latin rite much modified in a Ge'ez direction.

In the north it was the reverse. The formation of an indigenous Catholicism was hampered by the scarcity of reliable texts, and continually moved under the influence of Latin models.[2] None the less, de Jacobis nurtured the essential spirit, above all through the foundation of a national priesthood. His commitment anticipated by several generations Catholic practice elsewhere in Africa.[3] Obviously, the way was eased by the existence of the Orthodox Church, but this scarcely lessens the creativity of his approach, for the commonest missionary view was that traditional piety constituted their biggest barrier. De Jacobis saw deeper. Jettisoning European preconceptions about clerical training, he accepted Ethiopians as they came, and pressed them for the ministry with few alien trappings. He resisted an increase of foreigners, as one of his superiors reported:

This respectable and worthy colleague seems to have, with regard to the need of his mission, an idea which is not shared by his colleagues, and one which I, too, would not adopt: it's that indigenous priests could suffice to renew the face of Abyssinia, without its being necessary to have lots of European missionaries; and it's for that reason that he had written, about two years ago it seems to me, to not send any more.[4]

In the process a European missionary became Ethiopianized.

De Jacobis's policy was not without difficulties and contradictions. Full acceptance of the Ge'ez rite would have entailed recognizing the validity of Ethiopian holy orders. For this the missionaries were not prepared. The service of ordination was Coptic and no form of it proved readily available in Ethiopia. Careful examination of concrete

---

[1] Massaja to des Avanchers, Tetmara-Kafa, 22 Jan. 1860. See also APF, *SRC.AC*, vii. 106 ff.; Massaja to Prop. Fide, Sciap-Kafa, 13 June 1861.

[2] Korolevsky, *Living Languages*, 141–63, has an excellent discussion.

[3] J. Todd, *African Mission. A Historical Study of the Society of African Missions* (London, 1962), Chaps. II and X; Oliver, *Missionary Factor*, 215 ff. See also the now extensive Nigerian literature on Venn's celebrated policy: Ayandele, *Missionary Impact*; Ajayi, *Christian Missions*; and J. Webster, *The African Churches Among the Yoruba 1888–1922* (Clarendon Press: Oxford, 1964), 4 ff. Finally, also of relevance is C. R. Boxer, 'The problem of the native clergy in the Portuguese and Spanish Empires from the sixteenth to the eighteenth centuries', in Cuming (ed.), *The Mission of the Church and the Propagation of the Faith*, 85–105; reprinted from Boxer's *The Portuguese Seaborne Empire 1415–1825*.

[4] *Annales*, xvii (1852), 140; Poussou to Salvayre, 12 Feb. 1852.

cases suggested irregularities, which was only to be expected. The solitary nature of the episcopacy made ordinand supervision impossible. Moreover, succession gaps created backlogs demanding mass ordination, and this opened the way for extremely perfunctory observance of canonical regulations. Recent events had exacerbated the problem. Between 1803 and 1841 there was only the troubled reign of *Abuna* Qērelos, which lasted under fifteen years. Thus, by the 1840s an entire generation had passed without peaceful and regular government in the Church. The missionaries in their perplexity sought the guidance of Propaganda, which in turn looked to the Holy Office. No satisfaction was received.[1] By 1847 the mission was in a strained position, as de Jacobis explained:

One would not be able, Sirs, easily to form an idea of the difficulties and the embarrassment which we suffered on the subject of the ordination of the ecclesiastics . . . of whom the validity of the ordination, previously received, is at least doubtful. On the one side, we could not expose Divine worship to profanation, in permitting these priests to exercise the Holy Ministry, nor, on the other side, excite a public scandal which their suspension would have caused.[2]

Added complications came from the Ge'ez rite requirement of five clerics for the celebration of mass, for in no parish could there be mustered so many ordained by Roman bishops. Temporarily, then, the Eucharist was performed by Catholic priests assisted by men in Orthodox orders. The final solution, implemented with Massaja's arrival in 1846, was a complete reordination and the creation of a new Catholic priesthood. De Jacobis rejoiced; but his delight was not shared by his colleagues. Only the Neapolitan entered fully into the new fellowship. One follower recounts a visit to Massawa in which the Lazarist bishop was accompanied by two Ethiopians, one a priest. They were received to dinner by Fr. Stella and the Capuchin Felicissimo. Three places were set, for Europeans. De Jacobis took the food and left to share it with his Ethiopian colleagues.[3] Biancheri, consecrated coadjutor in 1853, viewed with gloom and despondency the prospect of becoming bishop of a diocese staffed by ill-educated

[1] Betta, 'Giustino de Jacobis', 311–12, n. 94: APF, *SRC.AC*, iv. 389 ff., Communication from the Holy Office to Prop. Fide, May 1844; 552 ff., de Jacobis to Prop. Fide, Guala, 25 Mar. 1846: *Annales*, xv (1850), 313–14; Biancheri to Sturchi, Rome, 24 Feb. 1850.

[2] *Annales*, xiii (1848), 67–8; to Conseil général, Propagation de la Foi (Lyons), Guala, 10 July 1847.

[3] CGL, 'Testimonies', *Abbā* Kidāna Māryām of Asmarā.

priests to be run under the Ge'ez rite. 'Judge', he cried, 'the crushing weight which bears down on my shoulders.'[1] The burden, so willingly carried by de Jacobis, became a stumbling block to his successors. Perhaps anachronistic in his extreme rejection of western methods, he had yet shown a holy and apostolic example. Insufficient respect for it cost the Catholic Church deep strife.

Massaja's attitude towards an indigenous priesthood was also creative. There was consensus amongst the Capuchins on the urgent need for a native clergy, whose efficacy in commending Christianity to their fellows was expected to be greater than the Europeans'. However, there was a radical divergence on how to bring this about. Elsewhere in Africa a sharp difference has been noted between Protestant and Catholic practice. The former quickly ordained Africans, minimizing educational requirements, while the latter, insisting on the same standards for black and white, imposed a long training. There has been a tendency to assume that the Roman pattern was immutable. We have already observed one exception, and have now to examine a second. For this classical dichotomy existed within the mission of south-west Ethiopia. While the subsequent disruption of Capuchin activity meant that the debate had little concrete issue, it is, none the less, of considerable theoretical interest. Basically, Massaja, following de Jacobis, fostered an extremely rapid formation of indigenous priests, while his sharpest critic, des Avanchers, advocated the western pattern.

Initially the Capuchins had the benefit of Orthodox clergy converted by the Lazarists. Because of stubborn adherence to their own rite, however, some of these men clashed with Massaja. He was not deterred and ordained several Gāllā and Amharā youths with no training whatsoever. Placed in responsible positions, they served faithfully and well. However, the Gāllā were redeemed slaves and their elevation drew a vitriolic attack from des Avanchers. Complaining to the Propaganda of the mission's condition, the Savoyard wrote that one of the causes:

is the mistaken course which Mgr. Massaja holds in the formation of the indigenous clergy—The ex-slaves always keep their primitive customs, but to place hands on children [enfants] scarcely 23 years old, who know neither how to read nor write, not even having the knowledge of our Holy

---

[1] *Annales*, xx (1855), 512–13; to Sturchi, Emqulo, 6 Jan. 1854. This difference in approach within the Lazarist mission was well remembered forty years later. CGL, 'Testimonies', *Abbā* James of Hālāy, *Abbā* Tasfā Ṣeyon of Hēbo.

Religion which one requires in Europe of a child taking its first communion. *It is to throw the Sacraments of the Church to dogs.* For how can these indigenous priests properly dispense the treasures of the Church?[1]

Massaja's approach was largely tactical. Faced with des Avanchers's alternative, the training of Gāllā priests in Europe, he agreed, in the long run.[2] Both men worked to this end. While Fr. Léon tried to produce Gāllā-language materials to aid the education of local clergy, Massaja worked for the establishment of a seminary in France.[3] Still the latter consistently defended his ordination of uneducated autochthons, and events justified him.[4] South-west Ethiopia was extremely difficult of access for Europeans. In 1863 Massaja crossed the Abbāy northwards, and was never able to return. 1878 saw the death of Mgr. Felicissimo, and the following year that of des Avanchers. Yet, when in 1902 Mgr. Jarosseau was able briefly to re-establish a European presence, the Catholic Church was alive in Kafā, and had expanded from the position left by Massaja in 1861.[5] The heroic and devoted service of four indigenous priests was responsible.

Through the apostolates of de Jacobis and Massaja the Catholic Church was established in Ethiopia, but it was largely the former who saw that the nascent organization was firmly rooted in its surrounding culture. The Lazarist proved himself wise and temperate in his relations with Ethiopian princes, and, although he was willing to call in as support the forces of European imperialism, he was quite able to survive without them. In short, he revealed qualities which were fully capable of exploiting the many and varied Ethiopian desires for a European connection. Yet the foregoing would give a misleading picture of the mission's situation, if no consideration were given to its potent forces of opposition. These forces crystallized around *Abuna* Salāmā.

Abuna Salāmā

Abuna Salāmā was one of the most controversial figures of the nineteenth century. A proud, difficult, and very young man, he was

[1] APF, *SRC.AC*, vi. 530ʳ; Limou-Enarea, 11 Mar. 1860. His emphasis.
[2] AG, OFM, H44, 2; des Avanchers to Massaja, Ghéra, 20 Sept. 1863.
[3] Ibid.; des Avanchers to Massaja and Coccino, Ghéra, 25 Aug.–: Massaja, *35 Anni*, viii. 7: Farina, *Lettere*, 280–3.
[4] AG, OFM, LA25, 5; Massaja to des Avanchers, Tetmara-Kafa, 22 Jan. 1860. See also *35 Anni*, v. 127 ff.; viii. 60–1: Farina, *Lettere*, 199–200.
[5] A. Jarosseau, 'L'Apostolat catholique au Kafa (Éthiopie) de 1862 à 1912', *Rev. his. miss.*, ix (1932), 94–101; and my thesis, Chap. V.

not the moral degenerate which the Catholic sources claim.[1] Indeed, few foreign sources show an adequate appreciation of his tenuous position. The erosion of imperial authority had destroyed the institutional basis of episcopal rule, while the rise of sectarianism had eroded its dogmatic and moral influence over much of the clerical élite. These developments condemned the bishop to the role of an intriguer, falling back on his popular mystique and charisma, his power of withholding ordination and of issuing limited anathemas, in return for temporary political alliances. Until the advent of Tēwodros, no politician was to offer him consistent, effective support.

Salāmā has been most noted for his anti-Catholicism. Three factors contributed. He had been educated at the CMS school in Cairo, where he developed a sympathy for Protestantism; the Catholics had vigorously opposed his election; and he saw in the missionary activities a clear infringement of his sovereignty. The controversy begins with his elevation at the extraordinary age of about twenty-one. The Catholic literature maintains that this was simoniacal;[2] but the charge is groundless as a careful examination of contemporary Propaganda and CMS sources reveals.[3] Indeed, until they discovered his educational background, the Catholics were favourably disposed, de Jacobis holding that his impressionable youth would make him amenable to toleration.[4] Fear of Protestantism, however, brought an attempt at coercing the Patriarch into dropping Salāmā. This failing, they tried to delay his departure for Ethiopia, but their efforts were countered by English support for the Patriarch, and merely aggravated the situation.[5] Through the CMS agent, British

---

[1] G. Lejean, *Théodore II. Le Nouvel Empire d'Abyssinie et les intérêts français dans le sud de la Mer Rouge* (Paris, 1865); A. d'Abbadie, *L'Abyssinie et le roi Théodore* (Paris, 1868); J.-B. Coulbeaux, 'Abouna-Salama', *Revue Anglo-Romaine*, i (1895), 625-36, 673-96. See also the writings of *Abbā* Takla Hāymānot. For Protestant views: Krapf, *Travels, Researches*; H. Stern, *The Captive Missionary . . .* (London, n.d.); Th. Waldmeier, *Erlebnisse in Abessinien in den Jahren 1858–1868* (Basel, 1869). Orthodox statements in C. Mondon-Vidailhet, *Chronique de Théodoros II roi des rois d'Éthiopie (1853–1868)* (Paris, n.d.), by *Alaqā* Walda Māryām; and Gabra Sellāsē, *Chronique du règne de Ménélik II roi des rois d'Éthiopie* (Paris, 2 vols., 1930-1), trans. Tasfā Sellāsē, ed. M. de Coppet.

[2] Pane, *Il Beato*, 352. See also 'Vicende', 456.

[3] CMS, C.M/045, 100, 102-3; Kruse to Secretaries, Cairo, 20 May, 17 June, and 17 July 1841: APF, *SRC.AC*, iv. 48 ff., de Jacobis to Prop. Fide, Cairo, 3 May 1841; 63, Cerruti to Fransoni, Alexandria, 26 May 1841; 73, Bourville to Fransoni, Cairo, 7 June 1841; 89, de Jacobis to Prop. Fide, Alexandria, 26 June 1841.

[4] Betta, 'Giustino de Jacobis', *Annali*, lxviii (1961), 168, n. 47: APF, *SRC.AC* iv. 63ʳ; Cerruti to Prop. Fide, Alexandria, 26 May 1841.

[5] See the references in footnote 3.

protection was obtained and the metropolitan sailed from Suez to Jiddah under the English flag.

With his arrival in Ethiopia, at the end of 1841, the bishop was plunged into controversy. The sects clamoured for recognition; Webē exploited him against *Rās* Ali; and he found the Catholics to be making progress. Through this morass he walked delicately. He tried to duck the theological issue, but aligned himself with Webē. Charges that the *rās* was Muslim were widespread, and it was easy for a Copt to fall in with the attempt to turn back the advance of Islam in Ethiopia.[1] Towards the Catholics he was firm, but moderate. He punished with closure the Adwā church in which Sapeto had said mass, and defended himself to Lefebvre:

> I have no intention . . . to prevent you from entering the churches; I only wished to prevent it that in the future a priest who is not of our communion should consecrate on our altars. I want to live in harmony with Europeans; but I will not allow them to mix themselves up in our religious government.[2]

It was a reasonable line, and Salāmā held to it firmly. Jurisdiction over the Ethiopian churches was his, and Catholic infringements were a constant complaint, reiterated over the years: 'Up to this moment the Roman Catholics have proved themselves my enemies. They desire to take possession of our churches, and should I prevent their doing so, they will place every obstacle in the way of travellers. . . .'[3] It was but one expression of his constantly frustrated efforts to establish a minimal sovereignty, the result of which was humiliation at the hands of dissident Ethiopians, and vilification from the Catholics.[4]

In February 1842, Webē was defeated by Ali at Dabra Tābor. The result was *Abuna* Salāmā's transfer to Gondar, under the control of *Rās* Ali, and a pronounced, if temporary, change in his attitude to the Catholics. Guarded hostility was transformed into overtures of peace. Uncertain of his new master, and fearful of the Gondar clergy, one foreigner turned to another for comfort. The bishop

---

[1] Abir, *Era of the Princes*, 110–16: APF, *SRC.AC*, iv. 179ᵛ; Blondel to Fransoni, Gondar, 1 Mar. 1842.

[2] *Voyage*, i. 311–12. See also MAE, *Corr. pol.*, i. 12; De Goutin to Ministre, Massouah, 1 Dec. 1841.

[3] PRO, FO 401/I, 176; Abuna Salama to Queen Victoria, 6 Apr. 1854. For the circumstances of this letter, see below, pp. 90–1.

[4] 'Vicende', 483–5; L. Fusella, 'Le lettere del dabtarā Assaggākhañ', *Rassegna di studi etiopici*, xii (1953), 94–5.

urged Fr. Montuori to remain in Gondar, although the Lazarist was determined to make good his escape while it was still possible:

After this disgrace [Dabra Tābor] I went to bid him good-bye [wrote Montuori] and on my assuring him of my pain on the question of the danger to which he had been subjected, he thanked me strongly and he told me that he was my friend, that our religions had been made one, and that if I wished, I could stay freely in the country.[1]

Following through in June 1842, Salāmā sought to alleviate the fears of the mission in Tegrē by sending gifts. De Jacobis replied in kind. The clergy of Adwā were instructed by their bishop to honour and respect the missionaries, and there was even a suggestion that the latter visit Gondar.[2]

The phase was short-lived. By September the metropolitan had come into conflict with the pro-Catholic *eçhagē*, and before the end of the year he instructed the clergy to refrain from contact with the mission.[3] Pressure was applied to the competing Tegrē princes, Webē and Arāyā, to force them to drop dabbling with the Catholics. On Webē's refusal, Salāmā redoubled his efforts. One last abortive overture of peace was followed in February 1844 by strong measures. The bishop explained himself to the CMS:

As to Yacob the Catholic, I, your beloved, will soon let him feel my power, for on his account I contended much with our beloved Oubea . . . I proclaimed excommunication in the market of Adowa that every one that enters into his house [de Jacobis's] . . . and hears his doctrine shall be expelled from the church. At this many of them who used to enter, forbore.[4]

Yet Gondar was too remote, and the control of the Tegrē princes over their Church was too tight, for more than harassment to result. This was particularly felt in the Aksum-Adwā area, from which, in any case, the mission had largely withdrawn. Still, before his return to the north, the bishop was able to trouble the new foundation at Gwālā.[5]

Meanwhile, Salāmā's position in Gondar had declined drastically. Constant quarrels with the local clergy on doctrinal issues became

---

    [1] *Annales*, ix (1844), 296; Montuori to Étienne, Khartoum, 29 July 1842. See also ibid. 288–9; Gallinier and Ferret to Bourville, Cairo, Sept. 1842.
    [2] De Jacobis, *Giornale*, ii. 86, 98–100: *Annales*, ix (1844), 276–8; de Jacobis to Étienne, Adowa, 19 Aug. 1842.
    [3] De Jacobis, *Giornale*, ii. 118, 140.
    [4] CMS, C.M/048, 60a; Abouna Salama to Lieder, n.d. [1844]. See also de Jacobis, *Giornale*, ii. 149, 153, 195; iii. 81–2, 133: and Methodios of Aksum, 'An Extemporaneous Account of Abyssinian Matters', *Abba Salama*, i (1970), 56–7.
    [5] De Jacobis, *Giornale*, iii. 236–7.

increasingly acrimonious. No secular support for the Alexandrian position was forthcoming, as Ali and his mother Manan curried the *eçhagē*. Moreover, Shawā was drawn into the controversy. Two points were at issue: Sāhela Sellāsē's rejection of the English presence, and the establishment of heresy in 1841. The bishop's account leans on the former:

> As to our love with you it is well known that our beloved Captain Harris, when he was in Shoa, we did for him all that we could, and sent particular men to fetch him, but Sahlasalāsi ... bound them, and we excommunicated him, and were angry at him, so that until now we are not reconciled.[1]

But it was the latter that had the real force. Salāmā attempted to gain restitution for the clergy displaced by the doctrinal *coup*. Excommunication made the Shawāns uncomfortable, but more serious was a refusal to consecrate ordinands and *tābot* (altar-pieces). By the end of 1845 Ali had been won to Sāhela Sellāsē's side, and the bishop's persistence resulted in a disgraceful banishment.[2] De Jacobis was shocked and saw in the ensuing outbreak of war the judgement of God:

> ... it seems that God wants to avenge the impious outrage even of his Unfaithful minister. The chief monk [*Eçhagē* Māhsantu], Wozor-Menen, Ras Aly, who have outraged the man whom they call their Bishop, God's representative on earth, have outraged God himself, and they are not slow in feeling the terrible effects of His anger.[3]

Tegrē was a more congenial clerical environment for the bishop but continuing attempts to thwart the development of Catholicism were only partly effective. Attacks on the Lazarists were interconnected with invitations to the Protestants. But the hostility of the secular élite dominated by Webē contained both. Salāmā maintained a desultory correspondence with Lieder of the CMS. In 1843 he had supported Isenberg's return, and the following year wrote to Aden with assurances that 'I am ready to forward your wishes in every way' and encouraging the establishment of a Massawa consulate '... because the french has one [*sic*]. ...'[4] The arrival of Plowden in

---

[1] CM/048, 60a; Salāmā to Lieder. For this event from the Shawān side, see above, Chap. III, pp. 52–3.

[2] Abir, *Era of the Princes*, 125–6; 'Nuovi Documenti', 384–7; 'Vicende', 476–9; de Jacobis, *Giornale*, iv. 12–13.

[3] *Lettres de Jacobis*, ii, no. 261; Gualà, 6 Nov. 1847.

[4] IO, *Political and Secret Records. . . . (Aden)*, xxviii. 156; *Abuna* Salāmā to Haines, Gondar, 12 May 1844. See also CMS, C.M/048, 60a.

1848 finally opened the way for the pursuance of an Anglophile policy.

However, this was slight compensation for the continuing defection of Orthodox parishes to the side of Rome. No definitive expulsion of the mission could be obtained. Webē's ascendancy over Tegrē in the early 1850s, however unsteady, allowed him to defy Salāmā. The prince went so far as to declare to de Jacobis:

> Abbuna Salama pretends that the spiritual jurisdiction in our country is solely His; however, about all that I know nothing. So I give very solemn directions to all the authorities, which are dependent on me, to never again get involved with, or further, these pretensions of the Abbuna against the Catholics. . . . I give complete liberty to all, as to the others, so also to the Catholics.[1]

His control, however, was less than complete. The mission's expansion was slowed, some converts returned, and material damage was inflicted.[2]

The bishop was also aware of Capuchin activities which he tried to curtail. In 1851 he sent a countermission, led by a Copt, to Enārya. Gallingly, it aborted in Gondar and took refuge with the Catholics.[3] Again in the same year he secured the defection of a Capuchin servant bearing money from Massawa to the south-west. Although some of the property was restored, the Catholics charged that Salāmā had held back the greater part. In retaliation, the metropolitan's friend was detained by the French consul in Jiddah. As a counter-reprisal the bishop's party seized and imprisoned Fr. Felicissimo at Adwā late in the year. Eventually, the affair blew over.[4] Webē secured the missionary's release, and the French relinquished their captive. It was but a further skirmish in Salāmā's continuing war with Catholicism. However, the incident served to reveal increasing foreign political involvement in Ethiopian religious affairs.

On the one hand, French support for Catholicism grew more intimate and concrete. On the other, Britain was becoming involved in the metropolitan's cause. As Plowden wrote: '. . . from his great influence in Abyssinia, the friendship of the Aboona Salama is, to me, absolutely necessary, and that friendship has hitherto never

---

[1] APF, *SRC.AC*, v. 543^r; de Jacobis to Prop. Fide, Halai, 11 Jan. 1852.

[2] Takla Hāymānot, *Abuna Jacob*, 175-6.

[3] De Jacobis, *Giornale*, iv. 200: CMS, CA5/016, 113; Krapf to Venn, Massoa, 2 Mar. 1855.

[4] For the Catholic side see *Rev. his. miss.*, xvi (1939), 582-6. Counter material is contained in PRO, FO 401/I, nos. 288, 309, 311, 363, 386.

wavered, serving me well in maintaining a delicate and critical post. . . .'[1] Salāmā's appeal to Victoria: 'to take me under your protection'; received the assurance 'that Her Majesty's Government are watching over his interests'.[2] Immediately, this meant representations in Rome, which were too late to affect the events which were their occasion. Ultimately, it led to Maqdalā. For British involvement in Ethiopia grew out of the friendship of bishop and consul. The rise of Kāsā, and Salāmā's consequent reinstatement in Gondar, opened the door to Protestant forces; and shut out the Catholics, pursuing them with persecution and martyrdom. And yet, in the end Salāmā's efforts were reduced to nought, while the foundations of a Catholic Church, however small, survived.

[1] PRO, FO 401/I, no. 288; Plowden to Malmesbury, Massowah, 15 Feb. 1853. See also W. Plowden, *Travels in Abyssinia and the Galla Country with an Account of a Mission to Ras Ali in 1848* (London, 1868), 91–2.

[2] PRO, loc. cit.; no. 363, Abuna Salama to Queen Victoria, 6 Apr. 1854; no. 364, Clarendon to Bruce, FO, 22 July 1854.

CHAPTER V

Tēwodros
'Out of the Dust'

By the mid-nineteenth century Ethiopia's crisis had deepened. Neither the aspirations of Ali nor Webē had succeeded in creating a coherent national rule. Warfare was endemic: the lot of the people hard. Furthermore there continued to exist a strong consciousness amongst the Christian population of its inherent superiority, perhaps even of a civilizing mission. The dominance of the Yajju Gālā, despite their adherence to Christianity, was felt as an alien imposition from a culturally inferior people. Moreover, the religion of the Gālā was compromised. The Muslim élites of Wallo and Yajju retained strong influence in the court of Begēmder, contributing many of the *rās*'s senior advisers. In the early forties their influence was sufficient to attempt a link-up with external Islam, and this policy became known. Ultimately, however, renewal came as the response to external challenge. From the beginning of the century Ethiopia's Muslim neighbours had undergone a major revival. This was largely stimulated by the emergence of Mehemet Ali's Egypt as a modern state. Political and economic expansion marched hand in hand. For the first time a unified threat emerged from two directions when both the Red Sea and the Sudan fell under the same rule. Numerous border clashes, beginning in the 1830s, created the impression amongst both Ethiopians and westerners that Egyptian expansion might engulf the highlands. This fear was premature. No such intention was held in mid century, although in the 1870s the Christian state suffered its first attempt at conquest since the sixteenth century.

Meanwhile a more powerful, if latent, threat had developed from the western powers. European interest had developed from the early nineteenth century. Its expression was largely indirect. Some compatibility was felt with Ethiopian Christianity and the powers acted to restrain Egypt. However, national competition, foreshadowing imperialism, was active. Thus, while Britain and France could unite to oppose Muslim advance, they viewed each other's activities with suspicion. We have seen how this gave rise to an overall increase in foreign involvement. The French consulate was established in 1840 and the English in 1848. Yet the most important antecedents of this secular representation lay in the missionary presence. Catholicism was closely allied to the interests of France; Protestantism to the United Kingdom. European competition was largely directed to nullifying the influence of rivals, but out of this dialectic an attempt at conquest finally arose in the 1890s. Meanwhile the extent to which the West constituted a threat to national independence became apparent only with the massive expedition of Napier to Maqdalā. The overwhelming power of modern military technology was revealed. Earlier, however, negative consequences had been manifest in the divisive tendencies of foreign competition. This emerged clearly in French support for Tegrē independence against the British-supported Tēwodros, although its origins were yet earlier. In Shawā, and to a lesser extent Tegrē, the powers had foreshadowed their intentions of manipulating the components of national disintegration. Finally, however, it was the missionaries who had most strongly represented the foreign threat. Krapf had done so in Shawā. It was still more clearly shown by Catholic advances. If Orthodox Christianity was a touchstone of national identity, then the establishment of a European sect on the plateau was dangerous indeed. The extent to which the Lazarist mission was allowed to defy *Abuna* Salāmā constituted a fundamental challenge to the institutions of Orthodoxy. It is in this context that the emergence of Tēwodros must be seen; and against this background that his policies are to be understood.[1]

Religion was inextricably involved, not only through the missionaries, but also through the identification of Orthodoxy with Ethiopian national identity. Although the empire was clearly multinational and multi-religious, no other path to reunification existed than the one which lay through a revival of the Orthodox state. Only from this stage could the national institutions hope to evolve towards a more accurate reflection of internal diversity. Moreover, the first attempt at restoration was made by a profoundly religious man.

[1] Abir, *Era of the Princes*; S. Rubenson, *King of Kings. Tewodros of Ethiopia* (Addis Ababa, 1966); M. Morgan, 'Continuities and Tradition in Ethiopian History. An investigation of the reign of Tewodros', *Ethiopia Observer*, xii (1969), 244–69; and my two articles 'Tēwodros as Reformer and Modernizer', *Journal of African History*, x (1969), 457–69; and 'The Violence of Tēwodros', *Journal of Ethiopian Studies*, xi (1970), 107–25.

Tēwodros had been formed in the Orthodox tradition and was attached to it. His monastic education proved indelible, while his personal morality arose from the Gospel. Compassion, justice, and identification with the poor all characterized his early reign.[1] Further, his belief in his own destiny was apocalyptic and millenarian. By the adoption of his throne-name, he laid claim to a national prophetic myth, which had returned to vogue as early as the 1830s. It was nothing short of the proclamation that he would 'reign in Abyssinia for a thousand years, and in this period all war is to cease, and every one, in fulness, to enjoy happiness, plenty, and peace'.[2] Although the millennium may not have been taken literally, the opening of a new era was clearly announced. His conviction of divine election was further developed, as the following reveals:

My fathers the Emperors having forgotten our Creator, he handed over their kingdom to the Gallas and Turks. But God created me, lifted me out of the dust, and restored this Empire to my rule. He endowed me with power, and enabled me to stand in the place of my father. By His power I drove away the Gallas.[3]

The conflicts into which Tēwodros came with the Church, so important for a full evaluation of the role of religion in his reign, are not our concern here;[4] but rather the complex role of foreign missions. In considering his attitude to missions, some observers have spoken of a 'fanatismo religioso',[5] which flatly contradicts what was, in fact, a pragmatic approach. The Catholics constituted a threat to the sovereignty of indigenous religious institutions. Therefore, they were to be contained, but ultimately tolerated. Protestantism, on the other hand, through its twelve-year absence, had no established position. If it were made dependent on the Emperor, it could be exploited. Moreover, there was some identity of views between Tēwodros and the South German Pietists who came forward to serve him in the religious and secular renewal of his country.[6] However, it was Catholicism which was first affected by the new order constituted in 1855.

---

[1] M. Moreno, 'La Cronaca di Re Teodoro Attribuita al Dabtarà "Zaneb" ', *Rassegna di Studi Etiopici*, ii (1942), 151; *The Autobiography of Theophilus Waldmeier, Missionary* (London, n.d.), 73–4; Krapf, *Travels, Researches*, 458.

[2] Bruce, *Travels* (1790), ii. 64–5; Rubenson, *King of Kings*, 49–51.

[3] PRO, FO 401/I, no. 802; Tēwodros to Victoria, n.d.

[4] Rubenson, *King of Kings*, 68–73.

[5] Conti Rossini, *Etiopia e Genti di Etiopia*, 85; Ullendorff, *The Ethiopians*, 84.

[6] See below, Chap. VI.

The Lazarists Excluded

Between 1852 and 1855 Ethiopian politics were transformed. In a dramatic series of battles with the regional princes, *Lej* Kāsā of Qwārā established a military and political ascendancy such as had not been seen for a century. As it slowly emerged, his programme was seen to be the transformation of ascendancy into an institutionalized, centralized state. This state was then to undertake social and economic reforms which were to place it on a basis of equality with its contemporaries. The inspiration for national restoration was largely medieval, entailing the revival of Solomonic kingship, to which the Church was central, both organizationally as an extension of the court, and ideologically. By 1854, Kāsā had conquered both Gojjām and Bagēmder, imprisoning their princes or driving them to flight. He recalled *Abuna* Salāmā to Gondar, proclaimed himself *negus*, and began a reform of national morality.

Foreign missions reacted quickly. The Protestants, as we will see, took fresh hope from the bishop's restoration, and tried to capitalize on it. Despite his long-standing conflict with the metropolitan, de Jacobis too sought to turn the new order to the benefit of Catholicism. His outlook was not shared by his colleagues. Kāsā's early attitude to the Catholics is uncertain. However, the balance of the evidence suggests that, from the beginning, he associated himself with the doctrinal and institutional interests of *Abuna* Salāmā, but that his approach to the mission was flexible. Their fears of the former blinded most missionaries to the latter. Thus, as early as 1849, Fr. Stella wrote from Gondar of his apprehension at the emergent prince.[1] Equally, Biancheri, several years later, was terrified of Kāsā, whom he described as 'amicissimo dell'Abbuna Salama'. For fear of detention, he first withdrew from Gondar to Dabra Tābor; and then to the north.[2] Delaye, the French vice-consul at Massawa, reflected this view.[3]

De Jacobis, however, was always more open to the Ethiopian situation and more sensitive to the views of his converts. He sensed the pragmatism. Kāsā was indeed deeply respectful of the bishop, he claimed, but he had been kind to both Montuori and Biancheri. He went on: 'When we recently established our residence at Gondar,

---

[1] *Annales*, xiv (1849), 678; Stella to Salvayre, Gondar, 20 Feb. 1849.
[2] APF, *SRC.AC*, v. 633ᵛ; Biancheri, Halai, 12 July 1853.
[3] MAE, *Corr. pol. Ég. Mass.*, i. 382ᵛ; Delaye to Ministre, Massouah, 19 May 1853.

Kaçâh made himself our protector; so well that Gondar has been since then, for the Mission, an inviolable asylum.'[1] Hitherto, the prince, although attributing much of his success to episcopal support, had resisted all pressure to banish the Catholics from the central provinces. De Jacobis then continued with a passage which reflects the impact which the future Tēwodros had on his contemporaries: 'As for Kaçâh, visible instrument of Providence, I cannot prophesy his intentions, and, if I have praised him to you, it is because virtue is such a rare thing here, that merely its appearance immediately seduces us.'[2]

With this judgement, de Jacobis repudiated the views of his colleagues, and decided to obtain a closer look at the situation. He consecrated Biancheri as coadjutor to supervise the well-established missions of the north, and in February 1854 left for Gondar. He entered the city on 8 March.[3] Events there justified the pessimism of Stella and Biancheri. With Salāmā's arrival imminent, many former friends disappeared. The bishop had already turned developments to his own account, obtaining from Webē the expulsion of the Catholics at Hālāy.[4] Kāsā was campaigning in Gojjām and an emissary was sent to obtain his permission to rest in the town. The reply was rather non-committal, but affirmative.[5] Meanwhile the eçhagē and the local governor, Kantibā Hāylu, tried to persuade the mission to withdraw. To no avail.[6] In May, the Coptic metropolitan reached Gondar. At first he refused to enter the city if de Jacobis remained. The Lazarist, however, noted that Salāmā was moderate in exploiting his triumph.[7] As Kāsā was soon expected, the bishop relented awaiting the prince's decision. Fresh pressure was applied for a Catholic retreat.[8] However, to a letter of greeting, Kāsā had replied: ' . . . that he saluted me with distinction and without adding: Leave Gondar.'[9] De Jacobis was determined not to abandon the

    [1] *Annales*, xx (1855), 477–8; de Jacobis to Sturchi, Abyssinia, 2 Jan. 1854.
    [2] Ibid. 479.
    [3] Takla Hāymānot, *Abuna Jacob*, 184.
    [4] APF, *SRC.AC*, v. 797, Biancheri to Prop. Fide, Emqulo, 21 Apr. 1854; 802, Zaccaria Cahen to Prop. Fide, Moncullo, 26 May 1854: *Rev. his. miss.*, xvi (1939), 595–6; Delaye to Ministre, Massaouah, 24 Apr. and 18 May 1854.
    [5] Takla Hāymānot, *Abuna Jacob*, 185–90. This account is first-hand.
    [6] Ibid. 192–6: *Lettres de Jacobis*, ii, no. 346; Gondar, 17 May 1854: APF, *SRC.AC*, v. 803ʳ; de Jacobis to Prop. Fide, Gondar, 27 Apr. 1854.
    [7] De Jacobis, *Giornale*, v. 13–14: Takla Hāymānot, *Abuna Jacob*, 198–9: PRO FO 401/I, no. 374; Plowden to Clarendon, Massowah, 29 June 1854.
    [8] Takla Hāymānot, *Abuna Jacob*, 199–200.
    [9] *Lettres de Jacobis*, ii, no. 348; Gondar, 30 June 1854.

local Catholics. He may have dreamed of creating a *modus vivendi*, and perhaps, like St. Paul, he wanted to appeal to Caesar. But, as he put it himself, from the first meeting of Kāsā and Salāmā 'all was lost'.[1] A 'concordat', he continued, was established between Church and State, the essential article of which was a mutual recognition of autonomy. Catholicism was sacrificed; persecution began.[1]

Whatever his private attitude to the mission, it was clear to Kāsā that restoring Salāmā entailed great limits on the foreign religion. Alexandrian doctrine was proclaimed, and the edict applied not only to indigenous sectarians led by the *eçhagē*, but also to Ethiopian Catholics. The refusal of the latter to submit was taken as seditious, and they were harried as were the traditional dissidents. De Jacobis and his neophytes were detained. The former was placed in the custody of the *kantibā* to await exile to Sennar. The latter were turned over to Salāmā.[2] Prominent among the detained Catholics were the two Takla Hāymānots and Gabra Mikā'ēl. The missionary was banished at the end of November, followed eventually by his younger priests.[3]

Yet de Jacobis had not relinquished hope. He turned back from the Sennar border and made his way to Semēn. Kāsā might still relent; Webē could prevail. On 9 February the clash took place at Darasgē. The northerners were swept aside and the mission's last protector deposed. On 11 February, in Webē's church, Tēwodros was crowned and the myth proclaimed. Convinced now that the possibility of accommodation was slight, and that Webē's collapse was a defeat for Catholicism, the missionary's breadth of sympathy still forced him to admire the new order. He respected the public morality which was expressed in edicts against prostitutes, in the King's example of marrying with the Communion, and his active participation in the reconstruction of several churches.[4] Moreover, in the letter which recounted Webē's defeat, he was lavish in praise of the victor. Tēwodros, an 'extraordinary' man sustained by Providence, continued to distinguish himself 'with admirable laws and ordinances for public prosperity and morality'. Commerce and agriculture were to be nourished; military oppression restrained.

---

[1] *Annales*, xx (1855), 526–7; de Jacobis to Étienne, Gondar, July 1854.
[2] Takla Hāymānot, *Abuna Jacob*, 209–13.
[3] *Lettres de Jacobis*, ii, no. 352; to Biancheri, Gondar, 21 Nov. 1854.
[4] De Jacobis, *Giornale*, v. 34, 52. See also Rubenson, *King of Kings*, 44; Zanab, *Cronaca*, 150–1; and 'Nuovi documenti V', 409.

The slave trade was abolished, and the Emperor's private slaves freed. His adherence to Salāmā was justified by reference to Constantine: 'I hide the faults of my Bishop with my Royal Mantle.' Moreover, 'he has made known his great pleasure at having us with him in his country, and several times requested the Bishop to release our Confessors'. Victory had been accompanied by 'very commendable acts of generosity and religion'. Webē was treated with respect, half the booty given to the Māryām Church, Darasgē. A general pardon was issued.[1]

What sealed the mission's alienation from Tēwodros was the fate of Fr. Gabra Mikā'ēl. Gabra Mikā'ēl was at least sixty. The most distinguished of the Catholic clergy, he exercised influence in Gondarē clerical circles. Kāsā and Salāmā were eager to win him over, or break him down. The Catholic made the mistake of challenging the new authorities, thus making the question, in part, a political one.[2] The readiness with which his colleagues were released suggests that he too might have taken exile. But from his defiance there was no backing down. He was mercilessly beaten; then, gravely weakened, was dragged round to follow the court. On 28 July 1855, he succumbed, his death a witness to the apostolate of de Jacobis, and a reproach to the bishop and Emperor.[3] This incident had a profound effect upon de Jacobis. Describing Gabra Mikā'ēl's persecution, he saw Kāsā transformed from Constantine to Julian the Apostate. He continued to believe that the Emperor had been sympathetic, but his need of legitimacy drove him into alliance with Salāmā.[4] The breach was complete. The Catholics, acting on their disenchantment, began an active opposition.

Yet the possibility of an arrangement had been real. Tēwodros tried to exploit most opportunities offered by the foreign presence. He was much stricter in controlling it than Webē had been, yet his moderation towards Catholicism was real. It was not his fault that his view of toleration was very different from the Roman one. This was shown in the case of Fr. Giusto da Urbino, the only Capuchin then in the central provinces. Fr. Giusto's missionary zeal was

---

[1] *Lettres de Jacobis*, ii, no. 357; Abbenat Semien, 7 Feb. 1855 (a mistake for the 17th).

[2] Conti Rossini, 'Vicende dell'Etiopia', 523: PRO, FO 401/I, no. 448; Plowden to de Jacobis, Gondar, 27 June 1855.

[3] 'Vicende', 523–5; Takla Hāymānot, *Abuna Jacob*, 238–9; PRO, FO 401/I, no. 448.

[4] *Lettres de Jacobis*, ii, no. 360; Abyssinie, 13 Sept. 1855.

slender and a deepening interest in Ethiopian culture and languages had brought him to rebel against Massaja, his superior. The Capuchin was offered the possibility of remaining if he refrained from proselytization. Hitherto engaged in precious little religious activity, he now opted for exile.[1] In May 1855 he was set on the road for Khartoum. Yet it had been a meaningful offer of toleration, if not of liberty. It was, then, a tragedy that Tēwodros and the Catholics were driven to conflict. For the former, it ruined his chances of profitable relations with France; while the latter became absorbed in a futile attempt at counter-revolution.

Catholics in Opposition

With his coronation the Emperor elaborated an imaginative foreign policy. His intention was to treat with the powers as equals, obtaining from them recognition, support against the Muslims, and much-needed assistance for the modernization and development of his country. Following the general lines already developed by Webē and Sāhela Sellāsē, Tēwodros's approach was distinguished by its breadth of objectives, its greater vigour, and its wider framework. Russia and Prussia were turned to, although Britain and France, already established in the region, naturally predominated. Anglo-Ethiopian relations in the 1860s have received almost obsessive attention.[2] Equally important, from the King's standpoint, was his overture to France. In mid-1855, at the same time as he opened negotiations with Consul Plowden for the sending of an embassy to London, he wrote to Delaye, the French vice-consul at Massawah. He protested that the Catholic expulsion was in no way to be taken as an action inimical to France. Rather, he sought friendship. He guaranteed protection for such French workers and travellers as might be sent to Ethiopia, and invited a reciprocal assurance for his own subjects abroad. The vice-consul rejected the letter out of hand and wrote Plowden so to inform the King.[3] The first attempt, as all subsequent ones, foundered on France's identification with the fate of Catholic missions.

[1] PRO, FO 401/I, no. 448; Plowden to de Jacobis, Gondar, 27 June 1855: APF, *SRC.AC*, v. 965; d'Urbino to Prop. Fide, Cairo, 22 Aug. 1855: Massaja, *35 Anni*, iii. 118–19: and Conti Rossini, 'Lo Ḥatatā Zar'a Yā'qob e il Padre Giusto da Urbino', *RRAL*, S5, xxix (1920), 213–23.

[2] See Rubenson, *King of Kings*, 64–5, 84–9, for a recent and useful summary.

[3] *Rev. his. miss.*, xvi (1939), 599–602; Delaye to Ministre, Massouah, 23 July 1855. See also *Annales*, xx (1855), 578–9; Biancheri, 16 June 1855.

While from his side Tēwodros remained open to friendly relations, the Catholics sought a rival candidate to receive French attention. Their first choice was the pathetic *Aṣē* Yohannes III, whose authority and influence had ever been slight. His chief qualifications were his Solomonic descent, and a strong leaning to Catholicism. Persuaded by Fr. Gabra Mikā'ēl to enter the Roman Church, he now wanted to make the pilgrimage to Jerusalem and Rome. In support of this desire, de Jacobis wrote to his mission society contacts in Paris and Rome, to the Propaganda, and to the French Foreign Office. In a long memorandum of February 1856, the missionary revealed a striking *naïveté*. Yohannes, he claimed, was the only candidate likely to succeed Kāsā, should anything happen to the latter. His potential was grandiose: '. . . what he lacks to be a perfect Prince, a practical knowledge of European civilisation is for you, Excellency, to give him. In allowing him to travel to Paris, you will thus make for Abyssinia its Peter the Great, its Civilizer. . . .'[1]

In response to this, and earlier letters protesting persecution, the Quai d'Orsay sought mitigation through representations in Constantinople, and with the Patriarch in Cairo. These measures failed. However, the shadow king was now taken up and a special subvention allotted to him. Furthermore, the vice-consul at Massawa 'had been invited to suggest what other marks of interest the Imp.al Govt. might be able to accord to this legitimate inheritor of the throne'.[2] Fortunately the matter came to an abrupt end when Yohannes joined the court of Tēwodros, and renounced formal adherence to Catholicism.[3]

The lines of a much more substantial policy were already being laid. Independently of each other, de Jacobis and the new Vice-Consul Chauvin-Beillard turned to Webē's successor Negusē. The two men understood each other well. The missionary was convinced that Beillard '. . . is the man whom we needed', one whose reports would reveal the true situation,[4] while the consul constantly sympathized with de Jacobis, supporting him against Biancheri and

---

[1] MAE, *Corr. pol. Ég. Mass.*, ii. 81ᵛ; de Jacobis to MAE, Abyssinie, 24 Feb. 1856—'Rapport sur des mesures à prendre pour garantir la sûreté des Catholiques en Abyssinie. . . .' This letter was published in *Rev. his. miss.*, ix (1932), 419–24 and ff. See also *Lettres de Jacobis*, ii, no. 374: *Annales*, xxiii (1858), 351–2: and APF, *SRC.AC*, v. 1028.

[2] MAE, *Corr. pol. Ég. Mass.*, ii. 109; Ministre to Chauvin-Beillard, July 1856.

[3] Ibid. 285ʳ; de Jacobis to MAE, 26 Oct. 1858. See also 'Vicende', 513–14; and Stern, *Wanderings among the Falashas . . .* (London, 1862), 212–13.

[4] *Lettres de Jacobis*, ii, no. 371; Emcullo, 17 June 1856.

Stella, who, he believed, were working against the mission's true interests.[1] Their approach developed on closely parallel lines, assisted by common objectives and close contacts.

Negusē was Webē's nephew. He claimed the succession in Semēn and, by extension, in Tegrē. Given the recent upheavals and continuing disturbances, he had a certain legitimacy. Moreover, following his victory of 1855, Tēwodros directed little attention to the north, and failed to create a serious administration there. Rather, he concentrated on Shawā and Wallo. Negusē seized his opportunity and rebelled. The imperial appointees proved unable to contain him, although some parts of Tegrē remained loyal throughout the insurrection. It was clear, however, even to himself that Negusē could not withstand unaided the Emperor's armies. Consequently he sought external help, and support for Catholic missions became the cornerstone of his policy. As Tēwodros had pre-empted the allegiance of the Orthodox Church, a pro-mission line was politically logical and cost little.

In 1856 the northern prince wrote to France. After greetings and a description of his threatened position, he went on: 'Help me then according to your wisdom and prudence; send me help, for a battle which is approaching. May your aid reach me no later than September! Until then I will try to avoid a general battle.' As for the key point in Franco-Ethiopian relations, the position of the mission, he claimed: 'At this moment, Abouna de Jacobis is my father; for the future I attend your counsel and your orders.'[2] He then indicated his intention of having the Lazarist bishop declared metropolitan of Tegrē, and offered to cede territory over which he had little control. Arms were not mentioned, but military advisers were sought.[3]

Beillard was convinced of Negusē's sincerity, and believed that his cultivation would provide freedom of activity for the Catholics, and counteract British influence with Tēwodros. It was, then, a disappointment to him when de Jacobis refused to intervene. As the consul knew no Ethiopian languages, he hoped for assistance in translation, but, remembering his rebuke in 1845, the Lazarist repudiated even this minimal participation in political affairs.[4]

[1] *Rev. his. miss.*, xvi (1939), 609–10; Beillard to Ministre, Massouah, 25 Apr. 1857. For the internal conflicts, see below, pp. 111–12.

[2] MAE, *Corr. pol. Ég. Mass.*, ii. 106ʳ; Négoussier to Napoléon, n.d. This letter was received at Massawa in June 1856.

[3] Ibid. 105; Beillard to Ministre, Massouah, 30 June 1856.

[4] Ibid. 104. For the 1845 incident see above, Chap. IV, pp. 68–9.

Nevertheless, Beillard recommended a positive response to the letter, and despite delays at the Foreign Office, began an ever-closer identification of French and northern interests.[1]

Throughout 1857 Negusē consolidated himself, becoming a serious challenge to the Emperor's claim that he had reconstituted the empire. In October the French vice-consul was invited to discuss closer relations. His report revealed the extent of the prince's ambition, for he now styled himself *negus*. The French warmed to this claim and developed a theory of double sovereignty: that of Emperor Tēwodros in central Ethiopia, and of King Negusē in the north. However, Beillard also noted his *protégé*'s military weakness.[2] De Jacobis continued to refrain from supporting the negotiations, although a number of his Ethiopian priests were intimately connected with the 'rebel'.[3] Nevertheless, he was fully committed to the view that in Negusē lay the mission's only hope of protection, and continually pressed his claims in correspondence with his mission society. Misled by his hopes, he maintained that Tēwodros had been 'abandoned by all', and that his rival had completely eclipsed him 'in the strength of his power as in the science of government'. Negusē, he said, '. . . has been given to us by Mary to protect us'. The missionary was particularly attracted by the clemency of the *negus*,[4] a fine quality which, alas, had the unfortunate consequence of lax military discipline. The argument was understandable. The prince had deposed the imperial governor in Agāmē, thus ending the local persecution of Catholics. Furthermore, he had granted temporal power to mission adherents, had Catholic priests at his court, and granted full rights to proselytize in Tegrē. However, a serious lack of realism was shown by the rhetorical question: 'King Negusē then, will he be for the renascent Catholicism of this country, the Constantine or Charlemagne of Abyssinia? We have every reason to hope so. . . .'[5] Still mindful of the disapproval expressed at his earlier initiatives, he wrote to Propaganda late in 1857, announcing

[1] MAE, *Corr. pol. Ég. Mass.*, ii. 105.

[2] Ibid. 151, Beillard, 13 July 1857; 172–80, Beillard, 19 Oct. 1857.

[3] PRO, FO 401/I; no. 523, Barroni, 18 Sept. 1857; no. 537, Plowden, 15 Nov. 1857; no. 538, Plowden, 18 Nov. 1857. See also Lejean, *Théodore II*, 91–2.

[4] *Annales*, xxiv (1859), 72–89; Halay, 1858. See also Fusella, 'La Cronaca dell'Imperatore Teodoro di Etiopia in un manoscritto amarico', *Annali dell'Istituto Universitario Orientale di Napoli*, N.S., vi (1954–6), 92–3; and *Annales*, xxiii (1858), 444–9.

[5] *Annales*, xxiv (1859), 82–3.

Negusē's intention to send a deputation to Paris and Rome, and soliciting advice on an appropriate course of action.[1] He received no reply.

Meanwhile, the need to clarify its increasing communication with the British Government over Ethiopian affairs, reinforced by strong representations from the vice-consul, and strident calls for armed intervention from the ex-Lazarist Sapeto,[2] forced the Quai d'Orsay to define more closely its attitude. It was first noted that no response had been made to Negusē's overtures. In view of the rapidity with which Ethiopian princes had been known to rise and fall of recent date, caution was recommended. However, the interests of either religion or commerce might demand action: 'In this case, between the two chiefs presently disputing Amhara and Tigre we would be as justified in dealing with Niegoussier [sic] as the British Government is today in supporting Théodore Koçah.' An approach to Plowden through London was advised to secure Catholic relief from persecution, and Beillard was instructed to avoid close commitment. The British were informed of French concern for the protection of the mission.[3]

Meanwhile, France's representative in Ethiopia expressed increasing concern over Negusē's military position which was too weak to withstand an encounter with the Emperor. Moreover, the prince lacked firmness and decisiveness; and, despite his great veneration for de Jacobis, it was precisely here that Beillard found the missionary 'a great hindrance'. 'At the least sign of rigour,' he wrote, 'even of a just severity, he intervenes personally or by his vicars, soliciting, imploring, and finally procuring an indefinite pardon.'[4] Innocent as a dove, de Jacobis was not always wise as a serpent. While encouraging Negusē's clemency, he would have done well to urge firmness, for the vice-consul had learned that everything was pinned on French support. When visiting the 'rebel' camp the preceding October, Beillard had been asked for cannons, or men capable of making

---

[1] APF, SRC.AC, v. 1382^r; 25 Dec. 1857.

[2] Sapeto was becoming increasingly committed to Italian imperialism. He was largely responsible for the acquisition of Assab in 1869. C. Giglio, Etiopia—Mar Rosso (Rome, 1958), i, Chap. iv; Giacchero and Bisogni, Vita di Sapeto; and Sapeto, Assab e I suoi Critici (Genoa, 1879). See also MAE, Corr. pol. Ég. Mass., ii. 205–17; Sapeto to Gramont, Rome, 24 Jan. 1858.

[3] MAE, Corr. pol. Ég. Mass., ii. 244^v, 'Note pour le Ministre concernant les Affaires d'Abyssinie', 5 May 1858; and 248, Ministre to Beillard, 14 May 1858. See also PRO, FO 401/I, no. 550, Inc.; Walewski to Malakoff, Paris, 19 June 1858.

[4] MAE, Corr. pol. Ég. Mass., ii. 246–7; Massouah, 7 May 1858.

them, to support a march on Dambeyā. 'These men', he wrote, 'have been at the disposal of the Negus for four months, and nothing happens.' As Negusē was unwilling to force the issue the vice-consul could not support his desire to send a deputation to Paris.[1] In September 1858, however, Beillard was able to report success. At his urging, the northerners had advanced on and taken Gondar. This sign of determination and aggressiveness, although much mitigated by Tēwodros's prolonged absence on his greatest Wallo campaign, was sufficient in the vice-consul's mind to warrant the embassy to France.[2] At last he gained the support of de Jacobis, and only just in time, for close personal straits soon forced him to leave office.

Hitherto the missionary had been much keener on the deputation, hoping that its success would obviate the need for the stern measures advocated by Beillard. However, this was no fundamental disagreement, but merely a question of priorities, and with the latter convinced, the two fell into close line. At the end of October 1858, de Jacobis took the final plunge with an important memoir for the French Government. He did not do so without reluctance. His plea of December 1857 to the Propaganda for guidance had been bootlessly repeated the following June, and, although he seems to have been correct in interpreting silence for tacit approval, the loneliness of his decision was distressing.[3] Moreover, Beillard's departure lent urgency. He began with the view 'that the regeneration of Abyssinia can only be brought about by means of a rapprochement with the civilized powers of Europe'.[4] He then described how Negusē, 'as remarkable for his military valour [!] as for the justice of his views', was following the course of his uncle Webē in seeking relations with France. De Jacobis then revealed that he had advised the prince about the embassy whose sending he now announced. Probably on the missionary's suggestion the deputation was visiting Rome as well as Paris and in the former would declare Negusē's veneration and attachment to the see of St. Peter. Furthermore, it was to declare his intention 'to embrace Catholicism as soon as the political

[1] MAE, Corr. pol. Ég. Mass., ii. 246–7; Massouah, 7 May 1858.

[2] Ibid. 274, Beillard, 16 Aug. 1858; 281, Beillard, 21 Sept. 1858.

[3] APF, SRC.AC, vi. 124–5; 10 June 1858. See also Lettres de Jacobis, ii, no. 383; 8 Nov. 1858.

[4] MAE, Corr. pol. Ég. Mass., ii. 283ᵛ–6; 'Mémoire sur l'ambassade envoyée à sa majesté Napoléon III, empereur des français, par Négoucié, roi d'Abyssinie', 26 Oct. 1858. (Published in Rev. his. miss., ix (1932), 539 ff.) See also APF, SRC.AC, vi. 196–8; de Jacobis to Prop. Fide, 30 Nov. 1858.

position of the country permits him, without compromising the peace of Abyssinia'. It was a vital qualification. Whether it was sufficient to call into question his sincerity, or merely reflected political wisdom, was never put to the test. In Paris, the embassy would make assurances of their friendship and desire for alliance. They would invite suggestions on how best they could serve French interests. However, the real meat of their mission was to solicit arms ' . . . and even, if it is possible, . . . auxiliary troops'.[1] In reporting these objectives, de Jacobis tacitly endorsed them, and, although he stressed that the arms were to be used defensively, he had become committed to Negusē's military victory. Therefore it was the more remarkable that following his triumph Tēwodros should show himself lenient towards the Catholics.

There is no need for detail on the course of the embassy's activities.[2] De Jacobis had been well informed. In Rome the ambassadors did indeed profess Negusē's obedience to the Sovereign Pontiff, and received the Propaganda's assistance for their trip to Paris.[3] There they were well received and given audience with Napoleon III. No military help was promised, but French interest was quickened by an offer of territory. They replied with the mission of the Comte de Russel.[4]

At the same time as Negusē's emissaries were negotiating in Paris and Rome, missionary enterprise was capitalizing on his pro-Catholicism in another direction. The Capuchin Léon des Avanchers concluded with him a treaty of friendship and commerce on behalf of Sardinia.[5] The origins of this projected alliance lay in a famous letter from Negri of the Piedmont Foreign Office to Massaja of January 1857, in which Massaja's support was solicited for commercial expansion. He was further invited to provide political intelligence, and, if possible, to negotiate treaties. The missionary,

[1] MAE, *Corr. pol. Ég. Mass.*, loc. cit.
[2] A number of accounts have been published. See: L. Fusella, 'L'ambasciata francese a Negusē', *Rassegna di Studi Etiopici*, vii (1948), 176–91; Sapeto, 'Ambasciata Mandata nel 1869 [*sic*] dal Governo Francese a Negussiè Degiazmate del Tigrè e del Samièn in Abissinia . . .', *Bollettino della Società Geografica Italiana*, SI, vi (Florence, 1871), 22–71; S. Russel, *Une Mission en Abyssinie et dans la Mer Rouge* (Paris, 1884); Lejean, *Théodore II*.
[3] APF, *SRC.AC*, vi. 240–1; Emnāta Māryām to Card. Barnabo, Rome, 11 Feb. 1859.
[4] Ibid. 280–337 *passim*; various letters from Sapeto in Paris of Mar. and Apr. 1859.
[5] E. Martire, *Massaia da Vicino* . . ., 338–41. See also Giglio, *Etiopia—Mar Rosso*, i. 54–9.

himself from the area and closely attached by sentiment and service
to the House of Savoy, warmly welcomed the overture, only regret-
ting that for some time his mission would be too isolated to serve.
He had few doubts on the desirability of a close European connection
with Ethiopia, and the benefits which it would bring to his work.[1]
Fr. Léon fully shared these views, and in his capacity as representative of his bishop acted for him. The initial Sardinian reaction was
to reject the treaty, because of her overwhelming commitments in
Europe. Besides, as Negri wrote, his government considered ' . . .
that King Negoussié does not seem to be invested with that incontestable sovereignty which is required'.[2] When the Piedmontese had
second thoughts it was too late.[3]

The Capuchins were not alone in attempting to bring the crypto-
Catholic Negusē within the Sardinian orbit. Italian nationalism was a
strong influence within the Lazarist mission as well. Sapeto had long
resented French protection, and left the mission to serve the cause
of Italian nationalism and imperialism. His friend Fr. Stella was
like-minded, and underwent a similar development. Meanwhile he
strongly supported Fr. Léon's negotiations, and tried, independently,
to have a Sardinian consulate established in Ethiopia.[4]

The net result of these Italo-Tegrē activities was slight. Nevertheless, they reflected Catholic Europe's interest in Negusē as an opportunity to gain influence in the Red Sea. The projected Suez Canal
had revived interest in the area and Sapeto was a leading propagan-
dist for the cause.[5] The immediate result of this interest was several
attempts to supply arms to the northerners.[6] Although the identity
of those involved is mysterious, and their further connections yet
more so, definite links existed between one gun-runner and Stella.

Arms were the key. The urgency with which Negusē sought them
arose from his deep insecurity. His embassy had been a qualified
success, but warm expressions of friendship would not stop bullets.
In October 1859 the prince again wrote acknowledging French

[1] Farina, *Le Lettere del Cardinale Massaia*, 212–29, for the letters of Negri and
Massaja.   [2] Martire, *Massaia da Vicino*, 350.

[3] Giglio, *Etiopia—Mar Rosso*, i. 58; ii. 1–4.

[4] Martire, *Massaia da Vicino*, 351–2 and ff.; Giglio, *Etiopia—Mar Rosso*, i.
64–8. Stella subsequently left the mission altogether for a colonization scheme.
A. Issel, *Viaggio nel Mar Rosso e tra i Bogos (1870)* (Milan, 2nd ed., 1876).

[5] Sapeto, *L'Italia e Il Canale di Suez* (Genoa, 1865).

[6] Lejean, *Théodore II*, 101–2; PRO, FO 401/I, no. 603; Barroni to Plowden,
8 May 1859; MAE, *Mém. doc (Afrique)*, lxi. 47; Negusē to Napoleon III, 13 July
1860.

kindness to his ambassadors and beseeching support. He addressed the Emperor as 'elder son of *our* Holy Church', and repeated his request for a consul to whom he would grant all those rights which, he pointed out, Tēwodros had refused to Plowden.[1] The heart of the letter was a request for artillery, in return for which he would cede off-shore territories:

At the same time I take the liberty of soliciting from the Emperor's generosity twelve cannons with a company of gunners;—To this end I am sending you this letter begging you also to accept as perpetual sign of my gratitude the island of Zulla or Ras Dumaira.

By October 1859, Gilbert had arrived to take up Beillard's post. There was no break in policy. Gilbert vigorously followed his predecessor's path, and renewed the close relationship with de Jacobis, whom he commended to his superiors. He reported that Negusē had proclaimed the Lazarist metropolitan of Tegrē and Semēn, and was convinced that 'without doubt' he was Ethiopia's most powerful prince.[2]

The missionaries, better informed, saw differently. De Jacobis continued to press the prince's claims, but he did so out of concern not confidence. Learning that a French embassy was on the way, the missionary again wrote urging that France's broader interests, and more particularly those of his mission, required acceptance of the cession of territory. Only in this way, he believed, could British supremacy be challenged.[3] If de Jacobis was uneasy, Biancheri was pessimistic and des Avanchers sceptical. From his position of detachment in Bogos, the Lazarist coadjutor believed that Negusē had little chance, and that the mission's commitment to him had alienated many people. Moreover, he pointed out that a considerable number of Tegrē nobles were frankly opposed to the 'rebel'.[4] Des Avanchers went further. Of Tēwodros's ability to crush Negusē, he had no doubt. If, therefore, Sardinia still wanted to develop her Ethiopian interest, it must be prepared to support him with arms.[5]

On 12 December 1859 Russel arrived at Massawa. His embassy was a fiasco. Far from strengthening the northerner, it led quickly to

---

[1] MAE, *Corr. pol. Ég. Mass.*, ii. 331–2; Negussé to Napoleon III, 13 July 1860. My italics.   [2] Ibid. 328ᵛ; 18 Nov. 1859.

[3] Ibid. *pol. Ég. Mass.*, ii. 340–2; 9 Dec. 1859.

[4] APF, *SRC.AC*, vi. 417; Karen, 18 Nov. 1859. Cf. 'Vicende', 529–32 for Takla Hāymānot's account of some of Negusē's internal difficulties.

[5] APF, *SRC.AC*, vi. 293–4; des Avanchers to Card. Pref, Kurata, 1 Apr. 1859; Martire, *Massaia da Vicino*, 342–3; des Avanchers to Cavour, Kurata, 2 Apr. 1859.

his utter collapse, for it forced Tēwodros to deal with the challenge once and for all. Russel's brief was to investigate possibilities for French annexation, to reciprocate Negusē's embassy, and, if possible, to communicate to Tēwodros France's commitment to the cause of religious liberty.[1] While Russel and his party climbed the plateau to effect its rendezvous, the Emperor moved on Tegrē. With his arrival, the façade crumbled. By late January Russel was in Hālāy, but Negusē had fled. Partisans of Tēwodros then surrounded the town and its small Catholic mission. Accepting the assurances of de Jacobis that the party would attend the King's wishes, the imperialists released Russel from close surveillance. He immediately absconded, leaving the missionary to face the consequences. Fortunately, Tēwodros was not hostile, and de Jacobis enjoyed a sufficient reputation in Tegrē for his release to be secured. In March he was back at the coast. But there was no hiding the ruin of the Franco-Catholic political line.[2]

Collapse was rapidly followed by a host of other changes. Plowden, who had lurked so much in the background, was assassinated in February 1860 by an ally of Negusē. On Tēwodros's withdrawal from Tegrē, the 'rebel' tried hopelessly to re-establish himself. But his cause had lost all credit. In a letter to de Jacobis, he put a fine gloss on his desperate flight: 'If I did not fight with him, it is because I wanted to follow the counsel which you had given me, counsel which I have found full of moderation and wisdom.'[3] Two letters of July and August 1860 attempted to rally French support, but to no avail.[4] Meanwhile, de Jacobis died. Seeking relief from the oppressive heat at Massawa, in July he returned to the plateau. On his way he suffered a stroke and quickly passed away.[5] From the beginning of his apostolate, he had encouraged Franco-Tegrē relations, and became one of their principal architects. As such, he was partly serving the

[1] See Russel, *Une Mission en Abyssinie et dans la Mer Rouge, 23 octobre 1859–7 mai 1860* (Paris, 1884), particularly 263 ff.

[2] See Russel, *Une Mission: Annales*, xxvi (1861), 46–88 passim, several letters from Fr. Delmonte: MAE, *Corr. pol. Ég. Mass.*, iii. 15–22 passim; Gilbert and Russel: *Lettres de Jacobis*, ii. 414, 417; to Delmonte, 22 and 28 Feb. 1860. See also Rubenson, *King of Kings*, 78–9 for a useful summary and references to the British and Ethiopian sources.

[3] Quoted in *Annales*, xxvi (1861), 101; Delmonte to Étienne, Emkoullo, 31 Mar. 1860.

[4] MAE, *Mém. doc. (Afrique)*, lxi. 47; Niguse to Napoleon III, 13 June 1860; ibid. 52; Niguse to Napoleon III, 12 Aug. 1860.

[5] *Annales*, xxvi (1861), 118–26; Delmonte to Étienne, Emkoullo, 3 Aug. 1860: Takla Hāymānot, *Abuna Jacob*, 271 ff : Pane, *Il Beato*.

interests of the northern princes. He shared with them the belief that Ethiopia would benefit from contact with European civilization, although his view of its implications differed from theirs. His Catholicism naturally brought him to channel the aspirations for foreign connection towards France. With reason, he was convinced that his mission would benefit more from that power than from Britain, the only real alternative. In this, of course, he narrowed the interests of his *protégés*, who were without preference. However, nascent Catholicism suffered little for its association with French interests. Rather the reverse. Its usefulness to the Ethiopian élite lay precisely here, and won it toleration. Between 1840 and 1855 on this basis the foundations of indigenization were laid, while from 1855 to 1860 a position of strength was built up in Bogos. When checks came, they were the product of resurgent nationalism, and as much a reflection of the mission's religious advance as of its political power.

Negusē was deeply distressed at the loss of de Jacobis and wrote to the Emperor Napoleon: 'I had much chagrin at this and, moreover, I fear there is none other like him. I hoped that this holy person, who only knew how to follow the truth, would continue to be a precious witness for me in my relations with the Europeans who arrive in my country.'[1] In December 1860, Tēwodros re-entered Tegrē. Within a month he finally trapped his quarry. In an awesome vindication of his military reputation he shattered the opposing army, and assigned his rival to a lingering death.[2] To their surprise, the Catholics did not suffer from their patron's removal. Although Tēwodros was fully aware of the mission's involvement, to the extent of securing arms, he was clement. He maintained his original line, that proselytism be forbidden but that the religious freedom allowed to Muslims and Falāshās be extended also to Catholics.

In 1859, Léon des Avanchers had visited Tēwodros with impunity and discussed with him both political and religious questions. His interpretation of imperial policy was somewhat narrow:

King Theodore would be most happy to contract an alliance with a European government, but he will not hear of religious liberty, still less of

---

[1] MAE, *Mém. doc. (Afrique)*, lxi. 52^r; Niguse to Napoleon III, 12 Aug. 1860. See also APF, *SRC.AC*, vi. 627^v; Negusé to Delmonte, 19 Sept. 1860.

[2] MAE, *Corr. pol. Ég. Mass.*, iii; 94, 30 Jan. 1861; 96, 1 Feb. 1861; Gilbert to Thouvenel: PRO, FO 401/1, no. 692, Inc. 11; Playfair to Anderson, Aden, 5 Feb. 1861: 'Vicende', 532–3: Fusella, 'Cronaca . . . Teodoro', 92–5.

Catholic priests and missions; he wants in Ethiopia but one religion, . . .
one bishop, and one King—for this he has worked for 5 years. . . .[1]

By liberty, of course, the right to convert was intended. From his
insistence on the Orthodox Church as the backbone of his nation,
Tēwodros never wavered; but his approach to the established
Catholic parishes was far more flexible than the Capuchin believed.
Replying to a letter from Gilbert, the Emperor informed him of his
intention to seek the friendship of all European nations. He repudiated any involvement in de Jacobis's detention at Hālāy and asserted
rather that he had immediately ordered his release ' . . . and allowed
[him] to reside in his dominions as should be most convenient to
himself'.[2] Gilbert then pressed for a definition of Tēwodros's policy
on liberty of conscience and worship. Although a full assurance was
in fact received, the vice-consul was disappointed at the continuing
ban on proselytism. Completely ignoring the mission's opposition,
the Emperor was courteous. It is clear that his overriding concern
was to attract European participation in national development.
His statement on the mission was precise:

Brothers in the Gospel, in the Cross, in Baptism, in the Unity and Trinity
of God, are sons of Jesus and consequently our brothers:—I can give you
the assurance, then, that neither your people nor those of our people who
profess your faith will ever be molested or tormented in the countries of
which Divine Providence has made me the master; for not only Christians
our brothers, but also Muslims and Jews can live in our countries on
condition that they behave in conformity with the laws of the country and
obey the wishes of the Sovereign. But if there are people who want to
teach us another faith, I will inform you that we have a Bishop and a
clergy and that we cannot renounce the belief of our fathers. . . .[3]

He acted on this declaration. A governor of Agāmē was appointed,
well disposed towards Catholicism. 'From that time until today they
[the Catholics] were without disturbances', wrote Takla Hāymānot,
'because they found favour with the head of Agamé, Sebhàt.'[4]
In 1862 Delmonte noted the Emperor's toleration and described the
mission's existence as 'tranquille'.[5]

[1] Martire, *Massaia da Vicino*, 342; des Avanchers to Cavour, 2 Apr. 1859.
[2] MAE, *Corr. pol. Ég. Mass.*, iii. 53ʳ; Bell to Gilbert, Tanta, 13 June 1860.
[3] Ibid. 111ʳ; Tēwodros to Gilbert, n.d. Compare this clearly articulated policy
with the much more vacillating line of Tēwodros's successor, Yohannes IV:
Aleme Eshete, 'Activités politiques de la mission catholique (lazariste) en Éthiopie
(sous le règne de l'empereur Johannès) 1868–1889' (Paris; typescript, 1970).
[4] 'Vicende', 532.
[5] *Annales*, xxx (1865), 61; 15 Dec. 1862.

PLATE V

a. The Church of Gwālā, near Addigrāt

b. The bell tower at Darasgē Māryām

An Indigenous Church

With the defeat of Negusē, Catholicism temporarily ceased to be of political importance. A strong order had been established, which though lenient towards the mission's position, prevented any further expansion within the Ethiopian kingdom. The Lazarists were thus confined to the northern fringes of the plateau. Between 1855 and 1860, the principal development had been the founding of work in Bogos. The death of de Jacobis ushered in a period of deep uncertainty, lasting for at least ten years. In fairly quick order, his three successors died without time to create and implement a consistent line. However, certain tendencies emerge. The dominating problem became the position of the indigenous clergy. For varying reasons, the subsequent bishops failed to establish rapport. Discord was prominent.

De Jacobis saw Bogos as a side issue. Biancheri, on the other hand, distrusted the object of his colleague's mission, and sought to develop work in precisely those areas where a native priesthood would not be a foreseeable issue. Bogos fitted his purpose. Consequently his commitment to it before de Jacobis's death, and his subsequent difficulties with the Ethiopian Catholics were expressions of the same attitude. In 1851, Bogos had been scouted.[1] The following year Stella settled in the region of present-day Karan and established a Church. Continuing slave raids from the Sudan drew him into political activity to defend his adherents. Success greatly increased his prestige, and eventually he seems to have become the political leader of the area.[2] At first, de Jacobis was bitterly opposed.[3] But Stella enjoyed substantial support,[4] and following a visit by Biancheri in 1853, de Jacobis became reconciled to this new departure, although he never directed any attention to it.[5] As early as 1857 Chauvin-Beillard painted a dark picture of the differences between Biancheri and his superior. In the latter, he claimed, resided the entire Catholic and French mission in Ethiopia. For, he continued: 'The Mission of Boghos and Mensah is above all a scission of the Abyssinian Mission,

[1] Sapeto, *Viaggio e Missione Cattolica*.

[2] Giglio, *Etiopia—Mar Rosso*, i. 64–8; Methodios of Aksum, 'Extemporaneous Account', *Abba Salāmā*, 58–9.

[3] *Lettres de Jacobis*, ii, nos. 319, 322, 324; to Étienne, 14 Dec. 1852, 21 Apr. and 4 June 1853.

[4] *Annales*, xvii (1852), 140–1; Poussou to Salvayre, 12 Feb. 1852.

[5] *Lettres de Jacobis*, ii, no. 326; APF, *SRC.AC*, v. 713; *Annales*, xx (1855), 495–6; Biancheri to Sturchi, Emqulo, 6 Jan. 1854.

a protestation against its Vicar General. These big words are not mine, I got them expressly from Mgr. Biancheri, who is not difficult to get talking.'[1] De Jacobis was thus increasingly isolated.

His last letters are dominated by a concern for the fate of his clergy should Biancheri succeed him, as he knew he must.[2] With the Comte de Russel came a reinforcement, Fr. Delmonte. De Jacobis hoped to pass on his convictions and spirit to the newcomer, whose indispensable quality was that 'He loves the Abyssinians.' Delmonte was appointed Procurator, but it was quite impossible that Biancheri's position should be affected, in spite of his personal reluctance to assume the office.[3] He had been consecrated with right of succession and had twenty years in the field. Events following de Jacobis's death justified his anxiety. The Ethiopian priests rebelled against Biancheri, as they had done six years before during their leader's absence in Gondar.[4] They petitioned the Propaganda for a 'Patriarch' who would act in humility, patience, and love. They complained that they were forced into great physical hardship, and that their spiritual needs were neglected. Biancheri, they alleged, was interested only in Bogos.[5] Hard times lay ahead for the Catholics of Agāmē and neighbouring provinces.[6]

Shortly after his appointment Biancheri left for Europe. In Paris, he pressed upon his Superior General his conviction of his complete unsuitability. Yet despite Étienne's recommendation that he be permitted to resign, nothing was done.[7] Meanwhile Delmonte had re-established hierarchical authority, and the priests returned to discipline.[8] De Jacobis's work had been a great deal more than the creation of a personal following, and it was within the broader context of obedience to Rome that the rebellion had taken place. Towards the end of 1863 Biancheri returned. He had learned nothing about treating the clergy. Rather, he was prepared to write them

---

[1] *Rev. his. miss.*, xvi (1939), 609; Beillard to MAE, 25 Apr. 1857; see also APF, *SRC.AC*, vi. 573-4: Biancheri, Karen, 15 June 1860.

[2] *Lettres de Jacobis*, ii, nos. 402, 412, 417, 421; Oct. 1859–May 1860.

[3] APF, *SRC.AC*, vii. 44; Biancheri, 5 Sept. 1861.

[4] 'Vicende', 507.

[5] APF, *SRC.AC*, v. 664-9, 20 Sept. 1860; vi. 615-19, 15 Oct. 1860. See also Lejean, *Théodore II*, 103-4.

[6] *Annales*, xxix (1864), 169; xxx (1865), 100: MAE, *Corr. pol. Ég. Mass.*, iii. 75-91 *passim*; *Mém. doc. (Afrique)*, lxii. 78-9.

[7] APF, *SRC.AC*, vii. 312; Étienne to Card. Pref, Paris, 9 Apr. 1862.

[8] Ibid. 392-3, 574-7, various letters from clergy of Agāmē, Alitēnā, and Hālāy; vii. 353, Delmonte, 16 July 1862.

off and start anew with a seminary at Massawa, strictly controlled by Europeans.[1] The idea was utterly foreign to the spirit of de Jacobis, and temporarily lapsed with Biancheri's death on 11 September 1864.[2] He was the last of the pioneers.

Biancheri was succeeded by Bel, a man without previous experience in Ethiopia, but of some standing through his posts as Superior of the Lazarist House in Beirut, and Visitor of the Province of Egypt and Syria. He was the first Frenchman appointed.[3] Had he enjoyed any length of time, he might have established a new approach, which, capitalizing on the foundations laid by de Jacobis, could have led to further progress. He belonged to a new generation of clergy, aggressive and concerned with the establishment of European standards. His apostolate was marked by two issues: the Ethiopian clergy and Bogos. When Bel visited Karan in 1866, he was very negative about the situation, all impetus to baptism having long been dissipated.[4] However, from this time onwards, Bogos attracted much more attention from the Lazarist Vicars Apostolic. The consolidation of Stella's work in the late 1860s and early 1870s made the area a corner-stone against the hostility of Emperor Yohannes IV. These years, in turn, laid the foundation for the expansion of Catholicism which took place under the direction of the Capuchins at the end of the century.

If Bogos became one of the centres of Ethiopian Catholicism, the genuinely indigenous elements lay elsewhere. Work expanded precisely because the area was a backwater. It was the creation of an indigenous clergy which provided the native cultural elements. Bel was dedicated to this concept, but differed radically from de Jacobis in its application. The latter had gathered his disciples around him, and trained them in a highly informal and personal way. Bel believed that European education and training was the course of the future.[5] Yet his alienation from the clergy was a fact. They rejected him.[6] No reconciliation with the missionaries was effected until after the bishop's death in March 1868. Once again a

---

[1] Ibid. 523: Biancheri to Prop. Fide, Massua, 20 Dec. 1863.

[2] Annales, xxx (1865), 77 ff.; Delmonte to Étienne, 13 Sept. 1864.

[3] APF, SRC.AC, vii. 662; Étienne to Card. Pref, Paris, 29 Nov. 1864.

[4] Annales, xxxi (1866), 603 ff.; Bel to Paris, 25 Apr. 1866. See also Metodio da Nembro, La Missione dei Minori Cappuccini in Eritrea (1894–1952) (Rome, 1953), 248–9.

[5] Annales, xxxii (1867); 550–3, Bel to Étienne, 6 Jan. 1867; 203 ff., Bel to Génin, 11 Sept. 1867. See Massaja's criticism of Bel, op. cit. viii. 58–61.

[6] Annales, xxxiii (1868), 469–71; Delmonte to Étienne, 2 Apr. 1868.

modus vivendi was reached, with the readmission of the priests,[1] only to suffer a further disruption, this time from the top. Delmonte was appointed as Vicar Apostolic but before the news reached him he had died, on 19 May 1869.[2]

The troubled years of the 1860s might have been disastrous. So unsettled internally, the mission would have been sorely troubled by external threats. There were none. Tēwodros was little interested in Tegrē once he had defeated Negusē. The main political events of these days took place elsewhere. So it was that the inevitable adjustments, following the death of one who had so largely created the mission, were able to take place in conditions of reasonable tranquillity. De Jacobis had wrought no mass conversions. Instead, he left behind several thousands of Catholics organized in eight parishes, served by some twenty indigenous priests.[3] More than that, he had impressed upon his Church indelible Ethiopian elements. It is fitting that one of his most tangible monuments is a collective biography by his faithful disciples. In this work filial devotion combines with concern for Ethiopia's religious life.[4]

[1] *Annales*, xxxiii (1868), 479–90; Delmonte to Étienne, 26 Apr. 1868.
[2] Ibid. xxxiv (1869), 599.
[3] Ibid. xxxii (1867), 548; xxxiii (1868), 207–9.
[4] Takla Hāymānot, *Abuna Jacob*.

CHAPTER VI

Tēwodros
'The Slave of Christ'[1]

THE Catholic role under Tēwodros had been largely negative, blocking his connection with France, and supporting northern dissidents. The Protestants played a more complex part. Pilgrim missionaries trained at the St. Chrischona Institute near Basel became the Emperor's chief modernizing and reforming agents, while Henry Stern of the Falāshā mission helped precipitate the final crisis in external relations. Although his foreign policy was sweeping, from the beginning the King had a clear leaning towards Protestantism and England. This disposition had been cultivated by a number of his intimates; principally Plowden, *Abuna* Salāmā, and a Scots adventurer John Bell, who rose high in his service. Thus the new alliance of Church and State constituted in 1854 was distinctly favourable to Evangelical missions, and they were not slow in exploiting it. Nevertheless, considerable confusion surrounded this new formation, and its history was often troubled.

The only continuing Protestant links with Ethiopia were slight. Salāmā's correspondence with his CMS mentors in Cairo had slackened. On the other hand, Gobat became Anglican Bishop in Jerusalem in 1846, and from his position kept contact with Ethiopian pilgrims in the Holy City. In 1848, 1850, and again in 1852, he was requested by Ali and Webē to protect their nationals, and especially the established convent of Dayr as-Sulṭan.[2] Although the missionary's correspondence contains few references to his dealings with the pilgrims, he enjoyed sufficient influence to alarm de Jacobis into

[1] Zanab, *Cronaca*, 153; J. M. Flad, *Notes from the Journal of F.* [sic] *M. Flad, one of Bishop Gobat's Pilgrim Missionaries in Abyssinia* . . . (London, 1860), 50–1.
[2] Staats-Archiv des Kantons Basel-Stadt, *C. F. Spittler Privat-Archiv 653*, xxx/3; John Bell to Gobat, Devra Tabor, 28 Dec. 1848: CMS, C.M/o28, 69–70; Gobat to Venn, Jerusalem, Jan. and June 1850: PRO, FO 401/I, no. 249; Gobat to Malmesbury, London, 29 June 1852. FO 401/I contains considerable material on the Dayr as-Sulṭan controversy and is reprinted in E. Cerulli, *Etiopi in Palestina Storia della Communità Etiopica in Gerusalemme*, ii (Rome, 1947), with other documents. See also S. Tedeschi, 'Profilo Storico di Dayr as-Sulṭan', *Journal of Ethiopian Studies*, ii (1964), 92–157.

attempting to establish a counterweight through the offices of the Catholic Patriarch of Jerusalem.[1]

A new Protestant scheme for stimulating Reformation in the Orthodox Church was broached in 1852. On a visit to Basel, Gobat consulted with the celebrated philanthropist and mission benefactor, C. F. Spittler. Together they agreed to engage six graduates of the St. Chrischona Institute. Under the bishopric of Jerusalem these men would be sent to Ethiopia where they would again attempt to realize Gobat's 'colonization' scheme.[2] The only Protestant agent still in the area, however, was Krapf, now on the Kenya coast seeking a route to the Gāllā country. He heard of the plan through Isenberg.[3] Neither was enthusiastic. Dwelling on their own unhappy experiences they emphasized the dangers of political uncertainty and clerical hostility. Krapf unfavourably compared work in Ethiopia with that under Turkish rule, and recommended that any available trainees would be better employed in America.[4] However, Gobat persisted. In April 1854, a formal decision was taken by the Pilgrim Mission's supervisory committee to assign men to the Anglican bishop; and, in the same year, on his return to Europe Krapf had gathered sufficient intelligence in the Red Sea and Egypt to convince him that the new order in Ethiopia warranted at least a trip of investigation. He volunteered.[5]

Like the Basel Mission in its early days, the Pilgrim Mission supported no work of its own, but rather trained men for the employ of others. The two institutes were closely linked through the person of Spittler. Formerly a director of the Basel Mission, he had become convinced that a more practical and pietistic training was required, and thus founded St. Chrischona. Here candidates were instructed in such crafts as carpentry, weaving, and masonry, in addition to the more normal Biblical courses. Preparation for ordination was not part of the school's programme.

---

[1] *Lettres de Jacobis*, ii, nos. 275 and 353 of 27 Nov. 1849 and 17 Dec. 1854: and APF, *SRC.AC*, v. 528 of 8 Nov. 1852 and 869 of 17 Dec. 1854.

[2] *Spittler-Archiv*, v/10; Gobat to Spittler, Jerusalem, 9 June 1854: and ibid. xxx/1; Gobat to Spittler, Beuggen, 9 Oct. 1852. For the earlier idea of a colony see above, Chap. III, pp. 39–40.

[3] *Spittler-Archiv*, D3/6; Krapf to Barth, Rabbai Mpia, 2 Apr. 1853.

[4] Ibid.; D3/4, Isenberg to Spittler, Riehen, 25 Apr. 1853; D3/6, Krapf to Spittler, Tübingen, 11 Mar. 1854.

[5] Ibid. B9/3; 'Beschluss über die für Abessynien bestimmten Zöglinge der St. Chrischona', Riehen, Apr. 1854: CMS, C.A5/016, 108; Krapf to Venn, Tübingen, 5 July 1854.

Conversations in Basel, and subsequently Jerusalem, gave Krapf a clearer conception of his colleague's plans. He warmed, and described them to Venn:

He [Gobat] wishes, that the settlement of the mechanics (who are now at Jerusalem) should be formed at Gondar or in its vicinity. They should pursue their accustomed trades and endeavour to engage some young men whom they could instruct in their trades as well as in spiritual matters. As the establishment would require many servants, the Bishop thinks, that there would be at once a little congregation of Abessinians, in which the Word of God could be preached, and the light and example of true christianity be exhibited before the Abessinians, without attacking the Abessinian Church in a direct way, as the Missionaries ex officio and professo would do. He thinks that the Abessinians, especially the chiefs would receive and value christian mechanics, whilst they would on the outset refuse official Missionaries or priests.[1]

Endorsing the scheme, he hoped '. . . that in this manner the way might be paved for more open and direct Missionary labour hereafter'.

There is a strikingly modern ring in this strategy of adopting secular garb. However, in part, it is deceptive. The degree to which the Pilgrim agents viewed their work as mission in itself varied considerably from individual to individual. Although, as we shall see, some did not, most saw their skills as a prelude to more overt and traditional forms of evangelization. None the less, it was a bold plan, more forceful than the contemporary use of native artisans in Nigeria.[2] The new mission also retained the CMS emphasis on stimulating the Orthodox Church to internal renewal, but had the added advantage of a lay *raison d'être*.

In January 1855 Krapf left Cairo for Ethiopia, accompanied by Martin Flad and Māhdara Qāl, a native of Adwā, who had established a CMS connection in Cairo. In March their path crossed with that of de Jacobis, on his way to the coast. The irony was not lost on Krapf. Noting that seventeen years earlier the arrival of a Catholic missionary had coincided with the CMS expulsion, he commented that now the Protestants were re-entering 'under circumstances far different from the state of things in former times'. He went on: 'The contemplation of these remarkable changes strengthened our confidence in Him who finally will overthrow the schemes of all the

---

[1] CMS, C.A5/o16, 112; Krapf to Venn, Cairo, 15 Jan. 1855.
[2] Ajayi, *Christian Missions*, 11–12, Chap. 2, and 155–65.

enemies of the gospel. . . .'[1] Leaving their companion in his native town, the two Europeans pressed on to Gondar. On 19 April, they joined the royal camp at Jān Mēdā, Dabra Tābor, and were cordially received by Salāmā.

They discovered that their hopes based on the new relationship between Emperor and bishop were fully justified. In his first encounter with the missionaries the metropolitan described how 'King Theodoros was one heart and soul with himself, [and] that His Majesty assisted the Church in every way, which neither Oubie nor Ras Ali had done previously'.[2] Furthermore, he claimed, the Emperor was personally devout and dedicated to civic reform on the basis of Christian morality. Turning to missions, Salāmā welcomed Gobat's plan, and promised to commend it to Tēwodros, who, he believed, '. . . would readily accept it, as he was very fond of obtaining mechanics and artists, to civilize the country, and that His Majesty intended to write to England, France, and Germany, to invite artists [sic] to Abessinia'.[3] So far as their evangelical purpose was concerned, the bishop was less receptive. He was willing to extend full liberty of practice to the artisans, but suggested that the King would not hear of preaching, and spoke in such a way as to convince the missionaries that he shared this hesitation. None the less, although he did not 'encourage them expressly to come', the general tenor of his remarks was encouraging.[4]

On the evening of the 19th, Krapf and Flad were visited by John Bell. He informed them that the metropolitan advised their not raising religious matters with the Emperor, but rather they should stress the secular value of the proposed artisans.[5] Salāmā probably feared that Tēwodros, without experience of Protestant missions, would fail to appreciate the crucial differences which, he was convinced, distinguished one form of European Christianity from the other. It may also be that he displayed signs of the latent jealousies

---

[1] *Church Missionary Intelligencer*, vii (1856), 39, for Krapf's account. See also CMS, C.A5/016, 113; Krapf to Venn, Massoa, 2 Mar. 1855; and *Travels, Researches, and Missionary Labours*, 441. The manuscript diary of Krapf's trip, found in C.A5/016, 178, was first published in the *Intelligencer* and subsequently, in a slightly different edition, in *Travels*.

[2] *Intelligencer*, vii (1856), 89–90; Krapf, *Travels*, 452.

[3] *Intelligencer*, 90; Krapf, *Travels*, 453. See also *Spittler-Archiv*, D2/1; 'Neue abyssinische Mission. Untersuchungsreise im Jahr 1855, durch Miss. Dr. Krapf und Bruder Flad von der Chrischona,—beschrieben durch Letzteren', 5.

[4] *Intelligencer*, 92; *Spittler-Archiv*, loc. cit.

[5] *Intelligencer*, 89–90; Krapf, *Travels*, 454–5; *Spittler-Archiv*, loc. cit.

and suspicions which later played such a large part in his relations with the King. As a result of their forewarning, and despite protestations, the missionaries did not mention the essentially religious nature of their mission. Thus, in their audience the following day they clearly gave Tēwodros the impression that they were offering artisans to enter his personal service. Having rejected such humble crafts as joining, weaving, and masonry, in which Gobat's candidates had been trained, the Emperor asked the Anglican bishop to send only three, a gun maker, an architect, and a printer.[1] As for the craftsmen's faith, declared Salāmā, '. . . you will allow them to live according to their own persuasion'. And the King replied, 'In matters of faith I shall not interfere, as this is your business—whatever you tell me in this respect, I will do.'[2] Although the King revealed himself in a favourable and sympathetic light, the conversation had been distinctly inauspicious. Instead of obtaining permission to establish an independent lay colony free to propagate Evangelical principles, the emissaries had been induced to promise men for royal employment with no assurance that they could preach.

In his recommendations to Gobat, Krapf reflected both his belief in the progressive nature of the new Church–State alliance, and the unfavourable response which their request had met. The entire conception of the mission, he felt, would have to be changed, for the time was not ripe for open evangelistic work, even after the Chrischona manner. Meanwhile, they would have to be satisfied with supplying Tēwodros's needs, thereby creating a fund of good will on which they could later draw to establish a full-blown mission. He concluded:

. . . Mr. Spittler's plan must be very materially changed, as His Ethiopian Majesty does not exactly require priests or teachers of spiritual matters, but only and principally artificers or mechanics for the civilization and improvement of his country, which the Abuna said, must now become like one of [the] Kingdoms of Europe.[3]

Nor could Gobat draw much more comfort from the letter which the Emperor sent him. The only reference to religious affairs was a complaint against the divisive activities of Catholic missions, and a claim to have restored Orthodox unity through suppression of the sects:

---

[1] *Spittler-Archiv*, loc. cit. p. 6. The three trades offered by the missionaries were, of course, known in traditional society, and enjoyed no status or prestige.
[2] *Intelligencer*, 89–90; Krapf, *Travels*, 456.
[3] CMS, C.A5/016, 114a; Krapf to Gobat, Cairo, 1 Aug. 1855.

'thou knowest the state of our country in which thou hast been. We were formerly divided into three parties, but by God's power I have united them.' It is clear that Tēwodros's overwhelming concern was the introduction of foreign technology: 'One of the labourers shall bring the thing which ploughs with a fire-screw—for I have heard, that there is something which ploughs with a fire-screw (steam-plough).'[1]

The Protestants, then, were to fit into the King's broader plans for the renewal of his country. After decades of requests, at last an Ethiopian prince would receive foreign aid, humble though it was. As Gobat remarked, this response was neither encouraging, nor yet so unfavourable as to cause him to relinquish all hope. Quite apart from the financial difficulties which then beset him, Ethiopian conditions were not propitious. Yet there was no possibility of abandoning the men who had been waiting for some months in Jerusalem, nor of obtaining the specific artisans requested. Only a living faith could overcome these difficulties, and, at the least, one of the brethren could undertake to visit the country, distributing Amharic New Testaments there. The Anglican bishop then set before his seven candidates the conditions facing them. Mayer and Kienzlen remained very enthusiastic; Bender and Flad accepted them, but with some hesitations; the remaining three withdrew.[2] The differences within the group remained important. Basically, they set out on faith, not knowing what awaited them. They would try to disseminate Scriptures, establish themselves independently, and perhaps prepare the way for a Gāllā mission.[3]

Imperial Service

Under the leadership of Flad, they arrived in Ethiopia in May 1856. They remained for twelve years, ultimately achieving a unique and close relationship with the Emperor. Although official interest in them was primarily secular, they found that as they grew in the royal confidence, so their opportunities for evangelism increased. Outsiders did not view them with sympathy. The Pilgrim missionaries were Pietists of the South German school, and the simplicity of their beliefs and behaviour was frowned on by the more aggressive apostles of European capitalism. The celebrated Samuel Baker

[1] CMS, C.A5/016, 115a; Tēwodros to Gobat, 1855.

[2] *Spittler-Archiv*, xxx/1; Gobat to Spittler, Jerusalem, 3 Nov. 1855. See also ibid. xxx/6; Venn to Gobat, London, 18 Sept. 1855. Venn felt a mission impossible.   [3] Ibid. xxx/1; Gobat to Spittler, Beuggen, 26 May 1856.

visited the Matammā station, where he expressed contempt at 'these excellent but misguided people'.[1] Plowden took an equally lofty and patronizing view.[2] Nor were the French more favourable.[3] The Ethiopian sources largely ignore them.[4]

For fifteen months the brethren lived in a vacuum. Tēwodros was too preoccupied with military, strategic, and ecclesiastical affairs to devote them any attention, while the missionaries clung to the hope of independence. A temporary arrangement settled them in Dambeyā where much of their time was frittered away. On the positive side they found both bishop and Emperor welcoming. Salāmā they described as 'ein sehr lieber Mann',[5] while Tēwodros expressed great interest in their plans to distribute vernacular Scriptures. Already in 1855 Krapf and Flad had heard of his preference for Amharic in his devotions.[6] Now, in one of their first interviews with him, they presented printed books. Flad noted his reaction: 'On receiving them, to our great delight, he said, looking at the *Ethiopic* books, "What is the use of these?—the *translation* is far better."'[7] Subsequently they enjoyed several theological discussions, in which the King revealed a mind both quick and penetrating. On the other hand, Flad regretted that Krapf's advice had not been followed more closely. His companions were mistakenly construed as the requested artisans, and Tēwodros felt deceived on learning their real character.[8] Moreover, their non-conformity to Ethiopian religious practices brought them into some tension with the metropolitan, although warmth and amiability still existed.[9] They were more negative in judging the clergy than Gobat had been, for Flad believed that they were 'enemies of the truth'.[10] Nevertheless, the period of frustration yielded one contact of lasting consequence. Flad became involved with the Judaized Falāshā who were settled near Gondar, and, when the opportunity later arose, he entered his life's work of evangelizing them.[11]

In September 1857 the brethren capitulated, and wrote offering to the imperial service their skills in masonry, gardening, carpentry,

[1] S. Baker, *The Nile Tributaries of Abyssinia, and the Sword Hunters of the Hamran Arabs* (London, 1867), 504–7.
[2] PRO, FO 401/I, no. 492; 11 Nov. 1856.
[3] Lejean, *Théodore II*, 77–81.　　　[4] But see Zanab, *Cronaca*, 177.
[5] *Spittler-Archiv*, v/20; Kienzlen to Parents, Efag, 30 June 1856.
[6] Krapf, *Travels, Researches*, 452: *Spittler-Archiv*, D2/I; p. 3.
[7] Flad, *Notes from the Journal*, 33–4, late June 1856.
[8] *Spittler-Archiv*, D3/2; Flad to Krapf, Gondar, 26 Oct. 1857.
[9] Flad, *Notes*, 51, 56.　　　[10] Ibid. 42. See also 55, 68.　　[11] Ibid. 42 ff.

and leatherworking.[1] The only way forward, they were now convinced, was to gain the King's confidence. Still distracted by other
affairs, Tēwodros sent a non-committal reply interpreted by some as
a dismissal. On 10 November Flad met the King who again expressed
interest in the missionaries' skills, but still made no promises.
Permission, however, was granted to Flad for a trip to Jerusalem.
He had become seriously ill. Moreover, the mission had exhausted
its resources. As the Emperor had concluded his business with the
visiting Coptic Patriarch, the latter was now returning to Egypt.
Flad took the opportunity to accompany him.[2] They left on 7
December 1857.

In Jerusalem and Europe Flad obtained reinforcements in the
persons of Waldmeier and Saalmüller, who, from the beginning,
were prepared to work for the King. Moreover, a gunsmith, Schrol,
was found to join the enterprise; and Flad married. In Germany
he took up with Krapf the question of a new consulate for Ethiopia.
The Prussian court had expressed interest in Evangelical developments there, and its willingness to foster and support them with its
secular power.[3] Ultimately nothing happened, momentous European
events again distracting a lesser power from the African scene. Neither
Krapf nor Gobat was encouraged by the way things were going,
although both advised continuing and the latter felt that the brethren
revealed a 'better understanding of the Abyssinian people and of
their calling than earlier missionaries' and that their decision to join
the King was, for the time being, 'for the best'.[4]

In Flad's absence very important changes occurred which fundamentally altered the mission's position, establishing it on a more
intimate footing with Tēwodros. In May 1858 the King came to
Gondar where almost daily he dined with the missionaries. As his
beloved wife Tawābach was ill he asked them for medical assistance.
Kienzlen and Mayer were sent to attend the Queen, while Bender
remained in Gondar, looking after a school which they had begun
for Falāshā.[5] During the rains they accompanied the Emperor to

[1] Flad, *Notes*, 70–2 and ff.
[2] Ibid. For the Patriarch's visit see Rubenson, *King of Kings*, 70–1, and my
article 'Tēwodros as Reformer and Modernizer', *Journal of African History*, x
(1969), 463–4.
[3] *Spittler-Archiv*; B7/3, Krapf, Kornthal, 31 July 1857; D3/6, Flad, Kornthal,
31 May 1858.
[4] Ibid.; xxx/1, Gobat to Spittler, Jerusalem, 14 Apr. 1858; and D3/6, Krapf,
Kornthal, 10 May 1858.
[5] Ibid. D3/5; Kienzlen to Flad, Suramba, 3 June 1858.

Maqdalā in Wallo. Despite the death of his consort Tēwodros began to draw closer to the foreigners. Still they felt their position as insecure and their work 'hopeless'. With the bishop they were on very friendly terms. They performed a number of services for him, and discussed frankly their relations with the Orthodox Church. In particular they had established sufficient confidence to raise the question of sharing the Communion, although they refused oral confession, fasting, and the kissing of churches and crosses. A number of priests had mentioned the subject, but withheld for fear of Salāmā. Kienzlen decided to have it out with him. Initially the metropolitan insisted that their differences in belief barred them. The missionary pressed him, and he first charged that their view of the Eucharist was inadequate. Kienzlen then insisted that the Lutheran doctrine on the Real Presence was identical to that of the Orthodox. They went on to the Two Natures, and reached a saw-off in the statement that the One Christ was equally Divine and human. Practices were then raised: the veneration, but not worship, of holy relics and images; and fasting. On the latter, Biblical references were exchanged, Kienzlen gaining the upper hand with Matthew 6: 17–18. They then agreed that the divisions in Christian fellowship were attributable to neither belief nor custom, but the ambitions of the Patriarchs of earlier times who had set themselves apart from each other. Salāmā concluded: 'There used to be a good priest here, when another such comes he will give you the Communion, however I can do nothing because of the Abyssinians.'[1] At this moment, the bishop's lunch arrived. The missionary tried to withdraw with apologies, but was detained to share the meal. Although it was a fast Kienzlen was provided with milk and they joked about the rigours of abstinence. Finally, as companions they smoked cigars and the Protestant was dispatched with presents. Subsequently clergy were found in both Gondar and Maqdalā willing to admit them to the Eucharist without any pre-condition.[2] It was a remarkable and unique example of ecumenical fellowship. No other missionaries so completely entered the life of the Orthodox Church. Yet this halcyon phase did not last. Increasing tensions arose between Salāmā and Tēwodros, and the brethren drew toward the latter.

Complete confidence with the King came slowly. In September 1858

---

[1] Ibid.; Kienzlen to Spittler, Magdala, 30 Sept. 1858.
[2] See also ibid.; Bender to Spittler, Nevas Mautscha, Nov. 1858: and D3/2, Flad to Spittler, Gallabat-Matammah, 1 Mar. 1859.

they could still write of him: 'we can say nothing at all about our real purpose'. Nevertheless, a new appreciation was developing. 'He is', said Kienzlen, 'the only man in Abyssinia who possesses the fear of God.' Again they began to dine and converse. His character they found pious, merciful, kind, and dedicated to truth and justice, although in the dispensation of the latter he could be truly fearsome. They closely associated themselves with his political struggle. 'We too fight with the King against the Gallas, although not with spears and shields, but with our pleas to God that He might bring the King's enemies underfoot.' The Gāllā, they felt, were Ethiopia's greatest threat, for they wanted to make it Muslim.[1] At the end of the year a major break-through occurred. Conversations established firm common ground in the emptiness of 'outward ceremonies', and the supreme and exclusive authority of the Scriptures, which should be widely disseminated in Amharic. Convinced by the brethren's protestations of their total adherence to the Gospel, 'He exclaimed, "Now we are united; you are my children, of whom I am bound to take care. Let us partake of the Lord's Supper together to-morrow."' Kienzlen summed up: 'On that night we really made a covenant of friendship with him.' While the religious fellowship was undoubtedly profound, secular benefits accrued. A demonstration of rock-blasting, of great strategic importance in view of the extremely primitive communications then prevailing, won approval and rich honours. Further intimacies and tokens of confidence followed. Tēwodros visited their house, shared in their food, and confided to them: 'Do not believe I am an Abyssinian at heart; no, I am as one of you.'[2] Thus was won a position of great influence; but only by the forfeiture of another: 'We are on tolerably good terms with the Abuna, but he is a covetous man, and not very upright, moreover, he is rather jealous at seeing the King's favour for us, and his disposition to follow our advice.'[2] Subsequently the bishop forbade the Emperor to share the Communion with his friends.[3]

A vital change was occurring in Tēwodros's orientation. The new era proclaimed in 1855 obstinately refused to be born. No major reform or revolution could be effected while national disunity prevailed. Rebellion was endemic. Quite apart from Neguse's

---

[1] *Spittler-Archiv*, D3/5; Kienzlen to Spittler, Magdala, 30 Sept. 1858. See also ibid. Mayer to various, Begemder, 29 Oct. 1858.

[2] Ibid.; Kienzlen to Gobat, Gondar, 4 May 1859: printed in Flad, *Notes*, 81 ff.

[3] Ibid. D3/9; Saalmüller to Schneller, Magdala, 12 Oct. 1859, p. 38.

dealings with the French, other dissidents were entrenched in Wallo, Gojjām, and the Gondar region. The King failed to develop an approach adequate to deal with them.[1] Increasing frustration brought alienation from his own people. Moreover, the Church to which he looked for support in national restoration was insubordinate. Entrenched habits of independence, coupled with a clash of interest, put the two at loggerheads. In 1856 controversies had broken out in which Tēwodros accused the clergy of seditious disrespect, and sought to alleviate his tight financial position by restricting the Church's rights of tax exemption.[2] His boldness in campaigning throughout the year, and his refusal to permit his soldiers to support themselves by plunder, effectively created a standing army, which the State's traditional resources could not maintain. In his plight, the King challenged the Church. No real solution was reached, as clerical resistance enjoyed popular support. Tēwodros thus alienated the clergy without obtaining financial relief. However, *Abuna* Salāmā remained uneasily allied with the Emperor. He had suffered at the hands of the priests and retained a suspicion of them and a sympathy for the King's objectives. In this situation, what the Pilgrim missionaries represented to Tēwodros was hope, and an alternative solution. Modernization would begin in spite of his people's recalcitrance. Besides, they could provide the roads needed by his army. At the same time, they offered him a theology that was able to encompass both his hostility to the formal structure of Ethiopian Christianity and his deep religious faith.

In May 1859 Flad returned. He did not adjust easily to the mission's changed position. The brethren had clearly risen high in the royal favour, and increasingly identified their evangelical task with service to the King. Acceptance of the local situation was symbolized by the marriages of Mayer and Waldmeier to Ethiopian ladies. Strong feelings were expressed in the correspondence as Flad held out for a more traditional concept of missionary enterprise and deplored what he felt to be his brethren's moral lapses.[3] This difference was soon to lead Flad and his wife into the Falāshā mission.

---

[1] See my article, 'The Violence of Tēwodros', *Journal of Ethiopian Studies*, xi (1970).

[2] Ibid. See also Rubenson, *King of Kings*, 68–9.

[3] *Spittler-Archiv*; D3/2, letters of Flads, Oct. 1859, and Mayer, 25 Oct. 1859; D3/9, Saalmüller, 12 Oct. 1859, p. 26; and D3/12, Waldmeier, 10 Dec. 1859. The gunsmith Schrol died on the Ethiopian border.

Differences in strategy, however, entailed no political disagreements. To a man the missionaries placed their hopes on Tēwodros's struggle and his imminent reform of the Orthodox Church. 1859 saw the climax of his bitter campaigning in Wallo, and, stationed at Maqdalā, the brethren were well placed to observe the devastation. They recounted in some detail the mounting atrocities, yet consistently defended them. The principal grounds were the obstinacy of the Gāllā in face of the King's repeated offers of a settlement; and the clash of Christianity with Islam. They accepted the questionable allegation that the Wallo wanted to make Ethiopia Muslim.[1] Waldmeier, perhaps in exaggerated form, expressed most forcefully the effect of the King's charisma.

Where [he wrote] is another King to be found, who in spite of his power and greatness in self-denial disdains all comforts, luxury and good-living— he really lives very poorly, while he rewards and gives royally—who in living trust in God's help lays before his feet heathen and wild nations . . . ? We all firmly believe that the Lord has proclaimed this man with His strength, and that subsequently He will use him still more as an extra- ordinary instrument for the physical and spiritual well-being of his entire people.[2]

A similar judgement is implicit in the hopes which were pinned on his impending Reformation. Kienzlen had written: 'He has already begun to act as a reformer'; and Flad came to a similar view: 'If the King becomes master of his land; so it is to be believed, that he will undertake a reform of his Church and of the priesthood, monks, and debteras.' And it was surely this belief which led him, despite his fears for his colleagues, to the further one: 'The King's attitude to us lets us expect auspicious things for the future.'[3]

Nevertheless, their alliance with Tēwodros came at the moment of his people's disaffection. The great promise of 1854–5 had initially been followed by tangible results. The Emperor's more disciplined army did not plunder or oppress; and, at first, its ascendancy brought

[1] *Spittler-Archiv*; D3/2, Flads to Spittler, Makdela, 7 Oct. 1859; D3/2, Kienzlen to parents, Magdala, 10 Oct. 1859, p. 15; D3/9, Saalmüller to Schneller, Magdala, 12 Oct. 1859, pp. 24–5. See also 'The Violence of Tēwodros', loc. cit.

[2] *Spittler-Archiv*, D3/12; Waldmeier to Committee, Magdala, 10 Nov. 1859: as printed in *Missions-Magazin*, NF, viii (1864), 483–4. See also 'Reformer and Modernizer', loc. cit. 466; and above, Chap. V, pp. 96, 97–8 for a similar judgement by de Jacobis.

[3] Flad, *Notes*, 83; Kienzlen to Gobat, Gondar, 4 May 1859: *Spittler-Archiv*, D3/2; Flad to Krapf, and Flads to Spittler, Magdela, 3 Oct. and 10 Oct. 1859. See also *Missions-Magazin*, viii (1864), 486–7.

peace. Moral and administrative reform may also have alleviated the popular lot, although an investigation of this question remains to be undertaken. Above all, the Christian peasantry had a leader who symbolized their return to self-dignity, whose concern for public welfare was convincing, and who was assiduous and impartial in administering justice. This formidable position was dissipated through personal and political mistakes. From the beginning, a violent streak had existed in the Emperor's personality, which was closely related to an obsession with sovereignty. The peak of his success was an expedition of 1855–6 to Shawā which effectively reduced this province to central control for the first time in possibly two centuries. Yet, at the very moment of his widest rule, challenges were issued from Gojjām, Gondar, and the north. The first was never suppressed. In 1856 potential support from the Church was eroded by the ineffective threats designed to increase the State's income. Meanwhile Wallo rebelled and the King fixed on it. In the shadow of its resistance many other parts of the country began to fall away. In 1859 Shawā revolted, and the King responded with terrible vengeance. In retrospect, the missionary Saalmüller discerned this to be the turning-point.[1] The controlled, often calculated, violence of 1856 had led to horrible massacres in Wallo in 1858; and now, in 1860, Tēwodros turned on the people, and Saalmüller could speak of a 'universal disaffection'. Purges of his court were carried out, defections increased, and peasants were beaten when they got in the King's way. The remarkable and noble qualities which had stood out at the first continued, but now expressed themselves erratically; and, moreover, were countered by terrorism. Personal degeneracy accompanied this political switch, and drunkenness and concubinage increased. Tēwodros's position constantly declined until, by 1864, he held less than half of his former territories, and, by 1866, only a tiny portion. Thus, the missionary strategy of winning access to the people through royal support was unsuccessful.

However, in 1859 failure could not be anticipated. On the contrary, the missionary position appeared extremely favourable. Unlike their earlier isolation, the Chrischona men were now busily employed. Although Flad remained ill in Gondar, Saalmüller and Waldmeier repaired some of Tēwodros's thousands of broken muskets. The

---

[1] *Spittler-Archiv*, D3/9; Saalmüller to Schneller, Gaffat, 13 Jan. 1861. This development is examined at greater length in my article 'The Violence of Tēwodros', loc. cit.

others blasted a road at Chachaho, a key pass on the border of Bagēmder and Wallo which controlled the Dabra Tābor-Maqdalā axis.[1] The Emperor pressed them to construct a powder machine.[2] Again their requests for a more permanent settlement were finally answered. Despite the King's fears for their security and his frequently sending them to his stronghold at Maqdalā, they were given land just outside his administrative capital of Dabra Tābor at a place called Gāfāt in June 1860.[3] A number of houses were built in the European style, a large workshop erected, and a school founded in which both literacy and technical skills were imparted. Small though it was, a beginning had been made in the training of Ethiopians in modern techniques.

Missions to the Falāshā

Several other Protestant projects were now under way. The Pilgrim contact with the Falāshā had raised hopes of their conversion, opening another avenue of indirect influence into the Ethiopian Church. The Chrischona Institute felt unable to support such work, but Spittler's son was able to persuade the Church of Scotland's Jewish Mission Committee to take it on. Consequently, two Chrischona-trained men, Staiger and Brandeis, were appointed. They set off in 1860, but bad news from Ethiopia reached them in Alexandria, and their arrival was delayed till 1862.[4]

Meanwhile, the Revd. Henry Aaron Stern had started a Falāshā mission. Its early years were ill-starred for Stern's pomposity and contempt towards indigenous society offended not only fellow-missionaries, but also Tēwodros. He was a German Jew, converted

[1] *Spittler-Archiv*; D3/9, Saalmüller to Schneller, 12 Oct. 1859, pp. 21–3, 26; and D3/12, Waldmeier to Jager, Magdala, 14 Nov. 1859: Stern, *Wanderings Among the Falashas in Abyssinia together with a Description of the Country and its Various Inhabitants* (London, 1862), 103: PRO, FO 401/I, no. 597; Plowden to Malmesbury, 1 Mar. 1859: Th. von Heuglin, *Reise nach Abessinien, den Galla-Ländern, Ost-Sudan und Chartum in den Jahren 1861 und 1862* (Jena, 1868), 311. For the strategic importance of Chachaho see Gabra Sellāsē, *Chronique du règne de Ménélik*, 137, n. 3; and I. Guidi, *Annales Regum Iyāsu II et Iyo'as* (Rome, 1912), 251–2.

[2] *Spittler-Archiv*; D3/2, Flad to Krapf, Magdela, 3 Oct. 1859; D3/9, Saalmüller to Schneller, Magdala, 12 Oct. 1859, p. 39.

[3] Waldmeier, *Autobiography*, 63: *Spittler-Archiv*, D3/2; Flad to Gobat, Gaffat, 30 Aug. 1860.

[4] D. McDougall, *In Search of Israel. A Chronicle of the Jewish Mission of the Church of Scotland* (London, 1941), 96–8. See also Church of Scotland, General Assembly, *The Home and Foreign Missionary Record of the Church of Scotland*, xv (1860), 54–5; xvi (1861), 80, 268.

to Christianity, ordained in Anglican Orders, married to an English-woman, and now a British citizen. He seems to have been a fairly successful missionary, retaining respect for the Jewish religious tradition. He had earlier undertaken trips of exploration for his organization, the London Society for Promoting Christianity Amongst the Jews, and was now commissioned, on the basis of the reports disseminated by Flad and the St. Chrischona Institute, to investigate Ethiopian conditions. He arrived early in 1860.

Shortly afterwards the Emperor granted him an audience in which he expressed approval of Stern's intention to instruct and convert. He insisted, however, that Salāmā's consent was necessary.[1] The bishop was receptive. When he later came to write up his account, carried away by his rhetoric the missionary was patronizing towards Salāmā, but his contemporary letters reflected only a 'uniform kindness and toleration'.[2] The agreement that was reached for the proselytization of the Falāshā reflects the earlier attitude of Salāmā and Tēwodros towards the Catholic mission. Although they welcomed this effort to evangelize some of Ethiopia's non-Christian inhabitants, they were unwilling to allow the formation of a separate Protestant Church. They insisted that all converts be baptized into the Orthodox Church, on the understanding that they '. . . should not be obliged to conform to the rules and rites of his [Salāmā's] own community, but that they should have toleration without schism. . . .'[3] Stern hoped that this 'unfavourable' agreement might foster renewal within indigenous Christianity.

Stern's visit brought to a head the tensions within the Pilgrim Mission. As Flad was in the anomalous position of having no skills to offer Tēwodros, and moreover held a different view of missionary work, he was easily engaged to enter the Falāshā project, pending Gobat's approval.[4] Personal quarrels between Stern and the Chrischona artisans followed, which led the brethren to strong defence of their strategy: '*Our* calling', wrote Bender, 'to enlighten and teach through our conduct—*his*: to preach and found schools; *He* through

---

[1] Stern, *Wanderings*, 56–7.
[2] *Spittler-Archiv*, D3/2; Stern to Gobat, Chartum, 19 Dec. 1860. See also *Jewish Intelligence, and Monthly Account of the Proceedings of the London Society for Promoting Christianity Amongst the Jews*, xxvi (1860), 360; N.S. i (1861), 89–90: *Wanderings*, 112–14, 301, 306–7.
[3] *Wanderings*, 301.
[4] *Spittler-Archiv*, D3/2; Flad to Gobat, Gaffat, 30 Aug. 1860; and Stern to Gobat, Chartum, 19 Dec. 1860.

instruction to show forth; *we*, through work!'[1] The importance of
this discord was twofold: it alienated Gobat from his missionaries;
and offended Stern's most useful line of influence into the court.[2]
Gobat's disapproval did not persist, but the loss of his most useful
allies was, literally, almost fatal to Stern. Moreover, Flad's removal
from the artisan community left it leaderless, and greatly reduced the
effectiveness of its evangelism. Only under the extreme duress of the
later years of Tēwodros did the group draw closely together, and by
that time a united witness was born in such adverse conditions that its
failure was a foregone conclusion.

   With official permission, Stern set out on a tour in September
1860. Jandā, the seat of the Gondar bishops and a centre of the
Dambeyā concentration of Falāshā, was selected for a station, under
the direction of Flad.[3] At the end of the year, Stern left for England.
In the few years available to him, Flad and his co-worker Bronkhorst
succeeded in converting some fifty Falāshā and in establishing a
school attended by roughly an equal number of boys.[4] He chaffed at
the restriction imposed by the obligation of baptizing his converts into
Orthodoxy. He believed: 'It cannot be denied that, in a moral point
of view, the Abyssinian Christians are below the Falashas.'[5] Echoing
the cry of Catholic missions, Flad asked, 'Is there no hope for us, that
the English Government will help us to get religious liberty?'[6]

   The fervour of early converts, and their conviction that the coming
of Christ had obviated the need for propitiatory sacrifice, led to a
bitter controversy which reached the Emperor in October 1861,
precipitating a general crisis for all the Chrischona graduates.[7] The
occasion was most unfavourable. Failure to suppress internal revolt
was driving Tēwodros to distraction, exacerbated by the delays
which accompanied his long-awaited diplomatic offensive. Dissension
stirred up by the mission dissipated his early delight at the prospective
conversion of the Falāshā, and was a most unwelcome burden.

   [1] *Spittler-Archiv*, D3/2; Bender to Gobat, Windstrasse, 3 Oct. 1860. His
emphasis.
   [2] Ibid.; xxx/1; Gobat to Spittler, Jerusalem, 15 Mar. 1860; and B/10, ibid.
Beuggen, 18 May 1861.
   [3] For Stern's tour among the Falāshā see *Wanderings*, Chaps. XVII–XX.
   [4] See his letters to the London Society in *Jewish Intelligence*, N.S. i (1861), ii
(1862), iii (1863), and *Jewish Records*, nos. 13, 20 and 28–9 (1863). See also Flad,
The Falashas (Jews) of Abyssinia with a Preface by Dr. Krapf (London, 1869).
   [5] *Falashas*, 70.
   [6] *Jewish Intelligence*, N.S. iii (1863), 67.
   [7] See *Jewish Records*, N.S. nos. 28–9, 1863, 13–20.

Moreover, their leaders brought accusations of duress, which offended the King's opposition to forced proselytism.[1] He accused Flad of violating his commitment to religious liberty and open evangelization. He was, however, convinced by the defence put forward by one of the converts; and, accepting the missionary's good intentions, he permitted a return to his work. Final judgement on the theological issues would await consultation with Salāmā.[2] Meanwhile, the Gāfāt brethren also suffered. Several of them left their settlement to visit Flad in his crisis, and their departure was interpreted as desertion. They were seized, their property confiscated, and their servants severely beaten.[3] Their great value to the Emperor had been sharply lessened by the arrival of a number of adventurers who were equally willing to serve Tēwodros. Dissension and suspicion subsequently sown was not easily overcome.

Over a year later in November 1862, Staiger and Brandeis were finally received by the King, following a delay of six months. There was no sign of hostility, rather the reverse. Now extremely changeable in mood he effusively welcomed the newcomers and assured Staiger and Brandeis of his permission, but referred them to his bishop for definitive clearance. He expressed the hope that the Protestants would evangelize not only Ethiopia's Jews and Muslims, but also the Gāllās and other neighbouring pagans. He aspired soon to make this possible.[4] Salāmā also approved. 'However,' he declared, 'I do not like to have two creeds and two churches in Abyssinia; but if you teach like Mr. Flad . . ., and let the Abyssinian priests baptise your proselytes, you may teach wherever you like. . . .' He made it clear that his jurisdiction was over the Ethiopian clergy, but without precise geographical definition. However strained his relations with the Emperor, they were maintained at a certain level of propriety and on a mutually acceptable basis. Evangelization beyond the area effectively held by the Orthodox Church was a matter, he thought, for Tēwodros. As he wrote to the missionaries, 'If you go to another country—i.e. to the Gallas or Shangallas, where Christianity is not

[1] Ibid. 15-16; Flad's Journal, 25 July 1861.
[2] Ibid. 19-20. See also Flad, Zwölf Jahre in Abessinien oder Geschichte des Königs Theodoros II und der Mission unter seiner Regierung (Basel, 1869), 32, 42-6.
[3] Spittler-Archiv; D3/1, Bender to Gobat, Dschadschaho, 20 Nov. 1861; D3/11, Schimper to Gobat, Adoa, 6 Feb. 1862.
[4] Scotland, Missionary Record, N.S. ii. 81. See also ibid. 31, for a letter of Waldmeier; and Waldmeier, Erlebnisse in Abessinien in den Jahren 1858-1868 . . . Bevorwortet von Dr. L. Krapf (Basel, 1869), 17.

yet known, and where Abyssinian priests not yet are—you may do as
the king allows you.'[1] In December, Staiger and Brandeis settled at
Darna near Flad's station.

The new missionaries profited greatly from the Gāfāt community's
return to favour. This had been slow in coming, and was won at
considerable cost. Relations had been complicated by a fresh demand,
this time for the manufacture of heavy mortars. The project had first
been raised by a European unconnected with the mission.[2] Its appeal
to Tēwodros was immediate for it would allow the reduction of the
ambās which his opponents, notably in Gojjām, had fortified against
him. Artillery assumed almost the status of a 'final weapon', although
its introduction had a generally negative effect. Siege warfare was
not improved, while increasingly heavy matériel reduced the mobility
on which the Emperor's ascendancy had hitherto depended. The
Pilgrim missionaries resisted as long as safe, their pacific objections
fortified by complete ignorance of casting and design. Until now
their efforts had been directed to the construction of roads, vehicles
of transportation, and the dissemination of their technical skills to
the youths which the Emperor apprenticed to them. It was, however,
their very success in the pacific arts which encouraged Tēwodros to
exploit them to create a war industry. One member of the Gāfāt
colony had had military experience: Herr Moritz Hall, a Pole; and
another knew something of the manufacture of guns: Bourgaud, a
Frenchman.[3] The missionaries joined their secular companions, and
repeated failure culminated in success. The Emperor's joy was unbounded.[4] The Pilgrim missionaries re-entered the royal confidence,
and were exempt from Tēwodros's increasing hostility to Europe.
Until the destruction of their workshops and houses in the last year
of his reign, they retained the King's favour and their own freedom.

They continued to exploit their position to spread religious values.
They enjoyed full liberty to preach and teach the youths assigned to
them for training: Muslims, Falāshā artisans, and captured Gāllā
were all available. Their households were greatly extended and became

---

[1] Scotland, *Missionary Record*, N.S. ii. 81. *Shānqellā* is a pejorative term for
dark-skinned peoples, generally found in the western lowlands.

[2] *Spittler-Archiv*; D3/9, Saalmüller to Schneller, Gaffat, 13 Jan. 1861, p. 16;
D3/1, Bender to Family, Gaffat, 15 Jan. 1861: H. Dufton, *Narrative of a Journey
Through Abyssinia in 1862–3* (London, 2nd ed., 1867), 84–6.

[3] Dufton, op. cit. 83. Hall's descendants, still living in Ethiopia, claim that he
was both a missionary and a German.

[4] *Spittler-Archiv*, D3/12; Waldmeier to Chrischona, Gaffat, 24 Nov. 1862.

centres of worship and study. They also attended the Ethiopian churches on Sundays and feast days and addressed the people drawing on the Scriptural passages read in the services. Some of the clergy objected, but Salāmā supported them, especially Waldmeier whom he made trustee of his household property.[1] In short, Gobat's concept of a Christian colony was becoming a reality, in spite of his own misgivings. Only one convert of distinction was made before the work was overtaken: *Dabtarā* Zanab, the King's scribe. Information about him is very slight. He was converted by Kienzlen and subsequently instructed soldiers of Maqdalā in the Protestant faith. He also wrote the official chronicle of Tēwodros's reign, but there is no discernible foreign influence in it. It stops shortly after the reinforcement of the mission in 1859.[2]

By the beginning of 1863, things were looking up. The artisans again enjoyed the King's confidence, while the Falāshā evangelists worked with official toleration. However, before the year was out, a fresh crisis arose; one which, in fact, spelt the end of all real missionary work by either group. At the end of 1862 Stern had returned to inspect Flad's work and to bring fresh labourers, Mr. and Mrs. Rosenthal. The Gāfāt community took alarm at the news of his arrival. Stern was unaware of Tēwodros's deep dislike for him, and the brethren rightly feared that all missions would suffer from the ensuing trouble. They petitioned the Emperor to ban his entrance, but were refused.[3] At first their concern seemed misplaced. Stern spent the best part of a year at Jandā, where progress much encouraged him. Especially pleasing was the approval of *Abuna* Salāmā, won in the face of resentment from his own clergy.[4] Despite what had been a pretty constant friendliness from the bishop, limited largely by the nature of his office, Stern had come to trust him but slowly: 'I always regarded this ecclesiastic', he wrote, 'as an opponent to us and our mission, but his sedulous attention to my wants, removed the distrust which I always harboured towards him.'[5] The missionary soon paid terribly for his new-found confidence, and, caught up in

[1] See Dufton, *Narrative*, Chap. VI: and Waldmeier, *Autobiography*, Chap. VI; and *Erlebnisse*, 18–19: *Spittler-Archiv*, D3/1; Bender to Schlienz, Gaffat, 20 Jan. 1861. But see also MAE, *Mém. doc. (Afrique)*, lxi. 396; Lejean to Ministre, 21 Mar. 1863.

[2] *Spittler-Archiv*; D3/2, Flad to Gobat, Djenda, 3 Dec. 1861; and D3/12, Waldmeier to Schlienz, Gaffat, 14 May 1862. See also Waldmeier, *Erlebnisse*, 2; Flad, *Zwölf Jahre*, 16–17.

[3] Waldmeier, *Erlebnisse*, 4–5, 30.   [4] Flad, *Zwölf Jahre*, 42–3.

[5] *Jewish Intelligence*, N.S. iii (1863), 279.

Tēwodros's frustration in foreign affairs, spent over three years incarcerated on Maqdalā.

International Crisis

The King had long hoped for profitable relations with Britain. Bell, Plowden, and Salāmā had all encouraged him to expect British support both for his modernizing schemes and his defensive needs. While it is true that he also looked to France and the other Christian powers for the same ends, he had little encouragement in this direction, and consequently the bitterness of his disappointment was much less. In October 1862 Tēwodros finally made a decisive overture in foreign affairs by simultaneously writing to the principal powers.[1] Hitherto he had confined himself to slight correspondence and dealings with the consuls. Now came the definitive attempt, at the turning point of the Emperor's career. Success might stabilize the internal situation; defeat would pull out the last prop. He proposed to send embassies with the ultimate objective of obtaining military alliances and agreements for technical progress. The British incompetently refused to reply. The French repeated their demand that the readmission of the Lazarist Mission with full rights of proselytization must precede any further discussion of mutually profitable relations.[2] Both sides had their rights; the French could set what conditions they wanted, and Tēwodros was properly formulating his own internal policy. Nevertheless, he was profoundly disappointed at his rebuff by France. No answers are known to have come from the other powers. Impatience at the British delay festered to eruption.

Early in October 1863 Stern set off for Massawa.[3] North of Gon-

---

[1] PRO, FO 401/I, no. 802, Inc. 3; Theodore to Victoria, n.d.: MAE, *Mém. doc.* (*Afrique*), lxi. 105; Théodore to Napoléon III, 20 Oct. 1862. See also Rubenson, *King of Kings*, 83 ff.

[2] MAE, *Mém. doc* (*Afrique*), lxi. 398–9; Drouyn de Lhuys to Théodore, 24 Mar. 1863.

[3] This account is based largely on Stern's letter to his wife, Maqdalā, Apr. 1865. From this time, most of the letters from Ethiopia passed through British consular hands, and are to be found in the India Office, *Abyssinian Original Correspondence*, much of which was included in the Confidential Print, FO 401. See FO 401/II, no. 189, Inc. 5. A number of Stern's letters were published [*Abyssinian Captives, Recent Intelligence from the Rev. H. A. Stern with Extracts from Mr. Rosenthal's Letter* (London, n.d.)] and form the basis of his later work, *The Captive Missionary: being an account of the Country and People of Abyssinia Embracing a Narrative of King Theodore's Life, and His Treatment of Political and Religious Missions* (London, n.d.).

dar, he unexpectedly came across Tēwodros's camp. Although he had already obtained permission to leave, he was in a dilemma, occasioned by knowledge of the King's hostility and fear to offend through a seeming snub. In the event, he probably behaved wisely by entering the camp to pay his respects. He could not have felt so at the time, for his servants were brutally seized and beaten to death. The immediate charge was that Stern had approached the court with inadequate respect and preparation, but the real grounds lay deeper than that. Tēwodros's long-standing pique at the missionary was sharpened by his diplomatic set-back. The French reply had created deep suspicions, only too justified, that Europe considered him with contempt. Moreover, although still awaiting the British reply, he had little faith in its arrival. Stern, of course, represented no government. Yet his British citizenship was a real factor in the cruelty with which Tēwodros treated him. On seeing his servants beaten, the missionary had inadvertently made a gesture which was interpreted as a sign of contempt. This reinforced suspicions which ill-disposed Europeans had fostered in the Emperor's mind. After a beating, Stern was brought in chains to Gondar, where his papers were searched and incriminating documents found. Some passages in his book *Wanderings Among the Falashas*, which he had brought with him, were taken as derogatory of the King.[1] Furthermore, correspondence was found in which both Rosenthal and Paulina Flad had expressed decidedly disparaging views. They were all arraigned. Paulina Flad was directly released; but Stern and Rosenthal were chained, severely treated, and the latter thrashed on several occasions.

Salāmā, the British consul Cameron, and the Gāfāt artisans all interceded for the release of the two missionaries. For a time, the artisan intervention appeared hopeful; but on 2 January 1864, the decisive event occurred. Cameron was himself seized and put in chains. On receipt of a dispatch from Lord Russell in which his activities were strongly disapproved and orders to proceed to Massawa communicated, Cameron had sought the King's permission to retire.[2] This confirmed the Emperor's worst suspicions of British disdain, and the consul suffered the consequences. So, too, did

[1] Especially the King's humble origins and his violence, pp. 63, 80–1. Most offensive was probably the author's haughty tone, since the material was largely commonplace. However, as Tēwodros had become more insecure in the late 1850s, he had placed increasing emphasis on his claim to Solomonic legitimacy; and the humble origins of which he boasted in 1855 were less valued.

[2] PRO, FO 401/I, no. 837; Russell to Cameron, 8 Sept. 1863.

Stern and Rosenthal for their fate was sealed: four years' harsh imprisonment. The final victim of this collapse in Anglo-Ethiopian relations and of the deflation of Tēwodros's high hopes was *Abuna* Salāmā. The King no longer made a serious distinction between internal and external opposition. Stern suffered on both accounts, because he was British and because he derogated the King's sovereignty. On the latter point, Tēwodros had always been extraordinarily sensitive. Moreover, Stern's association with the bishop was also costly. Although exaggerated, there is a strong element of truth in Stern's claim that: 'All my trials and sufferings I may attribute to my intimacy with the Metropolitan (who has proved a true friend), and to the misrepresentations which were made to the King about me and our mission.'[1] Salāmā was the most powerful court figure to remain in conflict with the Emperor, and increasingly became the focus of royal hostility.

His protests at the imprisonment of Stern and Cameron associated him with their fate. Although never chained, his last three years were spent in close confinement on Maqdalā, his episcopal functions suspended.[2] Cameron related that on 12 May 1864, there was 'a Billingsgate scene' between Tēwodros and Salāmā, in which each accused the other of having supplied Stern with his information about the King's character and origins. The following day, after a period of acute physical suffering, Stern was forced into statements implicating the bishop.[3] They brought the final and complete rupture between Tēwodros and Salāmā. Despite a few subsequent efforts at a *rapprochement*, this was the end of the road. Tēwodros's conflict with the Church over its loyalty and tax privileges had intensified from its beginnings in 1856,[4] and the propriety with which he treated the bishop as late as 1862 could not contain the personal animosities and political suspicion which deepened over the years. The crisis of October 1863–January 1864 was the final turning-point in the Emperor's reign. Hereafter, its course was inexorably downward. The break with the Church was a sign, not a cause, of failure.

[1] PRO, FO 401/II, no. 85; Stern to wife, 12 Apr. 1864.
[2] The chronicle of Walda Māryām is particularly interesting here, for its author was a follower of the bishop who shared his detention.
[3] PRO, FO 401/II, no. 225, Inc. 3; Cameron to Shaw, Magdala Prison, 28 May 1865.
[4] See above, p. 125.

Missions Confined

When the initial crisis arose in October 1863, the Falāshā missionaries had been called to hear the complaints against Stern. They were quickly dismissed, but the Scottish Mission station was suspended, and Staiger and Brandeis joined Flad. However, the imprisonment of Cameron the following January brought an end to all missionary work, for the Jandā station was then closed, and the Europeans brought to the royal camp. Tēwodros's suspicions of Stern's colleagues being again relieved, the missionaries were released, but forbidden to return to the field. Instead, they were sent to join the community at Gāfāt, and increasing pressure was brought on them to join the work of the artisans. Although they resisted bitterly, protesting that their calling was evangelism, eventually they all succumbed. Their real vocation they expressed by maintaining a school and ministering to the converts who had been able to follow them.[1]

The effect of this, of course, was a restriction on missionary activities amounting almost to a ban. Yet it was not so much the product of a fundamental change in religious policy, as it was a reflection of the new crisis in national security. Already by the beginning of 1864 the King seemed bent on challenging Europe. Violence had become a major instrument of internal policy, it was now to serve external ends. Thus, the charges against Stern were secular, and the stations were closed for strategic reasons. They had become an annoyance, and, with relations with Europe declining, the King needed a close check kept on all foreigners, although this surveillance was discriminating. Flad recounted that, in February 1864, after the detention of Cameron had resulted in the chaining of most Europeans in the royal camp, the Germans were released to Gāfāt while the British (mostly Cameron's servants) were sent to Maqdalā.[2] The result, however, was to swing the home mission societies into a demand for government action. The Church of Scotland's General Assembly petitioned the Foreign Office to act for the release of the prisoners and the protection of their agents, and Stern's relatives and society were very active.[3]

---

[1] See Scotland, *Missionary Record*, N.S. iii. 225, iv. 224–5, v. 85, 341; *Jewish Intelligence*, N.S. v. 102–3, vi. 112–14: Flad, *Zwölf Jahre*, 55, 67–8.

[2] PRO, FO 401/II, no. 145; Flad to Rassam, 26 Jan. 1865.

[3] Ibid., no. 76; 'Excerpt from Minute of Meeting of the Church of Scotland's Committee for Conversion of the Jews, July 18, 1864'. See also J. Hooker, 'The Foreign Office and the Abyssinian Captives', *Journal of African History*, ii (1961), 245–58.

It is not clear to what extent the mission societies' influence decided the course of action. Yet it is ironical that the Government which had got itself into difficulties precisely because of its reluctance to become involved should end up sending an expedition costing about £9,000,000. It was a case of muddle, pride, and confused considerations of security forcing its hand. Religious pressures and political factions helped push the juggernaut into motion. Nor did the prodding come solely from Protestants. Catholics with Ethiopian experience were even more rigorous in their conviction that Tēwodros's treatment of the Europeans constituted a grave affront to the standing of the white race throughout the 'uncivilized' world and in their insistence that honour must be vindicated; for they lacked the caution induced by having men in detention. Nevertheless, Bishop Massaja, not one to shirk forward action, believed that diplomacy would suffice to secure the release of the prisoners.[1] This was the line adopted. Unfortunately, the emissary Hormuzd Rassam did not reach Tēwodros's camp until January 1866; security in Tegrē, the King's indecisiveness, and continuing confusion about the envoy's instructions all contributed to delay.[2]

Meanwhile the internal situation deteriorated. *Abuna* Salāmā enjoyed some degree of freedom and influence at Maqdalā and he exercised it to alleviate the physical condition of the captives. All the detainees—Stern, Rosenthal, Cameron, and eventually Rassam—testify to his efforts on their behalf. But, being himself in disfavour, he was unable to secure a release.[3] In July 1865 conditions again worsened with the escape from the fortress of the young prince Menilek of Shawā. The following day Tēwodros had a bitter quarrel with the bishop and placed him in even closer confinement. Terrible reprisals were taken amongst Ethiopian hostages. It now became impossible for Salāmā to assist in any way, and, for a time, the captives tried to help him.[4]

[1] For Massaja see MAE, *Mém. doc. (Afrique)*; lxi. 462–3, 'Mémoire . . . 25 juin 1865'; lxii. 56–68, 'Osservazioni . . .'. See also PRO, FO 401/II; no. 34, Inc. 4, Delmonte, 12 Apr. 1864; no. 167, Inc., Stella, 10 Apr. 1865: and H. Rassam, *Narrative of the British Mission to Theodore, King of Abyssinia; with Notices of the Countries Traversed from Massowah, Through the Soodân, the Amhâra, and back to Annesley Bay, from Magdala* (London, 1869), i. 28–9.   [2] Rassam, op. cit. i.
[3] Flad, *Zwölf Jahre*, 69–70: PRO, FO 401/II; no. 145; no. 175, Inc. 2, Rassam to Merewether, Massowah, 12 May 1865; no. 178, Inc. 3, Cameron to Rassam, 6 Apr. 1865; no. 189, Inc.
[4] PRO, FO 401/II: no. 266, Incs. 4, 7, 11 for accounts by Cameron and Stern, Maqdalā, July 1865. See also Walda Māryām, *Chronique*, 41.

In January 1866 Rassam finally arrived at the King's camp near Lake Ṭānā. At first it seemed he might succeed, for he was received with honour and kindness, although the King repeated the complaints against Salāmā, Cameron, and Stern, which he had set down in a letter of July 1865. He had claimed: '. . . I treated them with honour and friendship in my city. When I then befriended them, on account of my anxiety to cultivate the friendship of the English Queen, they reviled me.' He then charged that they had slandered his method of avenging the deaths of Plowden and Bell; and that Cameron had failed to bring the promised letter. 'What have I done', he cried, 'that they should hate and treat me with animosity.'[1] Rassam suffered a great deal of undignified treatment before he lost his conviction of Tēwodros's essential goodness. None the less, the Emperor's capriciousness was losing touch with reality, and it is increasingly difficult to discern the *rationale* behind his actions, although it should be noted that his cruelty retained some discrimination right to the end.

Tēwodros agreed to a release, and had the captives brought to Qoratā on Lake Ṭānā. Their joy was as unbounded as it was short-lived. After repeating his charges, the Emperor dismissed the party which set out for Matammā. Scarcely a day elapsed before they were back in custody, and again on the way to Maqdalā, now accompanied by Rassam. The quixotic King had been alarmed at a duality which emerged in British policy. The controversialist Dr. Beke had arrived at Massawa bearing letters from Gobat and the prisoners' families. Moreover, paranoia somehow led to the suspicion that Rassam was pirating the captives away. The arrest of the second British envoy marked the end of the road. Perhaps Tēwodros hoped that by holding Rassam he could extract further concessions; but he was acting on impulse, and when fresh offers were made he disdained them. He became ever more deeply ambivalent and less decisive.[2] In April 1866 Flad was sent to Britain to bear news of Rassam's captivity and to obtain the long-sought technical assistance. The Government acceded by sending workmen to Massawa, but the mission failed through Tēwodros's strange refusal to accept these fresh artisans. The British began to prepare for force, while

[1] PRO, FO, 401/II, no. 250, Inc. 2; Theodore to Rassam, 5 July 1865: Rassam, *Narrative*, i. 93–4.

[2] PRO, FO 401/II: no. 370, Cameron; no. 371, Rassam; no. 372, Inc., Stern; no. 389, Inc., Theodore to Relatives of Prisoners; no. 390, Inc. 2, Theodore to Victoria, 29 Jan. 1866.

Tēwodros was strangely apathetic on Flad's return. He was rapidly losing his hold.[1]

In Flad's absence, those colleagues of his nominally at large, Staiger and Brandeis, were brought under ever-increasing pressure, as was the Gāfāt community. To remain at large, the last of the missionaries were obliged to enter the King's service and to engage in the artisan work, now devoted almost exclusively to the manufacture of ever bigger mortars. Even Rosenthal and Stern attempted to escape from their imprisonment by this means, but Tēwodros's personal animosity to them was too great.[2] In February 1867 Staiger and Brandeis attempted to escape from Gāfāt, but their plans were betrayed to the King, who imprisoned them.[3] Two months later the workshops and houses were destroyed by royal order and the European colony removed to Dabra Tābor.[4] As recently as the turn of the year, Tēwodros had continued to show great interest in the activities of his artisans,[5] but his distrust of the Europeans had become all-consuming. At the end of April 1867, when Flad finally returned from England to the royal camp, the Emperor was alternately indifferent and defiant. As for the workmen Britain proposed to send, what did he care, for, he claimed, '. . . God has given me in Mr. Waldmeier and Saalmuller workmen who can do every work for me.'[6] Flad too became an artisan for resistance was mortally dangerous.[7]

Dénouement

Nothing remained of Tēwodros's rule, save the tiny area occupied by his army. All the provinces had fallen away, and the peasants rebelled in the most loyal areas, close to the royal forces. Atrocities mounted, only increasing defection. Yet no rebel dared face the

---

[1] Rubenson, *King of Kings*, 88: Flad, *60 Jahre in der Mission unter den Falaschas in Abessinien* (Basel, 1922), Chaps. V, VII–VIII: India Office, *Abyssinian Original Correspondence* (*AOC*), i. 325–34, Inc.; Flad to Rassam, Debra Tabor, 3 May 1867. I regret that I have not been able to harmonize my references to the India Office material with FO 401 where much of the same material appears.

[2] Scotland, *Missionary Record*, N.S. v. 277, 341, letters from Staiger and Brandeis.

[3] Waldmeier, *Erlebnisse*, 59–60: Scotland, *Missionary Record*, vi. 274 f., Staiger: IO, *AOC*, i. 126–8, Inc.; P. Flad to Haussman, 15 Feb. 1867.

[4] Waldmeier, *Autobiography*, 91 ff.: Fusella, 'Cronaca', 104–7: IO, *AOC*, i. 296–7, Rassam; 307–9, Blanc.

[5] IO, *AOC*, i. 129; P. Flad, 16 Feb. 1867.

[6] Ibid. 776–7; Flad to Merewether, 11 June 1867.

[7] Ibid. ii. 145, Flad to Rassam, n.d.; P. Flad to Rassam, 8 Jan. 1868; 506–7, Flad to Merewether, 3 Feb. 1868.

Emperor, for fear restrained ambition. Thus lawlessness was unchecked. Looking back on this period, Waldmeier, who was ever faithful to Tēwodros's better self, was moved to observe: 'I often wished I was chained with the other prisoners at Magdala, out of sight of the formerly good-hearted, but now so cruel, monarch.'[1]

On 25 October 1867 *Abuna* Salāmā died, the hardship of his detention aggravated by an attack of bronchitis. Tēwodros reacted with pleasure. The British party, and the missionaries, mourned the passing of a true friend. In retrospect, only Flad had harsh words for this much-maligned man. From the very start of his ministry, Salāmā had laboured under the severest difficulties, the fragmented political situation accentuating and reinforcing the fissiparous tendencies of the Church. No prince until Tēwodros undertook measures to reinforce episcopal authority, and it soon became clear that some of his policies would run counter to what the bishop considered the interests of his own Church. Through the difficult years of the 1840s and the early 1850s, Salāmā had tried unsuccessfully to introduce limited Protestant activity. When this finally became possible, the Emperor pre-empted his bishop, and, for a time, drove a wedge between him and the missionaries. Moreover, the Chrischona graduates found it difficult to trust an eastern prelate. It took the fellowship of suffering and imprisonment to overcome the suspicions of many; yet, even when written out of suspicion, the Protestant sources reflect constant, if aloof, episcopal favour. It was only Stern and Waldmeier who were continuously faithful to him, and even Stern remained critical of Salāmā's exercise of his office, perhaps with reason. Harsh conditions, widespread hostility, and still more bitter isolation, all reinforced normal human frailty. The bishop could be proud and inflexible, and in his situation a very good man might well have been crushed. No serious charges of immorality or laxness have stuck against him, although these were alleged.[2] In short, he was an unremarkable man with an extremely difficult task. From 1864 all differences sank before a wider union. The detainees have only good words for Salāmā's care and solicitude. His character received its much-deserved vindication.[3]

[1] Waldmeier, *Autobiography*, 93–6; Walda Māryām, *Chronique*, 62 ff.; Fusella, 'Cronaca', 107 ff.; Fusella, 'Le Lettere del dabtarā Assaggākhañ', *Rassegna di Studi Etiopici*, xii (1953), 90–1.   [2] See above, Chap. IV, pp. 85–6.
[3] Walda Māryām, 52: Rassam, *Narrative*, ii. 193 ff.: Flad, *Zwölf Jahre*, 7, 139: *Jewish Intelligence*, N.S. viii (1868), 29 ff.; ix (1869), 141: *Spittler-Archiv*, D3/12; various letters of Waldmeier, 10 Nov. 1859, 30 Sept. 1860, 24 Nov. 1862.

In October 1867 Tēwodros received news of the impending British military expedition. The letter brought by Flad in April of the same year had threatened force if the captives were not released, and the Emperor's indecision drew the inevitable response.[1] Under conditions of incredible hardship, Tēwodros removed his camp and his greatly prized mortars from Dabra Tābor to Maqdalā. To the joy of the missionary artisans, the mortars, which were the prime reason for the trip's delay were never used to kill. Throughout the long journey, from October 1867 to March 1868, the Emperor was possessed. He showed little interest in the rapidly approaching British forces and threw himself like a demon into the job of moving the heavy equipment along. He was increasingly abusive to his former friends. Yet, through all this, Waldmeier was faithful; faithful even to the point of daring to offer the criticisms which friendship demanded, but which he knew would only draw the King's rage. Waldmeier's fidelity was viewed with surprise, wonder, and suspicion by his fellow Europeans.[2] At times, the Emperor reciprocated, but, despite the fact that Waldmeier was afflicted with dysentery, Tēwodros drove him to work. In February 1868 when the missionary advised peace with the approaching British, the King drew his pistol to kill one of the last friends he had. But 'the Lord stayed his hand'.[3] Ultimately, Waldmeier's fidelity and commitment to peace received due recognition. Paulina Flad wrote to Rassam of his efforts to alleviate the situation: 'Mr. W., tho' he has been abused by His Royal Master with most odious abuse, some of which our European ideas of propriety would even forbid me to mention, bears no malice in his great magnanimous heart.'[4] Yet all efforts to influence the Emperor back to rationality were futile. Towards the end of March, Tēwodros reached Maqdalā. Two weeks later the British arrived. Battle was quickly joined and as quickly resolved. Tēwodros released the captives, and then, on Easter Monday, 13 April, died by his own hand. Extraordinarily, despite the King's bitterness towards Stern and Cameron, no European died in custody.

In the last days, while he awaited the British arrival, Tēwodros was charged by his clergy with having adopted the religion of the Franks

---

[1] Rubenson, *King of Kings*. See also T. Holland and H. Hozier, *Record of the Expedition to Abyssinia* (London, 1870); and H. M. Stanley, *Coomassie and Magdala: The Story of Two British Campaigns in Africa* (London, 1874).

[2] IO, *AOC*, ii: 270–4, Flad, 24 Dec. 1867; 634–5, Flad, 15 Mar. 1868.

[3] *Autobiography*, 97–101.

[4] IO, *AOC*, ii. 588, 24 Feb. 1868. See also Rassam, *Narrative*, ii. 206.

(the Europeans).[1] At first sight, it was a strange allegation. However, as Rassam makes clear, it arose out of the King's exempting his army from the traditional fasts prescribed by his Church. This had been done out of considerations of military necessity, but the clergy were right to see in it another expression of hostility to the traditional ordering of Ethiopian Christianity. Tēwodros had lost all faith in his Church: he had not lost faith in Christ. He wrote to Rassam:

I have been called by some of my priests 'Frank'. I am not ashamed of the name, because both you and myself believe in one Trinity, which is the foundation of the Christian faith. Had I been accused of being a Mahometan, or of any other sect of unbelievers, I should have acted differently towards those bad priests. I would rather lose my head than hold any other faith save that in Christ.[2]

Tēwodros had shown himself a man of deep and abiding religious curiosity. He welcomed and conversed with missionaries, both Catholic and Protestant. He had tried to build national unity through unifying and strengthening his own Church. This policy led him into conflict with the Roman Catholics and their proselytes, a conflict which bedevilled his relations with France. Meanwhile, he and Salāmā found that Protestants were willing to help strengthen national religious unity through the conversion of non-Christians to the Orthodox Church and through the dissemination of more modern religious attitudes. At the same time, Tēwodros became increasingly impressed by the need for spiritual reform, and some of his ideas, primarily Amharic literacy and a new Biblical emphasis, were encouraged by the Protestants. Increasing missionary intimacy with the Emperor, at a moment of Church-State conflict, meant temporary estrangement between the Protestants and the metropolitan. Yet as Tēwodros became frustrated at the course of his relations with Britain, with whom the missionaries were generally identified, so the tension between the latter and *Abuna* Salāmā was largely dissolved.

For all that they enjoyed the establishment's favour, the Protestants left little lasting mark on the country. The missionaries were all evacuated by General Napier, some unwillingly. The Church of Scotland suspended their activities. The London Society for the Promotion of Christianity Amongst the Jews soon resumed work,

---

[1] Walda Māryām, *Chronique*, 59 ff.; Rassam, *Narrative*, ii. 280; Waldmeier, *Erlebnisse*, 84–6.
[2] IO, *AOC*, ii. 1086; *Report*, Rassam to Stanley, 1 Sept. 1868.

but it proved extremely slow. It continues to the present but no subsequent missionary has achieved the distinction, or notoriety, of Stern. The Pilgrim Mission was more or less broken up. Bender and Mayer soon returned, but the former died, and the latter laboured among the Gāllā of Shawā in very isolated conditions.[1] The principal impact arose out of collaboration with the Emperor, and his schemes for modernization. In any measurable sense, their legacy was slight. It is extremely difficult to discern the fate of their trainees, or any continuing Evangelical ideas. Nevertheless, the Gāfāt missionaries played an honourable role in a revolutionary attempt at national renewal and unification. Their failure by no means discredited the value of their strategy in more favourable conditions.

[1] Scotland, *Missionary Record*, N.S. vi. 84; *Report of the London Society for Promoting Christianity Amongst the Jews*, 1869, 77–8; Flad, *Zwölf Jahre*, iv; and Waldmeier, *Autobiography*, Chap. XII.

CHAPTER VII

Aftermath

BY most standards, the missions discussed cannot be considered successful. Protestants failed almost totally; Catholics made only a modest start. The CMS attempt to engage the Orthodox Church in a process of dialogue leading to internal renewal and reform never got off the ground. Gobat's promising beginning was not developed, despite Krapf's Shawān attempts. When it came to the decisive test of unequivocal recognition of the indigenous Church as truly Christian, Isenberg drew back, and the whole basis of his mission fell out from beneath him. None the less, by the time of the Evangelical expulsions in 1842–3, their objective had shifted from Orthodox Christianity to 'heathenism'. For this they needed secure access; and they could not obtain it. Thus, their failure was partly connected with their inability to sustain their strategy, and partly due to factors beyond control. In view of this, the validity of their approach remains a matter for speculation. Its success seems unlikely, although not impossible. In modern times both the Church Mission to Jews and the Bible Churchmen's Missionary Society have maintained an Evangelical witness without separating their converts from the national Church through schism. None the less, the tensions, difficulties, and slowness inherent in such an approach in the mid-twentieth century do not suggest it could have fared well in the nineteenth. Certainly, much tact and patience were demanded; and it is their absence which marks most men.

Later Protestant activity drew on the CMS experience. We have seen the intimate links between Gobat and Krapf, on the one hand, and the Pilgrim and Falāshā missions, on the other. In our period, neither group used ordained men. The Chrischona artisan strategy was the most daring, and the Pietism from which it arose extremely interesting for its tactical flexibility. Much of this movement's teaching, above all its 'inward' emphasis, differs little from other radical Evangelical groups. But its willingness to adopt secular service as something approaching the essence of mission is very unusual in Africa in this pioneering period.[1] The adoption of lay vocations greatly facilitated the strategy of leavening the loaf, as it gave the missionaries a *raison d'être* which was meaningful to indigenous society. At the same time, they became as committed to an African political system, as many of their contemporaries were to a European one. Given the instability of these systems in general, and that of Tēwodros in particular, their work was overtaken. It remains one of the most promising, but unrealized, of all experiments in our area.

The Falāshā missions were the only ones to meet head-on the difficulties inherent in the indirect approach. They made converts to what was essentially Protestantism, yet channelled their adherents into the Orthodox Church. As we have seen, Flad's reaction was impatience. Protestants had been created, he reasoned, they ought also to have their own Church. It would have been the simplest solution, allowing lines to be drawn clearly. The Falāshā missions were not as prepared as either the CMS or the artisans to concentrate their efforts for the renewal of Orthodoxy and adopted their approach largely through the pressure of Tēwodros and *Abuna* Salāmā. Thus, the missionaries did not impress upon their followers the need for patience; rather the reverse. The fears of the Ethiopian clergy, that, by means of this Trojan Horse, the Protestants planned the subversion of the national Church, was not far wide of the mark. Consequently, while the Falāshā example illuminates the problem of Protestantism within Orthodoxy, the lack of commitment to the strategy on the part of the mission's agents leaves a final judgement unresolved.

Yet the London Society for the Promotion of Christianity Amongst the Jews was the only Reformation society successfully to establish itself. Its impact has been slight. Only a tenuous missionary connection was maintained between 1868 and the 1920s, and, although a distinguished indigenous leadership emerged in the interim, the total numbers affected have not been great.[2] Nevertheless, its limited

[1] Compare, for example, the opposite deduction reached from similar postulates by the Plymouth Brethren in Katanga at the end of the century. R. Rotberg, 'Plymouth Brethren and the Occupation of Katanga, 1886–1907', *Journal of African History*, v (1964), 285–97.

[2] The main reference works for the later development of Protestant missions are: *Light and Darkness in East Africa. A Missionary Survey of Uganda, Anglo-Egyptian Sudan, Abyssinia, Eritrea and the Three Somalilands* (London: World Dominion Press, n.d. [1927?]), ed. A. McLeish; and J. S. Trimingham, *The Christian Church and Missions in Ethiopia (including Eritrea and the Somalilands)* (London: World Dominion Press, 1950).

success revealed that European attention would be most profitably directed to the country's non-Christian inhabitants.

This was the pattern of the future. In the late 1860s, the Swedish Evangelical Lutheran mission entered what was to become Eritrea. Under the inspiration of Krapf they sought to proselytize the Gālā. Contact with this people proved elusive, and eventually the Swedes concentrated on creating a base within the Italian colony, ministering partly to its non-Orthodox inhabitants. Outside of Eritrea, and the slight ripples of influence emanating from it, Protestant missions played little role until the 1920s, when the Regent, Tafari Makonnen, began to patronize them. By 1935 eight organizations supported activity in the Ethiopian provinces: the Sudan Interior Mission, the Bible Churchman's Missionary Society, the Seventh Day Adventists, the United Presbyterian Mission of the USA, the Church Mission to Jews, the Evangelical Swedish Lutherans, the Swedish Mission-ssallskapet Bibeltrogna Vänner, and the German Hermannsburg Mission. Yet little impact was made; and practically none on the Orthodox population. Only during the Italian occupation did indigenous Protestant churches emerge, and then in the southern and western provinces.[1] To the present, dialogue with the Orthodox has remained hesitant or non-existent. Thus the original dream of stimulation to renewal has seen scant realization.

Catholic missions equally failed to establish a firm foothold within the Orthodox areas of the Ethiopian state. In the north Justin de Jacobis proved able to exploit Ethiopian pro-Catholicism. Unlike the Jesuits he discovered common ground with Orthodoxy, and, although he converted few clergy, his followers were distinguished in quality. Far from a Roman Church in Ethiopia, he helped found an indigenous Catholicism. Nevertheless, the bulk of adherents were found on the fringes of the plateau. The Lazarists had worked consistently northward, and, with the advent of Egyptian imperialism in the 1870s, increasingly became involved with alien political forces.[2] The establishment of an Italian colony in the 1890s embraced

---

[1] Not much literature exists on the subject in English, but for the SIM see H. M. Willmott, *The Doors Were Opened. The Remarkable Advance of the Gospel in Ethiopia* (London: SIM, n.d. [1960?]); and R. J. Davis, *Fire on the Mountains. The Story of a Miracle—the Church in Ethiopia* (New York, Toronto: SIM, 1966).

[2] Aleme Eshete, 'Activités politiques de la mission catholique (lazariste) en Éthiopie (sous le règne de l'empereur Johannès), 1868–1889 (études documentaires)' (Paris: typescript, 1970).

the majority of the parishes. Thereafter, their development fell into the more normal African pattern of interaction with imperial rule, no clearer indication of which could be given than the replacement of French Lazarists by Italian Capuchins under the pressure of a secular government in Rome.[1] The Lazarists retreated to the parched and isolated hill country of the Sāho, maintaining a small presence within the borders of Ethiopia, at Alitēnā. Although they nourished a distinguished Tegreññā Catholic Church, their impact was basically local.

In southern Ethiopia the story is similar. Genius and vigour secured the implanting of Catholicism in Kafā. The Capuchins shared the Protestant hope that conversion of the Gāllā would open the road to central Africa. Yet they scarcely contacted the pagan masses. Rather, an indigenous Church was reconstructed, the Europeans reaping where the medieval Orthodox had sown. The instability of the highland Christian state, followed by the exclusionist policies of Yohannes IV, cut the missionaries off from the Church they had nurtured. Not until the arrival of the Consolata fathers in the 1920s was missionary direction re-established. Meanwhile, the Capuchins had withdrawn to the eastern part of the country, where, around Harar they founded continuing work.

The outstanding aspect of both Capuchin and Lazarist missions is their use of an indigenous clergy. In the north, it was the secular Ethiopian priests who converted and staffed many of the parishes. It was in them that the national traditions most strongly survived despite the modifications of de Jacobis's policy by his successors, and the distortions brought by Italian imperialism. In the south, it was natives who made possible the rapid establishment of a Catholic presence; and it was they who sustained it in the long years of isolation. Basically, then, what success the Church of Rome enjoyed came from its ability to utilize indigenous Christianity. And it was here that Protestants failed.

Missions generated little, if any, social change within Ethiopia before 1941. Schools were few and scattered; likewise dispensaries. The second phase of development was postponed at least until the restoration of Hayla Sellāsē in 1941. Yet throughout the nineteenth century missionaries played the same secular role as elsewhere on the continent. Their position as interpreters of Europe to Africa, and

[1] Metodio da Nembro, *La missione dei Minori Cappuccini in Eritrea (1894–1952)* (Rome, 1953).

vice versa, established the worldly framework for their evangelistic activities. The Chrischona artisans excepted (and even they flirted briefly with Prussia), all groups resorted to imperialism to establish the pre-conditions for mission. Naturally, this varied greatly, growing with intensity as the years passed. Isenberg's rather delicate negotiations in 1838 were transformed into Krapf's seemingly anachronistic calls for armed intervention and aggression in the early 1840s. Within three years the Lazarists had induced Webē to solicit a 'protectorate' relationship with France.[1] Just over ten years later, the Catholics again attempted to create a French client state in the north. The Capuchins aided the Lazarists in their dealings with Negusē, merely seeking to substitute Sardinia for France.

One must again emphasize that no religious agent considered this to be his primary role. In their different ways, both Protestants and Catholics reflect the modern concept of the separation of Church and State, religion and politics. In a surprising way, the most radical was de Jacobis. The Pilgrim artisans threw off their European contacts in order better to serve an Ethiopian prince in the introduction of European technology and religious attitudes. The Lazarist bishop, however, made practically no effort at all to use alien cultural forms. Education, literacy, and medicine formed no part of his mission, and the contacts which he maintained in Paris and Rome, when exploited for secular ends, were confined to diplomacy and power politics. Yet some secular role seems all but inevitable. Thus, it is not to be dismissed *per se*, but judged from the standpoint of what was expected from the missionaries by Ethiopians, and the extent to which this expectation was distorted by European prejudice and preconceptions, or exploited to serve alien sectarian interests. Krapf's ferocious (and uncharacteristic) aggressiveness over the Shawā question stands condemned. Lazarist politics before Tēwodros appear as moderate; while their involvement with Negusē now seems unwise, and perhaps a damaging prelude to their conflicts with the Emperor Yohannes IV in the 1870s and 1880s. Capuchin attitudes appear distinctly imperialistic, yet were never seriously applied.

Only in one case can a mission be said to have suffered for its recourse to outside forces: the CMS in Shawā. Despite the mitigating factor of an internal religious crisis it seems clear that Harris's embassy distinctly contributed to discredit Krapf and undermine his

[1] See above, for Isenberg and Krapf, Chap. III, pp. 44, 47–8, and 51–3; and for de Jacobis, Chap. IV, pp. 68–9.

position. Yet this example may well be countered with the same mission's fate in Tegrē. It is just possible that, if Isenberg and Blumhardt had been able to secure substantial support for Webē against the Egyptians in 1838, their secular value would have outweighed their religious nuisance. Again, it is possible that the Chrischona artisans made a fundamental misjudgement in repudiating foreign politics and committing themselves to Tēwodros. As the gulf widened between Emperor and subjects, the missionaries lost practically all contact with the objects of their religious mission, the Ethiopian Church and people. Little, if any, influence survived the King's suicide. Catholics proved more adept. Despite their anti-Tēwodros activities they lost little.

One more example may serve to illustrate the complexities involved in this interaction of religion and politics. The Falāshā missionaries Stern and Rosenthal suffered terribly because they lived in the pre-partition period. The European presence was, perhaps, the major question of African politics in the mid-nineteenth century. Tēwodros perceived this most acutely, yet was in the unusual position of being unable to attract either the kind or amount of foreign involvement which he wanted.[1] He had been led to expect a great deal from Britain, and the contempt of its silence and indifference was first punished in the person of Stern. The hapless fellow had played no role in frustrating the King's ambitions, but he was harried none the less.

Thus, if missions helped serve the advance of imperialism, they often paid heavily for it. Stern simply foreshadowed what was to be widely observed later. In East Africa, by 1892 the CMS was urging the establishment of a British protectorate in Buganda because the arrival of colonial agents had fundamentally altered the local political situation, endangering the lives not only of missionaries but also of African neophytes. Yet, Bishop Tucker argued: 'Fifteen years ago our missionaries entered Uganda, carrying their lives in their hands, never looking for, never expecting, Government protection.'[2] In Nigeria, the fixing of British rule and the revolution in European attitudes which accompanied it, completely transformed and distorted the relations between missionaries and converts, setting back for several generations the creation of the indigenous Church which had been Henry Venn's objective.[3]

[1] See my paper 'Reformer and Modernizer', loc. cit.
[2] Quoted in Oliver, *Missionary Factor*, 155.
[3] Ajayi, *Christian Missions*, Chap. 8.

Max Warren has written that the 'ambiguity' of the modern missionary movement must be taken seriously 'without denying its spiritual significance'.[1] It is an apt view. Objectives were generally laudable. On the religious side, Protestants tried to inculcate more relevant, more contemporary attitudes; to refocus attention on the Church's Scriptural origins; and to bring about reform. Catholics sought the broadening of indigenous spirituality into universal fellowship and the introduction of greater organization and discipline. In their secular attitudes intentions were also worthy: literacy; advanced technology; the expansion of modern trade; the eradication of the traffic in human lives; and closer intercourse with the developed powers of the time: all these were legitimate and progressive. Yet missionaries arose from specific national traditions, and they never left them behind. Committed to expanding the Kingdom of God, they also furthered the Kingdom of Man.

[1] *The Missionary Movement from Britain in Modern History*, 15.

SELECT BIBLIOGRAPHY

I. UNPUBLISHED MATERIAL

A. ARCHIVAL

1. *Mission Societies*

i. Basel Mission, 'Evangelische Missions-Gesellschaft zu Basel':

B.V.31, Gobat; B.V.32, Kruse; B.V.39, Kugler; B.V.41, Lieder; B.V.77, Isenberg; B.V.110, Krapf; B.V.144, Blumhardt; B.V.209, Mühleisen.
Basically a supplement to the more extensive CMS material, from which it is independent, but to which it is parallel. A special feature is short biographies and posthumous correspondence *about* the missionaries.

ii. Church Missionary Society Archives, London:

Mediterranean Mission: M/E2 and C.M/o8, general; C.M/o13, Blumhardt, 1836–8; C.M/o18, 42a an important letter from Blumhardt, 20 Feb. 1838; C.M/o28, Gobat; C.M/o35, Isenberg 1832–40; C.M/o44, Krapf 1837–41; C.M/o45, Kruse 1826–61; C.M/o46, Kugler 1826–30; C.M/o48, Lieder 1826–61; C.M/o51, Mühleisen 1841; C.M/o52, Müller 1841.

East Africa Mission: C.A5/o13, Isenberg 1842–4; C.A5/o16, Krapf 1841–80; C.A5/o19, Mühleisen 1842–4.
The CMS Archives are extremely rich. Both journals and letters are to be found. The Isenberg, Krapf, and Gobat files are obviously most important; but all are useful.

iii. Congrégation de la Mission, Paris:

Lettres manuscrites de Mgr. de Jacobis: i. 1824–38; ii. 1839–60.
An important collection, forming the bulk of de Jacobis's correspondence with his society both in Paris and Rome. Both Italian and an execrable French were used. The letters are numbered, and many seem to have been removed. However, as the dates closely follow one another, either copies or communications from other missionaries are the probable explanation. Vol. ii contains a few letters of Sapeto. There is a duplicate collection at the Archivio della Procura Generale della Congregazione della Missione presso la S. Sede.

iv. Archives of the Sacred Congregation for the Propagation of the Faith, Rome, 'Propaganda Fide':

Scritture Riferite nei Congressi: iii, Etiopia, Arabia, Sokotora, 1721–1840; iv, Africa Centrale, Etiopia, Arabia, 1841–7; v, ibid. 1848–57; vi, ibid. 1858–60; vii, ibid. 1861–70.

A rich source containing the letters and reports, chronologically arranged, of both Lazarist and Capuchin missions, as well as occasional letters from interested laymen like d'Abbadie and Blondeel. There are also documents from consuls of the Catholic powers and letters from the Ethiopian princes Webē, Negusē, Goshu, and Berru.

Scritture Originali Riferite nelle Congregazioni Generali

Several volumes of this series, as cited, have been used for the eighteenth-century missions. There appears to be nothing of importance between 1800 and 1870.

v. Archivio della Procura Generale della Congregazione della Missione presso la S. Sede, Curia Generalizia C.M., Rome:

Giornale B. Giustino de Jacobis, 6 vols., typescript.

The first four volumes, covering the period Nov. 1839 to Sept. 1852, totalling 948 pages, provide a detailed view of developments in the 1840s. The earlier sections were also used as a copy-book, but contain no letters not available elsewhere. The location of the original is unknown. The typist was unable to read Ethiopian terms accurately, and there are some frustrating misprints.

Testimonies

A bound manuscript volume, no title, no date; containing interviews with companions and eye-witnesses of the life of de Jacobis, secular and clerical; the first interview is dated 11 July 1894, and the whole is clearly part of the beatification campaign; pages are unnumbered, but there are 337 of Italian material, 21 of French; quarto size. Amongst the leading informants are the priests Tasfā Ṣeyon, Kidāna Māryām, and the two Takla Hāymānots. At times formal and pedantic in structure, the material becomes highly moving when the witnesses speak freely.

vi. Archivum Generale, Curia Generalizia, Frati Minori Cappuccini, Rome:

H.44, Missio Gallas; 2, 3.
LA.25, Massaia, G., Card.; 1–9.

An extremely useful supplement to the Propaganda material, this material has not been heavily drawn upon for the present study. Its value lies primarily in its more detailed account of internal developments within the south-western mission. Several useful expressions of opinion on the approach to the Ethiopian rite.

2. *State and Government*

i. Bibliothèque Nationale, Paris:

Fond Éthiopien-Abbadie: no. 186, 'Mélanges religieux'; nos. 265, 266, 267, 269, 'Journal de voyage'.

Antoine d'Abbadie was the most notable lay Catholic traveller of the period. His greatest value lies in his information on south-west Ethiopia, outside the scope of the present study. None the less, his observations on religious developments are acute. No. 186 is an Amharic commentary on a pastoral letter from the see of Alexandria discussing the doctrinal question.

ii. India Office Archives, London:

Bombay Secret Proceedings. Lantern Gallery: selected volumes 159–206.

The reports of the Harris Embassy to Shawā. As the initiative for the embassy was largely Krapf's, and as its fate so closely affected his, the material is very important. Harris and his colleagues also observed local political and religious affairs, and corresponded with *Abuna* Salāmā.

Political and Secret Records. (Secret Letters Received) (Aden): xxvi (1842)–lxiii (1866).

Of relatively minor importance. Occasional reports relating to missionary and religious developments. 1844, letters from *Abuna* Salāmā.

Abyssinia Original Correspondence: i (1867), ii (1868), iii (1869–71).

A primary source for the detainees under Tēwodros. All correspondence, after detention, passed through consular hands. Much of it was reprinted in FO 401, to which I have been unable fully to harmonize my references.

iii. Ministère des Affaires étrangères, Paris:

Correspondance politique. Égypte. Massaouah: i (1840–53), ii (1854–9), iii (1860–74).

Fundamental for an understanding of the fate of Catholic missions. A considerable amount of this material was published in the *Revue d'histoire des missions*.

Correspondance commerciale. Massaouah: i (1840–59), ii (1860–85).

Of minor importance, but contains occasional political comments not found elsewhere.

Mémoires et documents (Afrique): xiii, Abyssinie, 1838–50; lxi, Abyssinie ii, 1839–66; lxii, Abyssinie iii, 1867–83.

Primarily drawn on for the Franco–Negusē correspondence.

iv. Public Record Office, London:

Foreign Office

FO 1/I–III, Abyssinia.

Less important for Protestant missions than the MAE material is for the Catholic. Nevertheless valuable.

FO 401/I–II, *Correspondence respecting Abyssinia, 1848–1868.*

Seems to contain everything of importance from the founding of the British consulate. Plowden was involved closely with Tēwodros and Salāmā; and his successor Cameron became the centre of the diplomatic crisis in 1864.

v. *Staatsarchiv des Kantons Basel-Stadt*:

C. F. Spittler Privat-Archiv 653: iii. Briefe von Spittler; v. Briefe an Spittler; B. Pilgermission im Ausbau; D.1. Pilgermission in Abessinien; D.2. Landbeschreibung; D.3. Briefe (etc.); D.4. Hinweis auf Apostel-strasse; xxx. Samuel Gobat-Zeller Bischof v. Jerusalem.

Important and basic. The relevant material is scattered through the different files. There are no journals, and the whole ends in 1862.

B. THESES AND PAPERS

ALEME ESHETE, 'Activités politiques de la mission catholique (lazariste) en Éthiopie (sous le règne de l'empereur Johannès), 1868–1889 (études documentaires)' (Paris; typescript, 1970).

BETTA, L., 'L'Inizio della Missione Lazzarista in Abissinia (1838–1842).' Thesis submitted to the Pontificium Institutum Orientalium Studiorum (Rome, 1950). Copy at the Curia Generalizia della Congregazione della Missione, Rome. This is an important study resting on an exhaustive use of Propaganda and Lazarist material, limited only by the rigorous hundred-year rule of the former.

CAULK, R. A., 'The Origins and Development of the Foreign Policy of Menelik II, 1865–1896' (University of London; Ph.D., 1966).

CRUMMEY, D. E., 'European Religious Missions in Ethiopia 1830–1868' (University of London; Ph.D., 1967).

DARKWAH, R. H. K., 'The Rise of the Kingdom of Shoa 1813–1889' (University of London; Ph.D., 1966).

MERID WOLDE AREGAY, 'Southern Ethiopia and the Christian Kingdom 1508–1708, with Special Reference to the Galla Migrations and their Consequences' (University of London; Ph.D., 1971).

TADDESSE TAMRAT, 'Church and State in Ethiopia 1270–1527' (University of London; Ph.D., 1968).

II. PUBLISHED MATERIAL

A. MISSIONARY SOURCES

1. *Primary*

i. *Periodicals*

Annales de la congrégation de la mission, ou Recueil de lettres édifiantes écrites par les prêtres de cette congrégation employés dans les missions étrangères, i–xxxiv (1840–69). Excellent material. Long extracts, lightly edited.

The Church Missionary Intelligencer, vii (1856). The original publication of the journal of Krapf's trip to Ethiopia in 1856. Differs slightly from the subsequent version in *Travels, Researches*.

Church Missionary Record, detailing the Proceedings of the Church Missionary Society, i–xv (1830–44). Rich and important.

Der evangelische Heidenbote. Herausgegeben von der Direktion der evange-lischen Missions-Gesellschaft zu Basel, i–xvi (1828–43). Parallels the CMS *Record* in the same manner as the archival material.

The Home and Foreign Missionary Record of the Church of Scotland. xv–xvii (Jan. 1860–Mar. 1862); New Series, i–vi (Apr. 1862–Mar. 1870). Rather short extracts from the letters of Staiger and Brandeis.

Jewish Intelligence, and Monthly Account of the Proceedings of the London Society for Promoting Christianity Amongst the Jews. xxvi (1860); New Series, i–ix (1861–9). Some letters of Stern.

Jewish Records. New Series, nos. 4, 13, 20, 28–9. A journal of Flad.

Magazin für die neueste Geschichte der evangelischen Missions- und Bibel-gesellschaften. Various volumes from xiii (1828); and Neue Folge, i–x (1857–66). Some later numbers contain Chrischona material.

Reports of the London Society for Promoting Christianity Amongst the Jews. 1861–9.

Revue d'histoire des missions. ix (1932), xv (1938), xvi (1939). Not, strictly speaking, a missionary periodical in the sense of the foregoing; but containing a wealth of primary material from the MAE.

ii. *Missionary books, articles, collections of letters, etc.*

BECCARI, C., *Notizie e saggi di opere e documenti inediti riguardanti la storia di Etiopia durante i secoli XVI, XVII, e XVIII . . .* (Rome, 1903). Vol. i of the series continued as *Rerum.*

—— *Rerum Aethiopicarum Scriptores Occidentales Inediti a Saeculo XVI ad XIX,* xiv, 'Relationes et Epistolae Variorum' (Rome, 1914).

FARINA, G., *Le Lettere del Cardinale Massaia dal 1846 al 1886, . . . Insieme ad alcuni documenti riguardanti il Massaia. Prefazione di S. E. Pietro Badoglio . . .* (Turin, 1936). The basic published collection.

FLAD, J. M., *Notes from the Journal of F. [sic] M. Flad, One of Bishop Gobat's Pilgrim Missionaries in Abyssinia. Edited, With a Brief Sketch of the Abyssinian Church, by the Rev. W. Douglas Veitch . . .* (London, 1860). A rare and valuable book.

—— *Zwölf Jahre in Abessinien oder Geschichte des Königs Theodoros II. und der Mission unter seiner Regierung . . .* (Basel, 1869). Written in close conjunction with Waldmeier's book published in the same year, Flad's interpretation of Tēwodros and Salāmā is rather different. Chap. VII is the first published version of Zanab's chronicle.

—— *The Falashas (Jews) of Abyssinia with a Preface by Dr. Krapf* (London, 1869).

—— *60 Jahre in der Mission unter den Falaschas in Abessinien. Selbst-biographie des Missionars Johann Martin Flad. Mit Einleitung und Schluss-wort von seinem Sohn Pastor Friedrich Flad* (Giessen and Basel, 1922).

GOBAT, S., *Journal of a Three Years' Residence in Abyssinia in Furtherance of the Objects of the Church Missionary Society* (London, 1834). Lightly edited, very valuable. An introductory section contains extracts from

Kugler's journal. This material was replaced in the second edition (1847) by material relating to Gobat's election as Anglican Bishop in Jerusalem.

—— *Samuel Gobat, Bishop of Jerusalem. His Life and Work. A Biographical Sketch, Drawn Chiefly from his Own Journals With a Preface by the Right Hon. the Earl of Shaftesbury* (London, 1884). Useful for the period not covered by the *Journal*.

ISENBERG, C. W., and KRAPF, J. L., *Journals of the Rev. Messrs. Isenberg and Krapf, Missionaries of the Church Missionary Society, Detailing their Proceedings in the Kingdom of Shoa, and Journeys in other Parts of Abyssinia, in the Years 1839, 1840, 1841, and 1842* (London, 1843). A model of the genre. Scrupulous, intelligent observers, the authors produced a work of lasting value not only for the fate of their own mission, but also for Shawā in the 1840s and the ethnographic situation in southern Ethiopia. A higher proportion of Krapf's material was published than of Isenberg's.

ISENBERG, C. W., *Abessinien und die Evangelische Mission. Erlebnisse in Ægypten, auf und an dem Rothen Meere, dem Meerbusen von Aden, und besonders in Abessinien. Tagebuch meiner dritten Missionsreise vom Mai 1842 bis December 1843. Nebst einer geographischen, ethnographischen und historischen Einleitung* (Bonn, 2 vols., 1844). Principally of value for the second CMS expulsion from Tegrē in 1843. References are to the English manuscript version in the CMS archives, C.A5/o13, 30.

JOWETT, WM., *Christian Researches in the Mediterranean, from MDCCCXV to MDCCCXX in Furtherance of the Objects of the Church Missionary Society. . . .* (London, 1822).

KRAPF, J. L., *An Imperfect Outline of the Elements of the Galla Language Preceded by a Few Remarks Concerning the Nation of the Gallas and an Evangelical Mission Among Them, by the Rev. C. W. Isenberg* (London, 1840). A pioneering linguistic work, with an important essay on missionary strategy.

—— *Travels, Researches, and Missionary Labours during an Eighteen Years' Residence in Eastern Africa. Together with Journeys to Jagga, Usambara, Ukambani, Shoa, Abessinia, and Khartum; and a Coasting Voyage from Mombas to Cape Delgado* (London, 1860). A very brief, retrospective account of 1837–43, followed by a detailed account of the visit to Tēwodros and Salāmā in 1855. A second edition (London: Frank Cass, 1968) contains an important introductory essay by R. C. Bridges, largely concerned, however, with Krapf's East African career.

MARTIRE, E., *Massaia da vicino con una scelta di cento e più lettere di Massaia e di altri . . .* (Rome, 1937). Less original than Farina, but important for des Avanchers and Stella.

MASSAJA, G., *I miei trentacinque anni di missione nell'Alta Etiopia. Memorie storiche di Fra Guglielmo Massaja* (Rome, 12 vols., 1885–95). Rambling reminiscences, often invaluable. Unfortunately, Massaja lost most of his notes on his expulsion from Kafā in 1861 and his account of earlier events must be used cautiously.

MASSAJA, G., 'Un Ami et bienfaiteur de l'Éthiopie: Justin de Jacobis. Lettre inédite de Mgr. Massaia', *Revue d'histoire des missions*, xii (1935), 608–25. A spirited, if misconceived, defence of de Jacobis against charges of political involvement made by the French Consul Lejean.

PACELLI, M., *Viaggi in Etiopia del P. Michelangelo da Tricarico, Minore Osservante, ne' quali si descrivono le cose più rimarchevoli, ed osservabili incontrate in quella regione sulle orme del Ludolf, De La Croix, ed altri celebri scrittori di quei luoghi* (Naples, 1797). A very rare and important source for the mission of Mgr. Tobias in the 1790s.

PRUTKY, REMEDIUS, 'Aethiopia. Descriptio Compendiosa Imperii Aetiophici [*sic*] et Relatio Missionam Aetiopiae et Aegypti, excerpta Partim ex Archivio Sac. Cong. de Propaganda Fide, Partim ex Archivio Dictae Missionis, Et de Successu Singularium Rerum Dictas Missiones Concernentium, Auctore Patre Remedio', *Le Missioni Francescane in Palestina ed in altre regioni della terra* (Rome): vi (1895), 270–4, 459–67, 720–3; vii (1896), 117–23, 258–61, 372–9, 474–7. General information of a geographical nature.

—— 'La francescana spedizione in Etiopia del 1751–54 e la sua relazione del P. Remedio Prutky di Boemia O.F.M.', *Archivum Franciscanum Historicum*, vi (Quaracchi, 1913), 129–43. An analysis and discussion of Remedius's account by Fr. Teodosio Somigli di S. Detole, the major Franciscan historian of seventeenth- and eighteenth-century Ethiopia.

—— 'L'Itinerarium del P. Remedio Prutky, viaggiatore e missionario francescano (Alto Egitto), e il suo viaggio in Abissinia — 21 febbraio 1752 — 22 aprile 1753', *Studi francescani*, N.S. xxii (Florence, 1925), 425–60. Another important study by Fr. Teodosio Somigli.

SAPETO, G., *Viaggio e missione cattolica fra i Mensâ i Bogos e gli Habab con un cenno geografico e storico dell'Abissinia* (Rome, 1857). With its firsthand account of the events leading to the founding of the Bogos mission, and an early retrospective view of the author's pioneering role, it is his most useful work for our purposes.

—— *L'Italia e il Canale di Suez. Operetta popolare.* (Genoa, 1865). Commercial and political propaganda.

—— 'Ambasciata mandata nel 1869 [*sic*] dal governo francese a Negussiè Degiazmate del Tigré e del Samièn in Abissinia . . .', *Bollettino della Società Geografica Italiana*, S1, vi (Florence, 1871), 22–71. A first-hand account.

—— *Assab e i suoi critici* (Genoa, 1879). Another imperialist tract.

—— *Etiopia. Notizie raccolte dal Prof. Giuseppe Sapeto. Ordinate e riassunte dal Comando del Corpo di Stato Maggiore* (Rome, 1890).

STERN, H. A., *Wanderings among the Falashas in Abyssinia together with a Description of the Country and its Various Inhabitants* (London, 1862). A second edition (London: Frank Cass, 1968) has an introductory essay by R. L. Hess.

—— *Abyssinian Captives. Recent Intelligence from the Rev. H. A. Stern with Extracts from Mr. Rosenthal's Letter* (London, n.d.).

—— *The Captive Missionary: being an account of the Country and People of Abyssinia, Embracing a Narrative of King Theodore's Life, and His Treatment of Political and Religious Missions* (London, n.d.).

WALDMEIER, Th., *Erlebnisse in Abessinien in den Jahren 1858–1868 von Theophil Waldmeier, Pilgermissionar. . . . Bevorwortet von Dr. L. Krapf* (Basel, 1869). A guileless, warm-hearted man, he was very sympathetic to both Tēwodros and Salāmā.

—— *The Autobiography of Theophilus Waldmeier, Missionary: Being an Account of Ten Years' Life in Abyssinia; and Sixteen Years in Syria* (London, n.d. [1889?]).

2. *Biographies*

D'AGOSTINI, D., *Storia della vita del venerabile Giustino de Jacobis, apostolo dell'Abissinia* (Naples, 1910).

ARATA, S., *Abuna Yakob Apostolo dell'Abissinia (Mons. Giustino de Jacobis C. M.) 1800–1860* (Rome, 2nd ed., 1934). Useful.

BETTA, L., 'La luminosa Figura del B. Giustino de Jacobis Apostolo dell'Abissinia', *Annali della Missione*, lxvii (1960), 203–10.

—— 'Il B. Giustino de Jacobis, Prefetto Apostolico dell' Etiopia', *Annali della Missione*, lxvii (1960), 288–313, 350–73; lxviii (1961), 154–206. The most original and important material from Fr. Betta's thesis is published here.

CLAUS, W., *Dr. Ludwig Krapf, weil Missionar in Ostafrika* (Basel, n.d.).

COULBEAUX, J.-B., *Un Martyr abyssin. Ghebra-Michael de la Congrégation de la Mission (Lazariste)* (Paris, 1902). Subsequently revised and published as *Vers la lumière. Le Bienheureux Abba Ghèbrè-Michael, prêtre de la mission martyrisé en Éthiopie* (Paris, 1926). Not, of course, a missionary biography, but one of a convert. Coulbeaux had access not only to the writings of Fr. Takla Hāymānot, Gabra Mikā'ēl's companion, but also the testimonies of other eye-witnesses.

COZZANI, E., *Vita di Guglielmo Massaia* (Florence, 2 vols., 1943); vol. iv in the series 'I grandi Italiani d'Africa. Collezione a cura del Ministero dell'Africa Italiana'. Rests on the published sources.

DEMIMUID, M., *Vie du vénérable Justin de Jacobis de la congrégation de la mission . . .* (Paris, 1905).

GIACCHERO, G., and BISOGNI, G., *Vita di Giuseppe Sapeto. L'ignota storia degli esordi coloniali italiani rivelata da documenti inediti* (Florence, 1942). Original, scholarly. Useful not only for Sapeto, but also for Stella.

GUNDERT, H., *Biography of the Rev. Charles Isenberg, Missionary of the Church Missionary Society to Abyssinia and Western India from 1832 to 1864* (London, 1885). Sympathetic and useful.

HERBERT, M. E., *Abyssinia and its Apostle* (London, n.d. [1867?]). The only de Jacobis biography in English.

LARIGALDIE, G., *Héraut du Christ. Le Vénérable Justin de Jacobis . . . D'après des documents inédits . . . Préface de M. E. Coulbeaux . . .* (Paris, [1910]).

'The Missionary Career of Dr. Krapf, Missionary of the Church Missionary Society in Abyssinia and East Africa, and Pioneer of Central African Exploration.' Pamphlet, reprinted from *Church Missionary Intelligencer*, February and March 1882, London.

PANE, S., *Il Beato Giustino de Jacobis della Congregazione della Missione. Vescovo Titolare di Nilopoli. Primo Vicario Apostolico di Abissinia* (Storia critica sull'ambiente e sui documenti) (Naples, 1949). The most exhaustive study ever undertaken; scholarly and sympathetic. With Takla Hāymānot's study, one of the two indispensable works. Marred, however, by lack of sympathy for the Ethiopian context, and ignorance of the more accessible Protestant works.

ROEHRICH, L., *Samuel Gobat, ancien missionnaire en Abyssinie et évêque anglican de Jérusalem . . .* (Paris and Basel, 1880).

TARDUCCI, F., *Il P. Giusto da Urbino Missionario in Abissinia e le esplorazioni africane* (Faenze, 1899). These are two separate, small studies; no connection is made between Fr. Giusto and African explorations. Rather slight, but with interesting family material.

VALORI, F., *Guglielmo Massaia* (Turin, 1957). Recent, heroic view.

B. CONTEMPORARY EUROPEAN

ABBADIE, ANTOINE D', *Voyage en Abyssinie. Communication faite à la Société de Géographie . . .* (Paris, 1839).

—— *L'Abyssinie et le roi Théodore* (Paris, 1868).

ABBADIE, ARNAULD D', *Douze ans dans la Haute Éthiopie (Abyssinie) . . .* (Paris, 1868).

ANNESLEY, G., *Voyages and Travels to India, Ceylon, the Red Sea, Abyssinia, and Egypt, in the Years 1802, 1803, 1804, 1805, and 1806* (London, 3 vols., 1809).

BAKER, S., *The Nile Tributaries of Abyssinia, and the Sword Hunters of the Hamran Arabs* (London, 1867).

BRUCE, J., *Travels to Discover the Source of the Nile in the Years 1768, 1769, 1770, 1771, 1772, and 1773* (Edinburgh, 5 vols., 1790). A second edition (Edinburgh, 7 vols., 1805), edited by A. Murray, contains additional biographical material and information drawn from Bruce's notes.

COMBES, E., and TAMISIER, M., *Voyage en Abyssinie, dans le pays des Gallas, de Choa et d'Ifat; précédé d'une excursion dans l'Arabie-Heureuse . . . 1835–1837* (Paris, 4 vols., 1838).

DUFTON, H., *Narrative of a Journey Through Abyssinia in 1862–3, With an Appendix on 'The Abyssinian Captives Question'* (London, 2nd ed., 1867). Before travelling to Ethiopia, the author corresponded with Chrischona seeking to join its mission.

HALLS, J. J., *The Life and Correspondence of Henry Salt, Esq. F.R.S. & His Britannic Majesty's Late Consul General in Egypt* (London, 2 vols., 1834).

HARRIS, W. C., *The Highlands of Ethiopia* (*being the account of eighteen months of a British Embassy to the Christian Court of Shoa*) (London, 2nd ed., 3 vols., 1844). However much a classic, badly marred by overwriting; and needs to be balanced against the original reports on which it is based. Also probably more dependent on Krapf than the author admits.

HEUGLIN, TH. VON, *Reise nach Abessinien, den Gala-Ländern, Ost-Sudan und Chartum in den Jahren 1861 und 1862* (Jena, 1868).

HOLLAND, T. J., and HOZIER, H., *Record of the Expedition to Abyssinia, Completed by Order of the Secretary of State for War* (London, 2 vols., 1870).

ISSEL, A., *Viaggio nel Mar Rosso e tra i Bogos (1870)* (Milan, 2nd ed., 1876).

JOHNSTON, CH., 'Six Months in Southern Abyssinia. A Journal of incidents occurring during a residence in the Kingdom of Shoa', *Hunt's London Journal*, 1844, 288–90, 305–7, 321–3, 338–41.

—— *Travels in Southern Abyssinia, Through the Country of Adal to the Kingdom of Shoa* (London, 2 vols., 1844).

KATTE, A. VON, *Reise in Abyssinien im Jahre 1836* (Stuttgart and Tübingen, 1838).

LEFEBVRE, TH., *Voyage en Abyssinie exécuté pendant les anneés 1839, 1840, 1841, 1842, 1843* (Paris, 6 vols., 1845–8).

LEJEAN, G., *Théodore II. Le nouvel empire d'Abyssinie et les intérêts français dans le sud de la Mer Rouge . . .* (Paris, [1865]).

Methodios of Aksum, Metropolitan, 'An unpublished document edited and translated into English ["An extemporaneous account of Abyssinian matters"]', *Abba Salama. A Review of the Association of Ethio-Hellenic Studies*, i (Addis Ababa, 1970), 15–66. Written under the Emperor Tēwodros, the document was produced by a Greek merchant with influence at Court. Rather eccentric and poorly dated, it is of value for its unusual standpoint.

PARKYNS, M., *Life in Abyssinia: Being Notes Collected During Three Years' Residence and Travels in that Country* (London, 2nd ed., 1868).

PEARCE, N., *The Life and Adventures of Nathaniel Pearce, Written by Himself, during a Residence in Abyssinia, from the years 1810 to 1819. Together with Mr. Coffin's Account of His Visit to Gondar. Edited by J. J. Halls, Esq.* (London, 2 vols., 1831).

PLOWDEN, W. C., *Travels in Abyssinia and the Galla Country with an Account of a Mission to Ras Ali in 1848* (London, 1868).

RASSAM, H., *Narrative of the British Mission to Theodore, king of Abyssinia. With notices of the countries traversed from Massowah, through* the Soodân, the Amhâra, and back to Annesley Bay from Magdala (London, 2 vols., 1869).

ROCHET D'HÉRICOURT, C.-E.-X., Voyage sur la côte orientale de la Mer Rouge, dans le pays d'Adel et le royaume de Choa (Paris, 1841).

—— Second Voyage sur les deux rives de la Mer Rouge dans le pays des Adels et le royaume de Choa (Paris, 1846).

RÜPPELL, W. P. E. S., Reise in Abyssinien (Frankfurt am Main, 2 vols., 1838–40).

RUSSEL, S., Une Mission en Abyssinie et dans la Mer Rouge, 23 octobre 1859–7 mai 1860 (Paris, 1884).

SALT, H., A Voyage to Abyssinia, and Travels into the Interior of that Country, Executed under the Orders of the British Government, in the Years 1809 and 1810 . . . (London, 1814).

STANLEY, H. M., Coomassie and Magdala: The Story of Two British Campaigns in Africa (London, 1874).

C. ETHIOPIAN DOCUMENTS IN TRANSLATION

BASSET, R., Études sur l'histoire d'Éthiopie (Paris, 1882).

BÉGUINOT, F., La Cronaca abbreviata d'Abissinia nuova versione dall'etiopico e commento (Rome, 1901).

CERULLI, E., Scritti teologici etiopici dei secoli XVI–XVII (Città del Vaticano, Biblioteca Apostolica Vaticana): i. Tre opuscoli dei Mikaeliti (1958): ii. La storia dei quattro concili ed altri opuscoli monofisiti (1960).

CONTI ROSSINI, C., Documenta ad Illustrandam Historiam. 1. Liber Axumae (Paris, 1909); 'Corpus scriptorum christianorum orientalium'.

—— 'La cronaca reale abissina dall'anno 1800 all'anno 1840', RRAL, S5, xxv (1916), 779–923.

—— 'Il libro delle leggende e tradizioni abissine dell'ecciaghe Filpos', RRAL, S5, xxvi (1917), 699–718.

—— 'Nuovi documenti per la storia d'Abissinia nel secolo XIX', RRAL, S7, ii (1947), 357–416.

FUSELLA, L., 'Le lettere del dabtarā Assaggākhāñ', Rassegna di studi etiopici, xiii (1954), 20–30.

—— 'La cronaca dell'imperatore Teodoro II di Etiopia in un manoscritto amarico', Annali dell'Istituto Universitario Orientale di Napoli, N.S. vi (1954–6), 61–121.

GABRA SELLĀSĒ (Guèbrè Sellasié), Chronique du règne de Ménélik II Roi des Rois d'Éthiopie. Traduite de l'amharique par Tèsfa Sellassié. Publiée et annotée par Maurice de Coppet (Paris, 2 vols., 1930–2).

GUIDI, I., 'Le liste dei metropoliti d'Abissinia', Bessarione, vi (1899), 1–16.

—— 'Uno squarcio di storia ecclesiastica di Abissinia', Bessarione, viii (1900), 10–25.

—— *Annales Iohannis I, Iyāsu I, Bakāffā* (Paris, 1903); 'Corpus scriptorum christianorum orientalium', Series Altera, v.

—— *Annales Regum Iyāsu II et Iyo'as* (Rome, 1912); 'C.S.C.O.', Series Altera, vi.

HAILU, G. Y., 'Un Manoscritto Amarico sulle Verità della Fede', *Atti del Convegno Internazionale di Studi Etiopici* (Rome: Accademia Nazionale dei Lincei, 1960), 345-52. The document is not actually printed, but is summarized and analysed.

HUNTINGFORD, G. W. B., *The Glorious Victories of 'Āmda Ṣeyon King of Ethiopia* (Oxford: Clarendon Press, 1965).

MATTHEW, A. F., *The Teaching of the Abyssinian Church as set forth by the Doctors of the Same. Translated by the Rev. A. F. Matthew with an Introduction by Canon J. A. Douglas* (London, 1936). This book arose out of a questionnaire drawn up by a scholar of the Church of England and submitted to the authorities of the Ethiopian Church in the 1920s. As such it is somewhat artificial, but interesting none the less.

MONDON-VIDAILHET, C., *Chronique de Théodoros II Roi des Rois d'Éthiopie (1853-1868) d'après un manuscrit original* (Paris, n.d.). The earlier chronicle dealing with the entire reign, the author, *Alaqā* Walda Māryām, was close to *Abuna* Salāmā, whose captivity he shared.

MORENO, M. M., 'La cronaca di re Teodoro attribuita al dabtarā "Zaneb" ', *Rassegna di studi etiopici*, ii (1942), 143-80. Although the author was a Protestant convert, there is no discernible foreign religious influence in the document. See Flad, *Zwölf Jahre*, for an earlier translation into German.

TAKLA HĀYMĀNOT, *Episodi della vita apostolica di Abuna Jacob ossia il venerabile Padre Giustino De Jacobis raccontati da un testimonio Abba Teclà Haimanot prete cattolico abissino. Confessore della fede. Traduzione dal francese par P. Celestino da Desio* (Asmara, 1915). For the present study, the most significant Ethiopian document yet published; and one of the most substantial products of nineteenth-century Ethiopian historiography. The book is the distillation of the memories of de Jacobis held by those of his disciples who survived him. Filial and pious in tone, this edition is the least desirable, being a translation of a translation.

—— 'Vicende dell'Etiopia e delle missioni cattoliche ai tempi di Ras Ali, Deggiac Ubie e Re Teodoro, secondo un documento abissino', *RRAL*, S5, xxv (1916), 425-550. Published and edited by C. Conti Rossini. Useful largely from the interpretative angle.

—— *Lettere di Abba Tecle Haymanot di Adua* (Rome, 4 vols., 1939); published and edited by Fr. Mauro da Leonessa; translated *Abbā* Gabrē of Hālāy. Vol. ii is the principal Italian translation of this collection of historical and religious treatises.

—— 'L'ambasciata francese a Negusē', *Rassegna di studi etiopici*, vii (1948), 176-91. Edited and published by L. Fusella.

D. SECONDARY MATERIAL, WORKS OF REFERENCE

ABIR, M., *Ethiopia. The Era of the Princes. The Challenge of Islam and the Re-unification of the Christian Empire 1769–1855* (London: Longmans, 1968).

AJAYI, J. F. A., *Christian Missions in Nigeria 1841–1891. The Making of a New Élite* (London: Longmans, 1965).

AYANDELE, E. A., *The Missionary Impact on Modern Nigeria 1842–1914. A Political and Social Analysis* (London: Longmans, 1966).

AYMRO WONDMAGEGNEHU and MOTOVU, J. (eds.), *The Ethiopian Orthodox Church* (Addis Ababa: Ethiopian Orthodox Mission, 1970).

BAËTA, C. G. (ed.), *Christianity in Tropical Africa. Studies Presented and Discussed at the Seventh International African Seminar, University of Ghana, April 1965* (London: Oxford University Press, 1968).

BAETEMAN, J., *Dictionnaire amarigna-français suivi d'un vocabulaire français-amarigna* (Dire-Daoua: Imprimerie Saint Lazare, 1924).

BARRACLOUGH, G., *An Introduction to Contemporary History* (London: Penguin Books, 1967).

BECKINGHAM, C. F., and HUNTINGFORD, G. W. B., *Some Records of Ethiopia 1593–1646. Being Extracts from The History of High Ethiopia or Abassia by Manoel de Almeida Together with Bahrey's History of the Galla* (London: Hakluyt Society, 1954).

BUDGE, E. A. W., *A History of Ethiopia, Nubia & Abyssinia (According to the Hieroglyphic Inscriptions of Egypt and Nubia, and The Ethiopian Chronicles)* (London, 2 vols., 1928); reprinted Anthropological Publications (Oosterhout N. B., 2 vols., 1966). Highly eccentric and unreliable.

CAIRNS, H. A. C., *Prelude to Imperialism. British Reactions to Central African Society 1840–1890* (London: Routledge, 1965).

CERULLI, E., *Etiopi in Palestina. Storia della comunità etiopica di Gerusalemme* (Rome, 2 vols., 1943–7).

CONTI ROSSINI, C., 'Lo Ḥatatā Zar'a Yā'qob e il Padre Giusto da Urbino', *RRAL*, S5, xxix (1920), 213–23.

—— *Etiopia e genti di Etiopia* (Florence, 1937). Possibly still the best general introduction to the subject.

COULBEAUX, J.-B., 'Abouna-Salama', *Revue anglo-romaine*, i (Paris, 1895), 625–36, 673–96. Disappointing.

—— *Histoire politique et religieuse d'Abyssinie. Depuis les temps les plus reculés jusqu'à l'avènement de Ménélick II* (Paris, 3 vols., 1928).

CROSS, F. L. (ed.), *The Oxford Dictionary of the Christian Church* (London: Oxford University Press, 1958).

CRUMMEY, D. E., 'Tēwodros as Reformer and Modernizer', *Journal of African History*, x (1969), 457–69.

—— 'The Violence of Tēwodros', *Journal of Ethiopian Studies*, xi (1970).

CUMING, G. J. (ed.), *The Mission of the Church and the Propagation of the Faith. Papers Read at the Seventh Summer Meeting and the Eighth Winter Meeting of the Ecclesiastical History Society* (Cambridge: Cambridge University Press, 1970).

DAVIS, R. J., *Fire on the Mountains. The Story of a Miracle—the Church in Ethiopia* (New York and Toronto: S.I.M., 1966).

DUCHESNE, A., *À la recherche d'une colonie belge. Le consul Blondeel en Abyssinie (1840–1842). Contribution à l'histoire précoloniale de la Belgique.* (Brussels: Institut royal colonial belge, 1953).

FRAZEE, C. A., *The Orthodox Church and Independent Greece 1821–1852* (Cambridge: Cambridge University Press, 1969).

GIGLIO, C., *Etiopia—Mar Rosso* (Rome: Ministero degli Affari Esteri, 2 vols., 1958–9). Three tomes in all, the work of which this is part forms vol. i in the series *Italia in Africa. Serie storica.*

GIMALAC, P., 'Le Vicariat apostolique d'Abyssinie (1830–1931)', *Revue d'histoire des missions,* ix (1932), 129–90. Useful.

GIRMAH BESHAH and MERID WOLDE AREGAY, *The Question of the Union of the Churches in Luso-Ethiopian Relations (1500–1632)* (Lisbon, 1964).

GUIDI, I., 'La Chiesa Abissina', *Oriente Moderno,* ii (1922–3), 123–8, 186–90, 252–6.

—— *Vocabolario amarico-italiano* (Rome, 1901): reprinted by the Istituto per l'Oriente, 1953.

HABERLAND, E., *Untersuchungen zum äthiopischen Königtum* (Wiesbaden: Franz Steiner Verlag, 1965).

HAMMERSCHMIDT, E., *Äthiopien. Christliches Reich zwischen Gestern und Morgen* (Wiesbaden: Harrassowitz, 1967).

HARNACK, A., *History of Dogma. Translated from the Third German Edition by Neil Buchanan* (New York: Dover Publications, 7 vols. bound as four, 1961).

HILL, R., *Egypt in the Sudan 1820–1881* (London: Oxford University Press, 1959).

HOOKER, J. R., 'The Foreign Office and the "Abyssinian Captives"', *Journal of African History,* ii (1961), 245–58.

JAENEN, C. J., 'Blondeel: The Belgian Attempt to Colonize Ethiopia', *African Affairs,* lv (1956), 214–18.

JAROSSEAU, A., 'L'Apostolat catholique au Kafa (Éthiopie) de 1862 à 1912', *Revue d'histoire des missions,* ix (1932), 94–101.

JESMAN, Cz., 'La situazione religiosa in Etiopia durante il regno di Teodoro', *Africa. Rivista trimestrale di studi e documentazione dell'Istituto Italiano per l'Africa,* xxiv (1969), 156–79. Misleading and inaccurate.

JOHNSON, H. B., 'The Location of Christian Missions in Africa', *The Geographical Review,* lvii (1967), 168–202.

KOROLEVSKY, C., *Living Languages in Catholic Worship. An Historical Inquiry* (London: Longmans, 1957). An interesting chapter (Part III, Chap. II) on the Ge'ez rite incorporating first-hand information from Fr. Korolevsky's participation in eastern affairs in Rome.

LEVINE, D. N., *Wax & Gold. Tradition and Innovation in Ethiopian Culture* (Chicago: University of Chicago Press, 1965).

LOW, D. A., *Religion and Society in Buganda 1875-1900* (Kampala: East African Institute of Social Research, n.d.).

LUDOLF, J., *A New History of Ethiopia. Being a Full and Accurate Description of The Kingdom of Abessinia, Vulgarly though Erroneously called the Empire of the Prester John* (London, 1682).

MARIO DA ABIY-ADDI' (Ayyala Takla Hāymānot), *La dottrina della Chiesa etiopica dissidente sull'Unione Ipostatica* (Rome: Pont. Institutum Orientalium Studiorum, 1956); no. 147, in the series 'Orientalia Christiana Analecta'. In addition to the main published sources, Fr. Mario had access to an important manuscript collection in private hands.

MARSTON, T. E., *Britain's Imperial Role in the Red Sea Area, 1800-1878* (Hamden, Conn., 1961).

MATHEW, D., *Ethiopia. The Study of a Polity 1540-1935* (London, 1947).

MCDOUGALL, D., *In Search of Israel. A Chronicle of the Jewish Missions of the Church of Scotland* (London, 1941).

MCLEISH, A. (ed.), *Light and Darkness in East Africa. A Missionary Survey of Uganda, Anglo-Egyptian Sudan, Abyssinia, Eritrea and the Three Somalilands* (London: World Dominion Press, n.d. [1927]).

MEINARDUS, O. F. A., 'Peter Heyling, History and Legend', *Ostkirchliche Studien*, cxli (1965), 305-26.

METODIO DA NEMBRO, *La missione dei Minori Cappuccini in Eritrea (1894-1952)* (Rome, 1953).

MICHAELIS, J. H., *Sonderbarer Lebens-Lauff Herrn Peter Heylings, aus Lübec, und dessen Reise nach Ethiopien; nebst Zulänglichen Berichte von der in selbigen Reiche zu Anfange des nächts-verwichenen Saeculi entstandenen Religions-Unruhe: aus . . . Ludolfs edirten Schriften und andern noch nicht gedruckten Documenten, zur gemeinen Nachricht . . .* (Halle, 1724). Much invaluable material on Heyling, but little on Ethiopia.

MORDINI, A., 'Il convento di Gunde Gundiè', *Rassegna di studi etiopici*, xii (1953), 29-71.

MORGAN, M., 'Continuities and Tradition in Ethiopian History. An investigation of the reign of Tewodros', *Ethiopia Observer*, xii (1969), 244-69.

MURAD KAMIL, 'Letters to Ethiopia from the Coptic Patriarchs, Yo'annas XVIII (1770-1796) and Morqos VIII (1796-1809)', *Bulletin de la société d'archéologie copte*, viii (1942), 89-143. Arabic texts only, no translations. A useful, but rather limited, introduction.

NEILL, S., *Colonialism and Christian Missions* (London: Lutterworth, 1966). Potentially an important interpretation, it basically reflects a rather traditional missionary standpoint.

OLIVER, R., *The Missionary Factor in East Africa* (London: Longmans, 2nd ed., 1965).

OTHMER, C., 'P. Liberatus Weiss, O.F.M., Seine Missionstätigkeit und sein Martyrium (3 März 1716)', *Archivum Franciscanum Historicum*, xx (Quaracchi, 1927), 336–55. An important study.

POLADIAN, T., *The Doctrinal Position of the Monophysite Churches* (Addis Ababa, 1963); subsequently published by E. Hammerschmidt in *Ostkirchliche Studien*, cxli (1965), 184–200.

POLLERA, A., *Lo Stato etiopico e la sua Chiesa* (Rome, 1926).

ROBINSON, R., GALLAGHER, J. and DENNY, A., *Africa and the Victorians. The Official Mind of Imperialism* (London: Macmillan, 1965).

ROEYKENS, R. P. A., 'Les Préoccupations missionnaires du consul belge Ed. Blondeel van Cuelenbroeck en Abyssinie (1840–1843)', *Bulletin de l'académie royale des Sciences coloniales*, N.S. v (1959), 1135–54.

ROTBERG, R., 'Plymouth Brethren and the occupation of Katanga, 1886–1907', *Journal of African History*, v (1964), 285–97.

—— *Christian Missionaries and the Creation of Northern Rhodesia 1880–1924* (Princeton, N.J.: Princeton University Press, 1965).

RUBENSON, S., *King of Kings. Tewodros of Ethiopia* (Addis Ababa and Nairobi: Haile Sellassie I University with Oxford University Press, 1966).

RUNCIMAN, E., *The Great Church in Captivity. A Study of the Patriarchate of Constantinople from the Eve of the Turkish Conquest to the Greek War of Independence* (Cambridge: Cambridge University Press, 1968).

SAMUEL, V. C., 'Proceedings of the Council of Chalcedon and its Historical Problems', *Abba Salama. A Review of the Association of Ethio-Hellenic Studies*, i (Addis Ababa, 1970), 73–93.

SERGEW HABLE SELLASSIE (ed.), *The Church of Ethiopia. A Panorama of History and Spiritual Life* (Addis Ababa: The Ethiopian Orthodox Church, 1970).

SLADE, R., *English-Speaking Missions in the Congo Independent State (1878–1908)* (Brussels: Académie royale des Sciences coloniales, 1959).

STOCK, E., *The History of the Church Missionary Society. Its Environment, its Men and its Work* (London, 4 vols., 1899–1916).

TADDESSE TAMRAT, 'Some Notes on the Fifteenth Century Stephanite "Heresy" in the Ethiopian Church', *Rassegna di studi etiopici*, xxii (1966), 103–15.

TAYLOR, J. V., *The Growth of the Church in Buganda. An Attempt at Understanding* (London: SCM Press, 1958).

TEDESCHI, S., 'Profilo storico di Dayr-es-Sulṭān', *Journal of Ethiopian Studies*, ii (1964), 92–160.

TELLEZ, B., *The Travels of the Jesuits in Ethiopia* . . . (London, 1710).

TODD, J. M., *African Mission. A historical study of The Society of African Missions whose priests have worked on the coast of West Africa and inland, in Liberia, the Ivory Coast, Ghana, Togoland, Dahomey and Nigeria, and in Egypt, since 1856* (London, 1962).

TRIMINGHAM, J. S., *The Christian Church and Missions in Ethiopia (including Eritrea and the Somalilands)* (London: World Dominion Press, 1950).

ULLENDORFF, E., *The Ethiopians. An Introduction to Country and People* (London: Oxford University Press, 1960).

—— *Ethiopia and the Bible. The Schweich Lectures of the British Academy 1967* (London: Oxford University Press, 1968).

—— and BECKINGHAM, C. F., 'The First Anglo-Ethiopian Treaty', *Journal of Semitic Studies*, ix (1964), 187–200.

WARREN, M., *The Missionary Movement from Britain in Modern History* (London: SCM Press, 1965).

WEBSTER, J. B., *The African Churches Among the Yoruba 1888–1922* (Oxford: Clarendon Press, 1964).

WILLMOTT, H. M., *The Doors Were Opened. The Remarkable advance of the Gospel in Ethiopia* (London: S.I.M., n.d. [1960?]).

INDEX

Abbadie, Ant. d', 52 n., 59; and founding of Gāllā mission, 60; on Ethiopian pro-Catholicism, 75
Abbadie, Arn. d', 45, 46, 59
abun, vii. See also bishop, Qērelos, Salāmā
Addigrāt (maps, pp. 28, 58), 30, 36, 38
Adoptionism, and Yaṣagā Lej, 24–5
Adwā (maps, pp. xii, 28, 58): CMS 1830–8, 35–6, 40–6; CMS 1843, 56; as a mission centre, 37; Lazarists and, 59–60, 88
Agāmē, district (maps, pp. 28, 58), 71, 102, 110, 112
Aichinger (CMS carpenter), 36–7, 41, 43
Akāla Guzāy, district (map, p. 58), 71, 78
Ali II, rās (ruler of Bagēmder, 1831–53): political events, 55–6, 63–4, 69; internal religious questions, 51, 70, 87, 89; and missions, 71, 72; writes to Gobat, 115. Mentioned: 66, 67, 68, 74, 92, 118
Alitēnā (map, p. 58), 79, 148
Amda Ṣeyon, emperor (1314–44), 16
anathema, see excommunication
Ankobar (map, p. 28), churches of, 50, 51
Arāyā, bālgādā, 67, 68; and Salāmā and Catholics, 88
Asfā Wasan, ruler of Shawā, 50
Avanchers, Fr. Léon des (Capuchin missionary): attitude to rites and indigenous clergy, 81, 84–5; diplomatic activities and views, 105–6, 107; on Tēwodros's religious policy, 109–10
Azazo (map, p. xii), 22, 24

Baëta, C. G., quoted, 3
Bagēmder, vii, 14, 25, 29, 95. See also Yajju
Baker, Samuel, quoted, 120–1
Basel Mission, 29, 116
Beillard (French consul), see Chauvin-Beillard

Beke, C. T., 139
Bel, Mgr. L. (Lazarist missionary), 113
Bell, J., 115, 118, 134, 139
Bender, Ch. (Chrischona missionary), 120, 122; on artisan strategy, 129–30; returns to Ethiopia, 144
Berru, dajāzmāch (son of Goshu), 73–4
Biancheri, Mgr. L. (Lazarist missionary): arrival, 67; in Bagēmder, 72; consecrated coadjutor, 96; hostility to indigenous clergy, 83–4, 111–13; Bogos mission, 111–12. Cited on: Yaṣagā Lej, 24, 74; Webē, 71; Tēwodros, 95, Negusē, 107
Bible Churchmen's Missionary Society, 145, 147
bishop, Orthodox: anti-Catholic, 8; influence of, 16, 22, 86; avidity for, 34; Webē's project, 66; Catholic schemes, 71, 72. See also Qērelos, Salāmā
Blondeel, Ed. (Belgian diplomat): and Gāllā mission, 60; in Gojjām, 73; view of Ethiopian sects, 75
Blumhardt, C. H. (CMS missionary), 43–6, 150
Bogos (map, p. 58), 71, 111–14
Boru Mēdā, Council of (1878), 20
Bourgaud, 132
Brandeis, F. (missionary to the Falāshā), 128, 131–2, 137, 140
Britain: Webē's interest in, 44, 67; India Govt. policy, 53; approached by Hāyla Malakot, 73; protects Abuna Salāmā, 86–7, 90–1; rivalry with French, 92–3; relations with Tēwodros, 99, 134–6; captives question and Maqdalā expedition, 137, 138, 139–40, 142
British and Foreign Bible Society, 11–12
Bronkhorst, C. (missionary to the Falāshā), 130
Bruce, J., 11, 13

Cameron, D. (British consul), 135–6, 137; also 138, 139, 142

To learn more, visit us
www.tsehaipublishers.com

www.tsehaipublishers.com

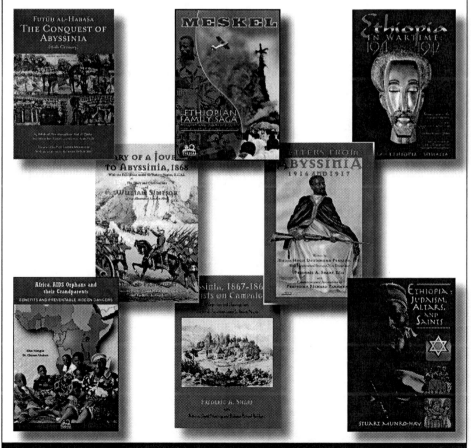

Printed in the United States
81007LV00004B/106-153